RE·ARCHITECTING TRUST

RE·ARCHITECTING
TRUST

THE CURSE OF HISTORY
AND **THE CRYPTO CURE** FOR
MONEY, MARKETS,
AND **PLATFORMS**

OMID MALEKAN

TRIPLE SMOKE STACK
NEW YORK

Published by Triple Smoke Stack, New York, New York.

Library of Congress Cataloging-in-Publication Data
is available upon request.

ISBN 978-1-7320273-2-9 (Hardcover)
ISBN 978-1-7320273-3-6 (Paperback)
ISBN 978-1- 7320273-4-3 (EBook)

Cover design by Paul McCarthy
Illustrations by Dorie Herman
Book design and page composition
by Karen Minster

www.omidmalekan.com

PRINTED IN THE UNITED STATES OF AMERICA

DEDICATED TO THE ORIGINAL
CYPHERPUNKS WHO STARTED IT ALL.

FOR MY DAD,
WHO TAUGHT ME TO ALWAYS
FINISH WHAT I STARTED.

Contents

Preface

Slouching Towards Digital Bethlehem

Look ahead. Take the most important economic, political, and social trends of today, all of which are driven by digitization, and project them forward. Assume that there is no great intervention on the horizon, no *Deus ex Machina* to save us from this folly. Behold our creation: a dystopian world where nobody trusts anybody because the lives of the many are controlled by the actions of the few—masked men hiding behind a silicon curtain pushing buttons. Terrible, yet somehow inevitable.

In this imagined future world, billions of people, from every country and almost every walk of life, now interact almost exclusively in the digital domain, a trend that began long ago and was accelerated by a pandemic. We communicate, work, play, shop, exercise, mingle, and learn together, as coordinated by the services of a handful of corporations in charge of search, social, e-commerce, and cloud. Due to their global footprint, these companies are arguably more powerful than entire countries, their algorithms more influential than many legal systems. Thanks to gig-economy services such as food delivery and rideshare, their algorithms also drive the offline economy. What you read, who you date, when you arrive, and how you feel is no longer in your hands.

People have a sense that these algorithms might be up to no good, but nobody can prove anything because the algorithms are opaque. Unlike any proper legal system, there is no transparency. Snippets of code enforce their will quietly and with little recourse. The people who operate them know how they work, but don't share that information. Instead they give speeches about social responsibility and bringing people together. They lack credibility and seem to have an ulterior motive. Not that anyone should be surprised. These are for-profit companies and their management doesn't get paid to make the world a better place. It gets paid to deliver financial results, and in this industry, that can mean doing the opposite. Feed users provocative content, hijack their attention, mine their data, increase the take rate, make bank.

Unhappy as we may be about this miasma, it's unclear who, if anyone, is responsible. Rolling back the digital tide is not an option and the services provided by these companies are useful. Without them, we'd still be using phone books and hailing taxis in the rain. It's hard to imagine life without them, or the same services being offered by a government as corporations have a long history of delivering results. Or at least they used to, back when they mostly manufactured products, and manipulating those products to make them more appealing was a virtue. But now we are the product, so we too must be manipulated, poked, and prodded like chattel then sold to the highest bidder. In this version of our digital future, Soylent Green really is people.

There are multiple reasons how we ended up here but an overreliance on advertising as a business model is a major one. All of that poking and prodding can take a dark turn when mass surveillance is required to make money and one group can pay to manipulate another. But there is no clear alternative because without advertising most digital content would be free. It would be one thing if creators and gig-economy workers could charge for their work directly and consumers could pay a tiny amount for every interaction, but the internet was designed to move data, not money. That crucial activity was booted to a handful of payment providers and card companies, most of which took advantage of this historical moment to become monopolies. Now they have us by our balances, collecting a toll on every interaction.

But they too cannot be blamed. We ran into their arms when we abandoned cash. Physical money had its drawbacks, but there was an elegance to it. Anyone could use it and every payment was both private and free. Cards and other forms of electronic payment are not so egalitarian. They charge high fees and collect data, and the companies that operate them now control the fates of entire industries. They also rely on the banking system, so those who don't have a bank account need not apply, literally.

What a dismal future indeed. Without anyone planning it, the world's digital and financial intermediaries are in charge of society. Entirely. They monetize the contributions of others and dictate social and political outcomes. Any idea deemed undesirable is quietly disappeared, demoted to the bottom of the search results, or refused a hashtag. Businesses that pay for positive reviews succeed while those that try to earn them don't. Payment processors pick winners and losers with the flexing of a fee. Impacting society through social activism or the political process used to be a heavy lift that required enough people to form a consensus. Now all it takes is a tweak of an algorithm by a few people in one company.

People across the political spectrum are upset by these developments. They demand government intervention but misunderstand the problem. They falsely assume that the algorithms are only out to get them, mistaking a structural issue for a partisan one. The real problem is one of power. Give anyone too much and they are bound to abuse it, a defect of human nature as true for a programmer as it is for a dictator. It matters little whether the people in question have ill intent. Their job comes with a powerful button, so they push it, day in and day out.

That kind of power used to only be considered appropriate for government officials, and only if constrained by transparency and due process. In the pre-web era, it would take an army of attorneys and years of litigation to deprive someone of their physical property. In this hypothetical *Meta Inc.* version of the Metaverse, depriving someone of their virtual property simply takes a T-shirt-clad CEO pushing a button. It doesn't even matter why. So long as the button exists, they will find a reason to push it.

Terrified of the power that these executives now possess (and also a bit jealous) the politicians try to push back. They hold hearings and threaten to break up the biggest companies. But they also misunderstand the problem, for it is architectural, not political. Yesterday's antitrust laws are not effective in the era of network effects. Diminishing the footprint of one corporate-owned platform simply enables the rise of another, a T-shirt-clad CEO replaced by one in a suit or a skirt. The problem isn't the people. It's the availability of the button.

Not that anyone trusts the politicians to deal with these issues anyway. Their credibility is also shot. Decades of economic mismanagement, growing income inequality, and bloated bailouts have taken their toll. It was one thing, all those years ago, when emergency tools for the creation and dissemination of money were created to deal with a global financial crisis. It was also understandable when those same tools were expanded to deal with a global pandemic. But in this future world they are deployed semipermanently to address more-ordinary issues: a fading market here, a bursting bubble there, an impending election somewhere, and exploding deficits everywhere. Manipulating money is also a button, and this one is showing its wear and tear.

The politicians used to tell us that the resulting economic fallout was transitory. Now they blame central bankers, who in turn blame economists, who argue that it wasn't their models that let us down, but rather the people who refused to act as predicted (and, by implication, directed). Not that this debate matters much. As the experts keep reminding us, modern money can only be issued by a government. Gold doesn't work online and digital currency that doesn't have a button does not, and cannot, exist. There used to be a small group of nerds and weirdos who argued otherwise, but we haven't heard from them in a long time. Maybe they changed their minds. Or maybe someone pushed a button.

The God in the Machine

Now look back. This part is actual history. In late 2008, in the middle of the Great Financial Crisis, an anonymous author writing under the nom de plume of Satoshi Nakamoto published a short paper on an email group dedicated to cryptography. A few months later, he (or she or they) released software that executed the ideas presented in that paper and—with the aid of a few others—began operating what we now know as the Bitcoin blockchain, although that word would not be invented until years later. Unbeknownst to anyone, a multitrillion-dollar industry was born.

```
I've been working on a new electronic cash system that's
fully peer-to-peer, with no trusted third party.

The paper is available at:
http://www.bitcoin.org/bitcoin.pdf

The main properties:
 Double-spending is prevented with a peer-to-peer network.
 No mint or other trusted parties.
 Participants can be anonymous.
 New coins are made from Hashcash style proof-of-work.
 The proof-of-work for new coin generation also powers the
   network to prevent double-spending.
```

1

Today, Bitcoin is taking the world by storm as a new kind of money, exciting the faithful, angering the skeptical, and bewildering everybody else. It's not alone, as there are thousands of cryptocurrencies out there, with more coming every day. Some resemble the original while others are notably different. All take advantage of a new technology, one uniquely capable of building trust in a digital setting and, by extension, eliminating buttons. But a close read of the Nakamoto paper—all eight pages of it—reveals that the original goal was something far less ambitious. The world was already digitizing, and a future where every interaction would require some kind of intermediary was on the horizon. The author was simply early in detecting the dangers of that development, as indicated by the opening paragraph of his paper:

Commerce on the Internet has come to rely almost exclusively on finan-
cial institutions serving as trusted third parties to process electronic
payments. While the system works well enough for most transactions,
it still suffers from the inherent weaknesses of the trust based model.

The "trust-based model" that Nakamoto referred to is one where people rely on someone or something to perform a function and *hope* that it does the right thing, with the very need for hope implying that it might not. This is in contrast to a trustless relationship, where reliable outcomes are guaranteed. Using a calculator is a trustless activity, whereas investing in a guy named Bernie is not. Alas, most of our financial system, not to mention the rest of the economy, is based on the trust-based model. Until very recently, there was no other way.

Having an intermediary facilitate between people is an ancient idea, spanning time from a tribal chief weighing in on a dispute to a legal system that arbitrates disagreements. Less extreme but more common are the countless government entities, corporations, platforms, and payment processors that facilitate our daily interactions with each other. For an intermediary to be effective, it needs to have the power to enforce its decisions, turning the most important intermediaries into central authorities. But the creation of such authorities—most of which are not trustless—has its own drawbacks. Two people transacting on the internet via a payment processor don't need to fully trust each other to do business, which is good, but they do need to trust the payment processor, which can be treacherous, not to mention expensive.

Despite the internet's original mission of breaking down barriers and connecting people directly, it could not function as incepted without central authorities. That's why almost every digital activity is now dominated by a few companies. We criticize them for their disproportionate power and profits, but still need them because most offline activity falls apart once it goes digital. Making a payment is a good example.

If you walk into a store and buy something with a physical dollar bill, the owner is reasonably confident that the money is authentic and the transaction irreversible. That's why currency in the form of physical objects like bills and coins has been popular throughout the ages. But what if you send an online merchant a digital payment in a text message? How do they know the money isn't counterfeit, or that the same dollars weren't simultaneously sent to somebody else?

Physical money works because it's difficult to create and counterfeits are easy to spot. Digital money, on the other hand, is just data, and data is the easiest thing in the world to create, not to mention edit, duplicate, and destroy. Creating counterfeit digital dollars could be as easy as a few strokes of the keyboard: copy and paste. Nakamoto honed in on this problem in the opening paragraphs of the paper. Digitization was appealing, but required new intermediaries to work, somewhat diminishing the appeal of going online in the first place.

But what if there was a technical solution to this unique problem of the digital era? What if we could create "a purely peer-to-peer version of electronic cash [that] would allow online payments to be sent directly from one party to another without going through a financial institution." In other words, what if we could address the shortcomings of a relatively new technology with an even newer one?

For a paper now associated with certain libertarian ideals and quoted by Bitcoin stalwarts as if it were their bible, the original Bitcoin white paper is surprisingly void of idealism. Even the title, "Bitcoin: A Peer-to-Peer Electronic Cash System" is mundane. For all the controversy over whether Bitcoin is actually money, or what role cryptocurrencies should play in our lives, the word *currency* only appears once in the paper, and only in reference to physical cash. The author seemed more concerned with solving a technical problem than starting an ideological movement.

And yet, the very first batch of Bitcoin transactions, the so-called "genesis lock," processed by Nakamoto in the opening days of 2009, included a clearly ideological reference to the ongoing bank bailouts. As can be seen by browsing the immutable and transparent Bitcoin blockchain, a not-so-secret text message embedded amidst the transaction details reads:

The Times 03/Jan/2009
Chancellor on brink of second bailout for banks

It's possible that the Bitcoin inventor referenced a newspaper headline as a sort of timestamp, to prove that the Bitcoin blockchain was launched on that day. But there were many headlines to choose from, most of which would have been less suggestive. Referencing the bailouts was probably no accident, leading us to ask "why." What happened in the months between publication of the mostly technical Bitcoin white paper and the launch of the more ideological Bitcoin blockchain? What happened was the greatest financial crisis in a century.

The mundane and mechanical problem of financial intermediaries being required for online commerce had exploded into an existential crisis for the online economy. If all digital commerce required intermediaries, and those intermediaries were prone to massive blowups, then the internet had a serious problem. Even when they weren't blowing up, these players could still corrode the integrity of our interactions. They could weaponize their size and profit off of everyone else's work in the best of times then hold society hostage and demand bailouts in the worst.

The rest of this story is blockchain history. Bitcoin, now more than a decade old, has not only survived but thrived, despite ongoing skepticism from many corners. The Bitcoin blockchain, the confusing mishmash of different technologies stitched together by a still unknown author to create peer-to-peer electronic cash, has proven effective and resilient. In over a decade of operation, that system has never been down, made a mistake, or needed a bailout. All despite the fact that, due to its open architecture and trillion dollars in value contained therein, it has been under constant attack.

Just as impressively, the ideas that enabled Bitcoin have by now been expanded and applied to almost every aspect of our lives, financial and otherwise. They have been used to improve the transfer of existing currencies and the trading of traditional securities. They have been used to automate manual processes and eliminate human error in contractual engagements. They have been used to build a different kind of banking system, one that is open, fair, and nondiscriminatory. They have been used to reinvigorate the worlds of art, music, collectibles, and gaming. They have reinvented what it means to be a member of a community and how groups of people from all over the world with shared values organize themselves to tackle specific tasks.

Best of all, they have been used to eliminate the availability of, or need for, the most destructive buttons. Contrary to what the powerful might think, power doesn't exist to serve them (regardless of their choice of attire). Power exists to fulfill a function, and the best and most useful systems, the ones that stand the test of time, are designed to defuse power. Not for any ideological reason, but because that which is decentralized is more stable and less likely to be manipulated, co-opted, or corrupted. Until very recently, there was no way of defusing power on the internet. But now, there's a blockchain for that.

The early pioneers of the crypto domain set out to create a new kind of payment system. To do so, they had to invent a new kind of money. To make that money valuable, they had to build a new kind of community. To make that community succeed, they had to build trust. The multifaceted nature of crypto is one reason why it is so confusing. There is no single answer to the question "what is Bitcoin?" It is a currency, but it's also an investment asset, payment system, digital platform, decentralized protocol, and a global community. It's complex yet elegant, which is one reason why so many are enthralled by it. It's far from perfect, but to the hundreds of millions of people all over the world who believe in it, it's better than what we have now. If you find yourself intrigued, but also skeptical and bewildered, then you've come to the right place.

My first book on blockchain technology was a nontechnical and non-ideological introduction to how it works. This book is about what it can change. It's ideological in the sense that I clearly believe in the potential for the technology to touch every part of our lives, but practical in accepting that—like life itself—predicting the ending is easier than knowing how we get there. To make my case for where I think we are going, I'd like to show you where we are coming from.

But first, we need to build a framework for how the world works, so we'll start off with our own genesis block.

RE·ARCHITECTING TRUST

0
TRUST

trust   verb
the act of weakening oneself to strengthen a group, at the risk
of someone else weakening the group to strengthen themselves.

Once, long ago, something remarkable happened between two people. We can only speculate on the conditions that led to this occurrence, because it predates written history, and there is no record. For all we know, it may even predate language, so the people that it happened to couldn't even describe it. But they surely felt it.

What happened was that two humans decided to trust each other. They chose to put aside their differences and cooperate, despite the natural tendency to do the opposite and compete. The unlikeliness of this decision must be acknowledged. Life was hard in this prehistoric period: the environment was harsh, resources were scarce, and dangerous predators lurked everywhere. Aside from mating, other people represented competition for food and shelter and danger from disease.

Why these two people made the peculiar decision to trust each other is only for them to know. Maybe one of them was born with a genetic mutation that made her less suspicious of others. Maybe the other had recently fallen and bumped his head. Maybe the weather was unseasonably pleasant, or they were both drunk. In any case, and despite all odds, two people decided to trust each other, and changed the course of history.

E Pluribus Unum—An Allegory

Trust led to success. The decision to cooperate allowed these two people to achieve more. They hunted more effectively and gathered more. They built a stronger shelter and took turns defending it. Other people took notice. The trusters looked happier and healthier and clearly had a better chance for survival and reproduction. Cooperation turned out to be beneficial, even for the selfish. Counterintuitively, the fundamental desire to live long and procreate was better served when people contributed to the well-being of others. Learning from this example, more people decided to put aside their base instincts and turn on the trust. Their success was contagious. The circle of trust was extended beyond those initial two and the first communities were formed.

Much like a virus or a meme, trust spread throughout the land. More and more people began forming bigger and bigger groups. Some of these groups even tried trusting other groups, forming a meta circle. The individual urge to compete was still present, but successful communities found harmless or productive outlets for it. They invented sports and competitive games that were as much a release valve for the baser desires as they were a form of entertainment. They even created team sports, the ultimate metaphor for the tug-of-war between cooperation and competition.

These were the most successful communities of all. There was less conflict and more abundance. Some people even tried expressing their competitiveness through their trustworthiness. They left their possessions unprotected and always volunteered to join the next hunting expedition. It wasn't that they didn't value their things or didn't like to rest. They just trusted other community members to not take advantage.

But therein lies the rub. Accidents of fate will swing both positive and negative, good and bad. Eventually, along came an individual who was not very trustworthy. Maybe he had his own genetic mutation, in the opposite direction. Maybe he too had bumped his head. Or maybe he was a mean drunk. Regardless, he didn't want to share his food or volunteer his time. Since everyone around him was so trusting, he could eat their food and take advantage of their work. He was a *free rider*, and so long as everyone around him was trusting, being a free rider paid off.

Free riding also turned out to be contagious. This individual wasn't the only ne'er do well in the bunch, and other would-be free riders noted his success. They began to emulate him. Now there were more lazy people, and less food. The rest of the community couldn't help but notice this breakdown in the framework. After all, each person's individual decision to set aside their baser instincts was predicated on the idea that others would do the same. The more free riders in the community, the less the incentive for others to work hard or share. As a result, nearly everyone began to pull back, and a virtuous cycle of camaraderie turned into a vicious cycle of mistrust. In this domain more than any other, a few bad apples really do spoil the bunch.

Similar reversals occurred in other communities, and hardship spread throughout the land. Nobody wanted to cooperate anymore for fear of a free rider showing up and taking advantage. With resources in ever scarcer supply, entire communities that used to cooperate with each other turned hostile. Majorities blamed minorities and the powerful abused the meek. When all was said and done, the cycle had completed, and nobody trusted anybody. So it went, and so it goes.

The Curse of History

While this allegory is anecdotal and oversimplified, we know it to be true because some version of this cycle explains everything from a successful marriage to a failed empire. Evolution selected for cooperative species long before anyone bumped their head, and the human version is further complicated by things like love, sex, family, culture, politics, and religion. Cooperation and trust are one thing when programmed into the DNA of a bee colony and another when filtered through a conscious mind and an aching heart.

Nevertheless, the cyclical nature of trust can be found throughout human history and in every aspect of our lives. It explains how we architect our institutions when a new framework arises and "re-architect" them when it fails. The cycle of trust explains why periods of tranquility are followed by periods of conflict, within a friendship or between nations. There is a deep appreciation for this cycle in our collective psyche, thanks to eons of societies that have tried to rein in free riding and enhance trust by inventing some new framework, then doing everything they can to make it last. Take a few ideas as disparate as religion, politeness, and a dance party, and the one thread that connects them is the attempt by a community to establish a trust framework and make it last. Why do people believe in supreme beings? Because doing so allows them to automatically trust others who believe in the same one. Why do people say please and thank you? Because doing so helps communicate the desire to build trust. Why do people take drugs, play music, and gyrate together? Because doing so helps them dissolve the ego (and with it, the temptation to free ride).

Despite these innovations and regardless of the setting, no framework lasts forever. This is the curse of history. The older any trust framework gets, the greater the likelihood of a breakdown. Trust has its own laws of thermodynamics, and energy must constantly be added to preserve it. But human beings are fickle and lazy. Two people who have only recently formed some kind of partnership—like a marriage or an LLC—are likely to start out on their best behavior. Success can thaw them out over time, however. Eventually one begins to slip, and the other fails to notice. By the time either one realizes what has happened, it might be too late. Familiarity really does breed contempt, but not because anyone wanted it to.

Part of the challenge of preserving any trust framework is the apparent contradiction at its core. To trust another person is to become vulnerable to them, and vulnerability is a form of weakness. But there is strength in numbers. Joining a new framework is the act of voluntarily weakening oneself to strengthen a community and thereby become stronger than would otherwise be possible. All for one and one for all, and all that. This is a paradox, one that constantly haunts us. Trusting other people means being weaker in their presence. And yet, the English word *trust* is derived from ancient terms for strength and solidity. So, we swing back and forth. We want to trust other people because we understand doing so will improve our lives, but we fear being taken advantage of. We enter new frameworks hoping for the best, then suffer when they break down. Thankfully, despite the constant cyclicality, we learn something new every time, so newer frameworks are different, and often better.

THE CYCLICAL NATURE OF TRUST

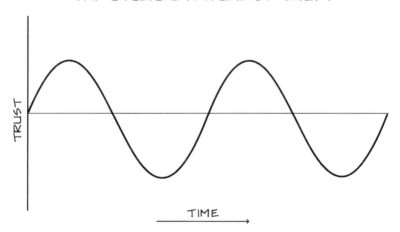

Across the span of thousands of years, trust has trended from the mystical to the scientific, and from the vague to the specific. People used to rely almost entirely on myths, and the commandments of supposed Gods, but now we have judges and lawyers (many of whom derive their legitimacy from myths and gods). We also have the benefit of hindsight, as history teaches us that periods of prosperity are usually defined by trust in major institutions such as governments, churches, and corpora-tions. Wealthy societies, from ancient Rome to present day Singapore, are understood to be *high trust*. The decline of major institutions—from the Catholic Church to Lehman Brothers—is usually precipitated by a loss of trust. Tellingly, the beginning of the end for both institutions was the fact that people trusted them too much.

The more trusting the members of a particular group—be they churchgoers or shareholders—the greater the temptation for that first breech. A prominent priest takes a strong interest in a young parishioner, and a powerful CEO fails to report an *honest* mistake. Both are trusted, so they get away with it. Then they do it again, this time more egregiously. Being human, they probably feel guilty. A part of them may even want to be caught. But this is a high-trust situation, where those around them will forgive, excuse, or otherwise pass on their transgression, so they won't be caught. The violation continues until it goes too far and can't be undone. Tragedy strikes. By then even the protagonists might be shocked by how far they've gone. If only someone had said something in the beginning. But alas, that first breach is always smaller than the last one, and now it's too late. Few people set out to become a free rider, yet many do. That's why the problem can never be eliminated. It can only be contained, and only for a while. Like the mythical devil, the greatest trick the curse ever played is convincing us that it doesn't exist.

Iteration and Innovation

Innovation has played an important role in how people and communities seek to build trust and preserve it with systemic solutions.

Consider the simple case of the written contract, which dates to at least the time of Plato.

Before its invention, people could only make oral contracts, agree-ments that needed impartial witnesses to be provable. Written contracts created a verifiable record of a promise and were therefore harder to violate. Although invented long ago, they continue to form the backbone of society, and it's hard to imagine a world without constitutions, employment contracts, leases, and user agreements.

But even with written agreements, the free-rider problem rears its ugly head. Though harder to do than with an oral agreement, written contracts could still be denied. A participant could claim that their signature was forged, or that the original contract had been modified without their consent. One solution is to (once again) require a third party to be present at the signing—a common practice today. Another option is to write two copies of the agreement on the same sheet of paper, then tear the document in half, with the counterparties each keeping one half. In the case of dispute, the two parties place the two pieces side by side, and if the teeth of the tear line up then the contract is authentic. As odd as this solution may sound, it was a common practice in Europe in the Middle Ages, and is where the word *indenture* from the Latin *dente*, meaning tooth, comes from.[2]

Another innovation in trust building is a legal system. Until very recently, contracts have been *dumb*, meaning that the contract itself cannot enforce anything. Participants holding torn pieces of an indenture could still violate its terms, justifying their actions on their interpretation of the text. Thus, a third-party intervention in the form of a court system that could be called upon to interpret contracts and enforce them, was created. Indeed, so-called *tripartite indentures* were written out in triplicate and signed before a court, with the court keeping its own copy. For this intervention to be meaningful, the court had to have power to dole out punishment. Like the documents themselves, the most effective punishments had teeth. Thus, the need for a powerful authority.

Authorities exist for many reasons, but one of the most important (and underrated) is the enforcement of trust. Two people who make a promise to each other are more likely to follow through with it if they fear punishment from someone more powerful than they are. That's the basic idea behind the *social contract,* loosely defined as an implicit agreement by a group of people to surrender some freedoms (like the freedom to break their word) in exchange for a more harmonious existence.[3] Social contracts are usually talked about in the context of political philosophy and are used to explain why people put up with government. But another way to look at them is as a means of preserving trust among disparate actors. Two people who don't know each other, don't believe in the same god, and haven't bumped their heads are more likely to trust each other if they both accept the legitimacy of the same ruler.

But now we have a second paradox. Trust built thanks to the existence of an authority comes at the expense of creating a free-rider temptation for the authority itself. In other words, two people who've signed a contract and opted into a legal framework enforced by a judge can better trust each other, but now have to fear abuse by the judge. After all, judges are people, and people are fickle. They can be corrupted or co-opted. What if the judge is related to one of the parties in question, or bribed by the other? Or what if the judge simply isn't any good?

One solution is to make the judge accountable to an even higher authority, one more powerful than they are. The judge may now be less likely to be biased or corrupted, for fear of punishment, but this solution simply moves the risk upstream. Lower-level judges have been rendered more accountable, which is great, but at the expense of an even greater free-rider temptation for the ones higher up. They too must be made accountable to a higher authority, so we have to add another layer. Eventually we end up with a hierarchy.

Hierarchies allow groups of people to build trust among themselves by putting their faith in someone above. They attempt to solve the paradox of trust by making every authority accountable to an even higher one. To preserve efficiency, the authorities get narrower as you climb, so an appeals court only bothers looking at the most important cases to come out of a lower court. As we'll see later, hierarchies are common in every aspect of human interaction where trust matters, particularly financial ones. They can be best understood as trust achieved at one level of interaction in exchange for the risk of exploitation from another.

The most successful hierarchies rein in the tendency toward corruption for the people at the very top by making them accountable to the bottom—as is the case in democracies where the most important judges are selected by elected officials. The Ideal Hierarchy of Trust illustration demonstrates the circular flow of this ideal hierarchy. But many hierarchies fail at this crucial last step of making the very top accountable to the bottom. The free-rider temptations at the very top are the hardest to rein in, so they end up with a dictator. Tellingly, their victims usually don't revolt, despite having strength in numbers. One reason why uprisings are so rare is the fear of a total breakdown and the resulting anarchy should the revolution succeed. Preserving trust at the lowest levels of the pyramid is so important that it makes people willing to tolerate a breakdown at the top.

THE IDEAL HIERARCHY OF TRUST

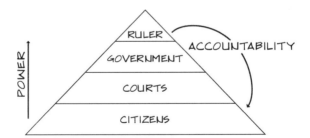

Incentives in the Mix

Incentives play an important role in the evolution (and undulation) of trust. People join existing frameworks and invent new ones because of the perceived rewards of being a part of a community. Other people try to take advantage of those frameworks (or break them altogether) because of the benefits to them of being a free rider. From a system-design point of view, neither group is irrational. Society may classify one group as "good" and the other as "bad," but those designations are based on cultural norms and ethics.

Trust is more complicated because human beings are calculating. A police officer who dedicates her life to the preservation of law and order and a career criminal are both acting selfishly in that each makes important decisions based on the perceived incentives of going down one path versus another. This is not to say that they are morally equivalent, or that there aren't other, more spiritual, consequences to being bad. But architecting a lasting framework requires a deeper appreciation of the human condition, one that goes beyond a children's book telling of cops and robbers. Good people can do bad things and the bad guys can feel like they have no other choice. For evidence, we can look to the world of organized crime, where criminal syndicates can have stronger trust frameworks than the law enforcement organizations they evade. So, a career mafioso refuses to rat on his colleagues despite the threat of going to jail, but an underpaid cop is easily bribed. *La cosa nostra*, but also, our thing.

Designing a lasting framework begins and ends with an understanding of the different incentives that people juggle when making decisions. Mobsters may need to be threatened with punishments such as asset seizures that hurt their immediate families, but cops also need to be paid well. Broadening out further, would-be criminals need to feel like they have opportunities for advancement away from the local gang, and cops need to feel a higher sense of duty.

A moralist might find such cold calculations uncouth. But life is hard, and most people exist at the intersection of multiple trust frameworks. They are citizens and employees and family members and have to consider the incentives for good or bad behavior in every context. Does cheating on their taxes help send their kids to college? Will sacrificing family time to work harder pay off? Is this hierarchy meritocratic? Is that framework going to last?

Incentives come in many forms. They can be implicit or explicit, fully spelled out in a contract or simply implied in a handshake. They can be short term or long term. They can be financial, structural, or cultural, as in cash in hand versus a promotion versus a certificate of recognition. They can also be intangible. Some people like to break into computer systems for fun. They don't break or steal anything because they aren't in it for the money, only the satisfaction of success, the kind one feels from solving a puzzle. Good security companies will often hire such people and let them do their thing to find vulnerabilities. Great security companies do that, and offer bounties to strangers, some of whom might be dangerous criminals.

The more important the desired outcome, the greater the range of incentives that need to be deployed. Incentives are the ultimate weapon in the never-ending tug-of-war of trust. They are more powerful than guns and bombs.

Putting It All Together

All of these concepts—the importance of trust, the struggle to achieve it, the temptation to free ride, the need for hierarchies, and the role of incentives—color every aspect of our lives. They determine winners and losers and help explain the general flow of history. Too often, they are only thought of when something goes wrong. Being first principles, they are more useful proactively, whenever societies need to undergo some kind of transformation.

Now is one of those times. The rise of computers and the advent of the internet have changed much of the world in the span of a few decades. Borders have dissolved and billions of people have been crammed into the same global village. Some of these changes, like the ability for anyone anywhere to access all the world's information, are great. Other changes, like the ability for anyone anywhere to access all the world's information, are terrible.

Our first instinct has been to try to cram this brave new world into our existing trust frameworks. We've asked corporations to control the flow of money, information, goods, and people, and for governments to oversee them. Both have done a poor job because neither was built to tackle the problems of today. Modern corporations were invented at the dawn of the industrial era. They are highly centralized and hierarchical because that is what it took to drill for oil or make refrigerators. Modern governments were also invented long ago, at a time when the mail took weeks to arrive, and many couldn't read.

The slow decay of our most sacred trust frameworks is apparent all around us. People used to trust major companies, but now fear them. They used to respect experts, but now mock them. They used to revere their government officials, but now loathe them. Tempting as it might be to think of the present moment as unprecedented, it's just the latest down cycle in the never-ending undulation of trust. The incentive structures of the corporate world are not effective in a digital era, so the free riders have run amok. Our governmental hierarchies are too slow to keep up with the times, so their responses tend to be reactive and seldom productive. Our collective ability to share information has surpassed our ability to process it.

The Change, It Had to Come

As these older institutions decline, a new class of trust frameworks begins to rise. Unlike their predecessors, they are natively digital, and designed to take advantage of a world where everyone has a connected device in their hand. They are naturally borderless because borders are just a restriction on physical movement, not information. They are fully transparent, because now that everyone has access to all the world's information, there is no excuse not to be. They embrace the promise of incentives and use mathematics and cryptography like rebar and cement—the strong foundation upon which everything else is built.

There are many things that are both unlikely and impressive about the Bitcoin solution, but the most important may be this: despite the hundreds of billions in value that it now contains and the tens of billions of daily transactions that it processes, nobody trusts anybody. The developers don't trust the miners and the users don't trust each other. And yet, it works. The ultimate achievement in trustlessness, one where nobody has to trust anybody, but everyone trusts the outcome. There are many interesting applications of such a technology, and together we will explore some of them, starting with money.

1
MONEY

money   noun

that which is nothing, then everything, then possibly nothing again.

What the Heck Is It?

The most ubiquitous things are the hardest to explain. Chief among them is money. Ask a child to explain money and she'll probably describe it as the thing you need to buy toys. Ask an adult and he'll probably tell you much the same, though perhaps with a lament. An economist will lecture on stores of value and mediums of exchange, while the historian will recall gold coins and coined guilders. The artist might describe it as the thing she'll never have, and the preacher may denounce it as the thing you shouldn't want. Money is a paradox, somehow easy to describe yet impossible to define. The dictionary says "something generally accepted as a medium of exchange, a measure of value, or a means of payment," but that too is more descriptive than definitive. For a topic so fundamental to our lives, thoughts, and even language, money is surprisingly difficult to pin down. Most of us can describe it at the drop of a dime, and clichéd idioms referencing it are a dime a dozen, but none of these descriptions deliver much bang for the buck. Except for one.

Money is a myth, a mass delusion that we all opt into to gain access to a powerful trust framework. Two people who have nothing in common can still do business so long as they believe in the same kind of money. Human culture is full of myths that help bring people together, but none are as widespread as money. There are billions of people all over the world who describe themselves as either Christian, Muslim, or Hindu. They worship different prophets and follow different texts, so there is a lot of disagreement. But the one thing they can all agree on is the purchasing power of the US dollar. Religion is a powerful myth, but it seldom goes unquestioned in the way that money does. Plenty of perfectly sane people identify as atheists. Only a madman would refuse to believe in money.

Money was invented thousands of years ago by independent societies all over the globe. It appeared in different forms at different times, but always to serve the same purpose. Why it was invented, or what came before it, is a subject of furious debate—partly because money is so old that we have few records about how society was organized before it appeared. Some believe that money was created to solve the inefficiencies of barter. Others argue that barter economies never existed, and that money was invented to settle the favors (and debts) that members of small communities constantly accrued against each other. Regardless, the one thing we do know is that few social technologies have been as transformative as money.

If the drive for survival and a better life is the fuel that drives the engine of commerce, then money is the oil that keeps that engine running. It can be thought of as a sort of bridge across activities and throughout time. Without money, it would be practically impossible for a worker to trade his or her labor today for a coat to be acquired next winter. With money, the same activity becomes trivial, as easy as swapping a few pieces of paper (or increasingly, bits of data). Despite its reputation in popular culture as something that tears people apart, money is the ultimate unifier. People of different ages, genders, races, nationalities, and religions can all provide economic value for each other so long as they believe in the same kind of money. The Catholic Church and the Secular Coalition for America have little in common, but they both accept donations in dollars.

Trust is fundamental to the success of any specific kind of money, also known as a currency. As stated by Yuval Harari, author of the best-selling book *Sapiens,* "money is the most universal and most efficient system of mutual trust ever devised."[4] What makes a dollar worth a dollar is the fact that so many people trust that it will continue to be worth a dollar. The circuity of this logic is by design and is the main reason why the myth of money is so pervasive. It doesn't matter what you, as an individual, think of any particular currency. So long as everyone else believes it to be valuable, you have no choice but to agree, lest you be cut out of the economy.

Many of the most important economic and cultural leaps forward throughout history have revolved around the improvement of money. But as a direct consequence, so have some of the most catastrophic setbacks. The Roman empire rose and fell in part due to increasing then decreasing trust in the currency of its emperors. Pre-war Germany descended into fascism in part because of the collapse of its currency while post-war America rose to superpower status in part because of the growing demand for hers. Money is arguably the most important trust framework in human interaction, and the stability of any society's currency is usually a good predictor of its overall health. You can't have a great society without also having good money.

But there is a catch. If money is the most powerful trust mechanism in society, then the management of a currency presents the ultimate free-rider temptation, the ultimate curse. One cannot exist without the other. Not all types of money need to have somebody in charge, but as we will see, there are practical benefits to using a currency that has a central issuer. Without knowing much else, we can fairly conclude that most issuers throughout history have succumbed to the curse. There have been many great currencies over the millennia. Most had some sort of central issuer. None survived to the present day.

There is something about successful currencies that allows them to rise to dizzying heights, stay there for some time, then fall into oblivion. The cycle revolves around trust, but the exact mechanics of how it works is complicated and, in some ways, unique to money. Before delving into it, we need to understand more about the basic properties of money, as well as its storied history.

The Core Characteristics of Good Money

Economists understand money through its uses, summarized as a unit of account, medium of exchange, or store of value. Put simply: money is used to price things, buy them, or save for future purchases. Although we can't be sure if barter economies existed before the invention of money, we can imagine how difficult life in a pre-money society would be. A farmer and a blacksmith could only do business if one wanted wheat at the same exact time when the other needed a spade—an unlikely situation given the usual delay between planting and harvesting. In the absence of this "coincidence of wants," the two parties would have to find an intermediary. Even then, doing business would be slowed by the need to price every good in terms of every other good, a spade costing ten bushels of wheat, and a bushel of wheat going for two bags of sugar, and a bag of sugar covering an hour of labor. Saving would also be difficult, as one could never be sure what good to save in that would be valued tomorrow while saving in any kind of perishable good has obvious drawbacks. Most of these economic frictions go away if everyone opts into the same myth of value transfer and preservation, ergo money.

While the uses of money describe the need for its invention, the characteristics of money explain the types that were invented. Almost anything could be used as money, and through the ages, almost everything—from grains to cowry shells to giant stones—has been used. The most successful types of money have shared a handful of characteristics: they have been durable, portable, divisible, fungible, and scarce. The best kind of money lasts for a long time, is easy to transport, can be broken up into interchangeable units, and most of all, isn't too easy to create. Most of the things that have been used as money have shared some of these characteristics, but few have managed them all. Grain is easy to carry around and divide into smaller pieces but doesn't last. Giant stones last forever, but they are not portable or divisible. Leaves are very portable, but the opposite of scarce, so money doesn't grow on trees.

Metals comprise a good balance of the successful characteristics of money, so most societies eventually evolved to using them. Some metals are more durable and scarce than others, and gold and silver have historically occupied the sweet spot of both. Those two metals, along with bronze, iron, tin, and copper, were used as money for thousands of years, sometimes simultaneously within the same economy. Today, we think of metal money as coins broken down into neat little denominations, but of course metal doesn't come out of the ground like that. How it got there is a fascinating study of an important dynamic when it comes to the evolution of money, the constant tension between trust and convenience.

The less processed or manufactured any kind of money is, the more trustworthy and, by extension, long lasting it can be. As with any other processed good, the manufacturing process is a trusted relationship. Users have to trust the manufacturer to do a good job and not take any shortcuts. But like any trusted relationship, there is a temptation for the manufacturer to do just that and free ride. The problem with money is that unprocessed money is hard to use. The best kind of money, the kind likely to gain widespread adoption due to network effects, is the kind that is easy to store and transfer. But altering money to make it more convenient can also alter its trust framework. The standardization of metal money with coinage touched every aspect of this dynamic.

From Chunks to Coins

The economic life of merchants and consumers in the days before the invention of metal coins was filled with anxiety. Not only did they have to worry about finding a seller for the good they needed to buy or a buyer for the wares they hoped to sell, but they also had to worry about the chunks of metal used to finish the deal. Every payment involved a painstaking process of determining both the quantity and the quality of the metal involved because, to paraphrase Shakespeare, not all that glitters is gold. Determining the real quantity of money was a problem of biblical proportions.

In the Book of Genesis, we are told about the time when Abraham— said to be rich in "cattle, silver and gold"—is forced to use some of his metal to purchase a burial plot for his wife. Once a deal is struck a payment needs to be made, so he is said to have "weighed out for him the price he had named . . . four hundred *shekels* of silver, according to the weight current among the merchants." That's the translation according to the New International Version of the Old Testament. Standardization by weight turns metal money into a currency. We don't know exactly how much silver Abraham paid, but there must have been some generally agreed upon unit of mass. Indeed, the New American Standard translation of the same passage states that he weighed the silver according to "the commercial standard," and the New King James version cuts to the point and simply says "four hundred shekels of silver, currency of the merchants."

Thus, the inconvenience of having to weigh metal money was an ever-present source of economic friction. Commerce before the invention of coins must have been cumbersome, with everyone having to either walk around with their own scale or worry about being cheated using someone else's. The word *shekel* comes from the Semitic root for "weighing," and appears throughout the Judeo-Christian Bible, as well as other ancient texts such as the Code of Hammurabi, as a unit of weight often applied to money. Present-day residents of that part of the world no longer weigh their money, but they do make payments in New Shekels, the official currency of the State of Israel.

The ancient Romans also struggled with having to weigh their money. Instead of shekels, they relied on a unit called the *libra pondo*—Latin for "a pound by weight." Contemporary Italians don't have to weigh their money either, but up until the introduction of the Euro not that long ago, they made their payments in *liras*. The French used a currency called the *livre* for the better part of a millennium, and the British still pay with *pounds*. *Peso* is the Spanish word for "weight." It has been a long time since Europeans had to weigh their money, but the importance of doing so has lived on in the names of some of their most storied currencies.

The advent of coinage, which showed up independently in the East and the West over two thousand years ago, solved this problem. The value of money was still derived from the scarcity of a metal, but quantity and quality were now standardized into discrete units that could be counted easily. The first known Western coins were minted by the Lydians of present-day Turkey. They were made of a naturally occurring alloy of gold and silver and stamped with the head of a lion to be easily identifiable. The first Chinese coins to achieve widespread adoption were made from copper and had a hole in the middle so they could be strung together. Both Eastern and Western societies experimented with coins in the shapes of tools or animals during antiquity, and other geometric shapes have been used throughout the ages. The most popular shape has been a circle, probably because they are easier to manufacture and carry around, and don't wear down as fast as coins with sharp angles. The present-day Chinese *yuan,* Japanese *yen,* and Korean *won* all trace their names back to the Chinese word for "round object."

As convenient as coins are, they raise the issue of who the issuer should be. It doesn't make sense for there to be too many, as the point is to achieve a society-wide standard. The primary issuer should therefore be big enough to mint the coins at scale, and powerful enough to punish anyone who might produce counterfeits. Although there have been various private issuers of metal coins throughout the ages, the most likely candidate has usually been the ruler of a society. Not only can a king or emperor demand that all of his subjects use his money, he can also amplify the network effect by paying salaries, collecting taxes, and even borrowing in his own coin. As a bonus, and to indicate that his coin is the official money of a region, he can stamp each coin with his seal or likeness, a practice still in use today.

Increasing Convenience, Corroding Trust

And so, the preference for a single standard leads to the centralization of money. But the convenience of having it comes at the expense of a major free-rider opportunity. Before the introduction of coinage, trust in metal money was diffuse as everyone had to practice the monetary version of "buyer beware." Once powerful entities such as the emperors of Rome created their mints, the trust of an entire empire—not to mention the neighboring nations that traded with it—was placed in a single issuer. As long as that issuer did not take advantage of their position, then trust persevered.

But alas, no issuer can resist the temptation forever, and the periodic violation of trust—the all-too-human indulgence in the ultimate free-rider temptation—makes for a fascinating read of European history across the span of centuries. Rome first began issuance of its popular *denarius* coin around the year 225 BCE. Each coin contained approximately 95 percent silver, a purity maintained for the first few centuries. According to the Book of Matthew, it was a denarius coin that Jesus was shown when he made his famous declaration to "render unto Caesar what is Caesar's" (but only after asking his audience "Whose head is this, and whose title?").[5] The silver content of the denarius declined steadily over the next few centuries, however, with the biggest drops coming during periods of shortage and war. By the time the Roman Empire collapsed, the silver content of its coin was barely 5 percent.

Violation of the trust placed in the issuer of money is so common throughout history that it has a name: *seigniorage*, technically defined as the difference between the face value of issued money and the cost of producing it. With coinage, any issuing authority can earn a profit by diluting the precious-metal content of each coin, but still stamping it as being the same monetary unit—a coin that barely contains any silver being issued as if it were pure. The ruse only works so long as users treat the debased coin as if it were no different from its predecessor, but trust, as history has proven time and again, is not so gullible.

Since money is only a myth, all values that are tied to it are relative. Unlike nature—which is built on exact ratios like two units of hydrogen to one of oxygen in water—monetary ratios are a social construct. A coin's actual purchasing power within an economy, along with its exchange rate for other types of money, is set by the market, and therefore always in flux. Put differently, currency values are also determined by the laws of supply and demand: supply as determined by the issuer, and demand as determined by trust. A coin that might fetch a goat today might not be enough to buy a tuft of wool tomorrow if enough people lose confidence in its value. Issuers of metal coins can enrich themselves by diluting the precious-metal content, but users can just as easily respond by demanding more of that coin in exchange for the same goods and services.

Such was the case for the Roman soldiers who demanded ever-greater salaries as the denarius coins they were being paid with declined in value. Their demand was met throughout the centuries, but that doesn't mean that the warriors in the latter days of the empire, who earned several orders of magnitude more denarii per day than their predecessors, were any richer.[6] The overall purchasing power of Roman coins fell with their silver content. The economic term for a loss of confidence in a currency— and the subsequent decline in its purchasing power—is inflation, and the end days of the Roman empire had plenty of it.

These historical tendencies—the formation of a money myth, the drive for standardization, monopolization of issuance, the exercising of the free-rider option, and the resulting inflation—take time to play out, often across the span of centuries. None happen in a vacuum, and cause and effect are often impacted by exogenous factors such as war, the discovery of new sources of metal, and politics. Things are further complicated by the fact that both the benefits and pitfalls of rising and declining purchasing power are felt unevenly by different parts of society. An emperor who dilutes his own coins sees only benefits at the outset, while the poor and powerless are the final victims.

If we zoom out far enough and plot the overall progress of money on a chart, what we find is a wave resembling a sin curve, with the horizontal axis representing time and the vertical one trust (as we saw in Chapter 0.) A new currency is introduced and slowly gains adoption. Its success brings new riches (not to mention new powers) to the issuer. The curse, complacency, and arrogance (or war or other exogenous events) lead to seigniorage, which eventually causes inflation and a decline in trust, so the money (and oftentimes, the ruler) are disposed of and society switches to a more trustworthy alternative. The value of money is closely related to the level of trust.

The one characteristic of money that doesn't cycle is convenience. Although the purity of money and its resulting purchasing power have always gone back and forth, the type of money that is dominant, from commodities to metals to coins to paper bills to electronic databases, only moves in one direction, with the most convenient type of money always prevailing.

In Paper We Trust

Despite the dominance of precious-metal money across the span of thousands of years it has been mostly abandoned as a currency. The culprit is the ever-present drive for greater efficiency and convenience. As useful as metal coins were compared to raw metal, they were nonetheless cumbersome to use. Using more money meant carrying around more weight, and everyone was a potential target for robbers. One solution was to deposit the coins at a secure location managed by someone used to holding large amounts of money, like a goldsmith (or a relatively new institution known as a bank) in exchange for a paper receipt that represented the right to collect those coins. Thus, the genesis of paper money.

Paper money first appeared in seventh-century China to save merchants the hassle of having to carry around ever-larger quantities of copper coins. Each piece of paper was regarded as a receipt or IOU and derived its value from the fact that it could be used to redeem coins at a future date. European travelers, such as Marco Polo, brought this idea back home with them and—aided by improvements in the development of paper and inventions such as the printing press—the concept of paper money as receipt for metal money eventually gained widespread adoption. The earliest European forms of paper money were known as banknotes, highlighting the fact despite being denominated in the prevailing currency, they really represented a claim on a financial institution, and were one step removed from the official units issued by the king.

Once again, the drive for convenience led to a shift in trust. Whereas metal coins only required trust in the issuer, the earliest forms of paper money required trust in the issuer *and* the storer. A bank holding user coins could be robbed, steal the coins for itself, or mistakenly issue more paper than it had coins in backing. The fact that paper money gained widespread adoption in spite of the shortcomings is a testament to the importance of convenience, and the risks users are willing to take to have it.

Along with ease of payments, the shift to paper money included other benefits. Thanks to their growing deposits of coins, banks were in an easier position to lend. Credit plays an important role in the economic growth of a society, so long as those who provide it do so responsibly. The history of money and credit are deeply intertwined. If we were to add a fourth function to money, it would be *facilitator of lending and borrowing*, something people have been doing with money as long as it has existed. Indeed, the alternative theory on the origins of money, the one that argues money rose not to solve the problems of barter but to make it easier to settle or transfer favors, is referred to as the *credit theory* of money. For as long as money has been a thing, those who have it have wanted to lend it to earn interest and those who don't have it have been willing to pay that interest to gain access to more of it.

Lending involves its own complicated trust frameworks, as we'll see later. For now, it's important to know that the general desire for credit creation on the part of both lenders and borrowers has had an important impact on the evolution and standardization of money. In the days of metal-backed paper money, banks that stored client coins were natural lenders. Most of the coins in their possession just sat there, so it wasn't that much of a stretch for them to lend some out from time to time. The interest they earned offset the cost of storage, and some of it was passed on to depositors to encourage them to keep *saving* at the bank.

The easiest way for a bank to lend coins was by issuing additional paper claims against the same bunch. Depositors were not directly impacted, because in their mind, each note was backed by a bag of coins sitting under the counter. It just so happened that some bags were simultaneously backing multiple notes. So long as all the depositors did not attempt to reclaim their coins at once, nobody had to be the wiser. Borrowers got to borrow, depositors (inadvertently) got to lend, and bankers got to profit. As an interesting side effect, the supply of money magically grew.

Here we must pause for a moment to explore the peculiar relationship between money and credit, along with their combined impact on money supply, or the total amount of money in circulation. This strange voodoo might be the most confusing monetary phenomenon of all, but understanding it is paramount for appreciating the design of our financial system. If we lived in a primitive economy with no banks or credit, then the money supply could easily be calculated by adding up all the physical units of a currency in circulation. But lending and borrowing complicate this calculation, particularly when an intermediary like a bank is involved.

If you deposit one hundred coins with a bank in exchange for a receipt that lets you reclaim them later, you still consider yourself the owner of that money, it's just that someone else is holding it for you. But what if the bank takes all your coins and lends them to someone else? Now they also possess that money—one set of coins, but two owners. Technically speaking, the borrower owns the money, and you own a promise from a bank, an IOU. But that's not how you (or any other depositor) think of it. You don't say to yourself "I used to have a hundred coins, but now I just have a promise." You think that you have a hundred coins in a savings account and live your life accordingly. Meanwhile, the borrower is out spending your coins. The rest of the economy doesn't know about any of this funky alchemy, so it treats you and the borrower as being more or less equal. You use the existence of your savings to court a spouse, and the borrower uses the funds to buy a house. But the money supply goes up, as the same coins are effectively counted twice. If taken too far, this process can lead to inflation.

Some people blame banks for this apparent sleight of hand, but the same thing would have happened had you loaned out the money directly. As we'll see later, banks simply make the process more efficient, allowing it to scale. The real culprit as far as supply is concerned is the mercurial nature of money, and our all-too-human tendency to conflate money, value, and wealth. Having a savings account is not the same as possessing cash, and money that is borrowed is different from money that is earned.

Nevertheless, people like to borrow and lend, and doing so increases the money supply. That's fine most of the time because money is a mass delusion anyway. The physical forms of it are just placeholders for the economic value that the members of a society are willing to provide for each other. That's why both the supply and purchasing power of a currency have a shifty quality to them. Economists today try to add some nuance to the measurement of supply by differentiating between *base money*, the original amount issued by an authority, and *total money*, which includes amounts loaned and borrowed. The latter is usually several orders of magnitude higher than the former.

Which brings us back to the business of banking, an important part of the economy, whether critics like them or not. The fact that, like money, banks rose independently in every part of the world is a testament to their importance. But their growth during the Middle Ages, along with the mainstream adoption of their notes as the prevalent form of money, created its own inconveniences and inefficiencies, leading to the next major evolution of money.

Enter the Central Bank

The proliferation of privately issued paper money created the need for a new type of standardization. The more banknotes gained traction in an economy, the harder it was to keep track of which receipts were backed by which coins held by which bank. This problem was particularly acute in regions where neighboring cities each had their own coins, banks, and paper money. The multitudes of money and institutions made it more cumbersome to verify authenticity and easier to pass counterfeits. Like the metal money that came before it, paper money was in dire need of standardization. Since most governments already maintained a monopoly on coin issuance, and the original point of paper money was to create a more convenient way to transfer ownership of metal, it made sense for the same governments that issued the coins to also issue the paper. Doing so required a central bank.

Central banks first appeared in the sixteenth and seventeenth centuries in Europe. They came in different types and served a variety of different though adjacent functions. The earliest central banks were private institutions, but were often granted a government charter. Some focused on the standardization of money across a region while others focused more on improving how commercial banks interacted with each other, or how the government borrowed money. Central banking came relatively late to the United States, resulting in a more fragmented banking system and a confusing mishmash of paper money as represented by different banknotes that dominated different regions. One explanation for the emergence of *dixie* as a nickname for the South is the popularity of a $10 note issued by a commercial bank based in the French Quarter of New Orleans in antebellum times (*dix* is French for ten).[7]

Regardless of their structure, central banks played a pivotal role in advancing the dual desires for convenience in payments with paper, but preservation of trust with metal. Paper is easier to carry around and pay in large denominations, but precious metals are more scarce. One way to combine those functions is to have the central bank store the metal and issue paper against it. Due to its affiliation with the government, the central bank can help assert the ubiquity of a single currency within an economy while preserving trust—not to mention the resulting right to seigniorage. In times of crisis, the central bank can even lend some of its massive metal stores directly to the government, secure in the knowledge that it's unlikely for all the holders of its banknotes to try to redeem them simultaneously.

Modern defenders of this structure for money, some version of which dominated from the Renaissance era until not that long ago, look back on it with fondness. They consider paper money backed by metal—often referred to as a *metal standard* or *hard money*—as the right balance between trust and convenience. But their nostalgia is a little revisionist. Like the private bankers who issued the first banknotes, central banks did not back *all* their paper money with metal. Some of it was backed by government debt, turning every holder of the currency into a (unwitting) lender to a monarch. Besides, just because paper money is supposed to be backed by gold or silver doesn't mean that the issuer of a currency can't resort to the usual shenanigans and succumb to the curse.

No ruler in their right mind would surrender the opportunity to generate profit by diluting their own money, and central banking as originally structured offered its own clever mechanism for doing so. Instead of having to dilute the precious-metal content of their coins, rulers could now simply change the redeemability of their paper. A simple decree that banknotes that used to be redeemable for ten ounces of silver are now only redeemable for nine is all it would take to effectively depreciate the precious-metal backing of a currency by 10 percent. Redemption could even be suspended outright during a crisis to devalue the currency even further. All the benefits of metal dilution without the burden of having to retool the mint.

One of the more fascinating consequences of the drive for convenience, one that accounts for so much of the evolution of money, is the periodic surrender of trust. As a rule, money that is easy to use is also easy to devalue, usually because of centralization of issuance. Intentional dilution of metal money was not possible in biblical times, because everyone was vigilant of the actual metal content of every lump. Coinage reduced the threat of some merchants being cheated by their customers but opened the door to all merchants being cheated by their ruler. Paper money made seigniorage even easier thanks to the possibility of variable redemption. The more widely accepted a form of paper money becomes, the greater the temptation for the issuer to reduce the amount of metal backing it. No wonder then that most of the paper money in existence today is backed by no metal at all.

Trust that for millennia was derived from a durable, portable, divisible, interchangeable, and scarce metal now comes from nothing more than a promise. An American $1 bill that used to have language on its redeemability for silver (a feature preserved until 1968) now says "Federal Reserve Note."[8] The technical name for this kind of money is *fiat money*, a nod to the source of its value, and a notable distinction from the metal-backed *representative money* that predated it. The word *fiat* in English is defined as "a formal authorization or proposition" and is derived from the Latin for "let it be done." The fact that such self-referential currencies make up the backbone of global commerce today is further evidence that the value of their predecessors was really more about the myth than the metal.

DIFFERENT TYPES OF MONEY

METAL MONEY	REPRESENTATIVE MONEY	FIAT MONEY
LUMPS OR COINS MADE FROM METAL	PAPER RECEIPTS OR ACCOUNTING ENTRIES BACKED BY METAL MONEY	PAPER RECEIPTS OR ACCOUNTING ENTRIES BACKED BY A PROMISE

The transition from representative money to the fiat variety took over a century to play out, had many fits and starts, and unfolded unevenly in different jurisdictions. One common theme everywhere was the volatility of the money supply in currencies tied directly to precious metals. Money that is backed by gold or silver can only have two sources of new supply: the introduction of additional metal reserves, which is rare, and credit creation, which is tied to the business cycle—in both directions. We've already seen how credit creation magically increases the money supply. The opposite is also true. Credit destruction, like the kind that happens during an economic downturn, reduces the money supply. The global migration to fiat currency was driven in part by the realization that an overly cyclical money supply can whipsaw the economy, as was the case for some of the worse economic downturns of the nineteenth and early twentieth centuries.

Money supply is an important variable when it comes to economic growth. Societies need to source new supply as their populations and economies grow—lest future generations not have access to any money at all. In a balanced economy, the money supply grows in line with economic need, not too slow to hamper commerce, but not too fast to cause inflation.

During the growth phase of a business cycle, this problem more or less solves itself. Optimism for continued economic expansion creates greater demand for credit from borrowers while also enabling a loosening of standards from lenders, creating a virtuous cycle of loans taken out, interest paid, and economic value created. The overall money supply grows alongside economic output, as currency earned in one business venture is invested into another. Banks play an important role in this process, as their willingness to create new money by lending out deposits is a reliable source of credit. Savers understand that a portion of their deposits is now being lent out and accept the arrangement, because they earn interest, and are confident that most loans get repaid during an expansion.

But the older an expansion gets, the greater the risk of a boom turning into a bubble. Emboldened borrowers chase riskier ventures, while eager bankers lower their lending standards or lend out a greater portion of their deposits. Savers, who by now have grown complacent after years of steady income, look the other way. The money supply grows and grows, fueling a virtuous cycle of wealth creation, until a tipping point is reached.

All good things must come to an end, and nothing ends quite like an economic boom. As greed turns into fear, often on a dime, the cycle reverses. Borrowers who have been investing in unproductive ventures start to default on their loans. Banks facing losses tighten credit requirements, forcing other types of economic activity into decline, and creating shortfalls for even more borrowers. Asset prices fall, putting pressure on the debt associated with them, leading to even greater depreciation and default. News of slowing economic activity (or, as was famously the case on Black Tuesday in 1929, a crashing stock market) leads to panic. The next blow arrives when savers, fearful about the safety of their deposits, seek to withdraw their money from the bank at the same time. The final crescendo is the ugly specter of a bank run, as panicked savers desperately line up to reclaim money that is no longer there.

The rest of the story is a familiar tale of several of the industrial era's worst recessions, up to and including the Great Depression of the 1930s. Economists today see much of what went wrong then through the lens of monetary history. As banks that were unable to meet all of their withdrawal requests began to fall like dominos, the overall supply of money collapsed, leading to significant declines in both wages and asset prices. Strict adherence to a metal standard meant that central banks could do little more than stand by and watch. When a currency is directly tied to a metal, there is not much a government can do to alleviate the rapidly declining supply of money. The scarcity of metal that is often thought of as a benefit during the good times turns into a liability during the bad.

A money purist may argue that this is not a problem. The job of the central bank is to preserve trust in money, not its overall supply, or the banking system that amplifies it. Speculators who borrowed too much and savers who risked too much get what they deserve, and there is no reason why bad banks shouldn't be allowed to fail like companies in any other industry. The resulting economic decline may even be a reward for those who didn't get sucked into the mania, as they can buy assets and hire workers on the cheap.

As valid as this argument may be to some, it represents a rather limited (not to mention cold) worldview, particularly in the face of a crippling downturn like the Great Depression. Economics doesn't exist independent of the political sphere, and politicians often win or lose elections based on economic outcomes. Being in charge of economic policy, many used the Great Depression as an excuse to empower their central banks to try to smooth out the business cycle, mostly by controlling the money supply.

To fulfill that mandate, central banks slowly abandoned their strict adherence to a metal standard. Doing so enabled them to become so-called "lenders of last resort," a complicated interaction with commercial banks that allowed the central bank to slow the rate of credit contraction (and resulting drop in money supply) during a crisis. To understand the process, and its impact on the evolution of money, we need to understand a bit more about the business of banking.

A Rising Tide Lifts All Ships, Most of the Time

One of the major functions of a commercial bank—beyond playing intermediary between borrower and saver—is to facilitate a naturally occurring mismatch in time frames. Savers, such as a consumer saving for a rainy day, want immediate access to their money should they need it. Borrowers, on the other hand, such as a farmer taking out a mortgage, prefer to borrow for the long term. Commercial banks try to cater to both sides. A successful banker knows how to balance the proper mix of *demand deposits* and *loan maturities* to give everyone what they want, usually by juggling a complicated mix of deposit types (checking, savings, certificate of deposits) and loans (lines of credit, business loans, mortgages) so there's always enough cash on hand to pay out anyone making a withdrawal, but not too much to reduce the bank's income.

But the best laid plans of bankers and men often go awry, particularly during a crisis. Banks don't fail just because too many savers try to withdraw their money at once. They also fail because they can't demand that all their borrowers pay off their loans on short notice. This means that during a crisis even a responsible bank whose borrowers are *eventually* good for the money can fail.

If an economy follows a metal standard, there is not much that the central bank can do about this problem. There is only so much gold in its vault, and all the paper money that it backs has already been issued. But if the central bank is authorized to create additional money out of thin air, then it can step in and give a troubled commercial bank an emergency loan. The extra cash is used to meet withdrawals and a crisis is averted. This is not a handout, however, as the commercial bank usually must pledge some kind of asset, like quality mortgages given to trustworthy borrowers, as collateral.

This is the concept of the central bank as "lender of last resort," and is as much about psychology and confidence in the banking system as it is about loans and collateral. Savers who understand that their bank has protection during a crisis are less likely to withdraw their money in the first place, reducing the risk of bank runs. To prevent commercial banks from abusing this privilege, the central bank can charge a punitive interest rate and demand the highest quality collateral.

Better yet, it can try to prevent a banking crisis from starting in the first place by requiring every commercial bank in its jurisdiction to always keep some of its cash on reserve with the central bank. Doing so prevents private banks from lending out all their deposits. Since the central bank is now heavily involved in how commercial banks behave, it can also control the interest rates at which they borrow and lend, introducing yet another tool for managing the business cycle. And since the central bank is effectively responsible for the banking system, then it might as well be given the power to regulate all commercial banks. Most of these actions are still technically possible under a metal standard, but constrained. Trust derived from the overall amount of metal in the vaults of both commercial and central banks comes at the expense of flexibility. Promises and decrees are more malleable.

There are a few other benefits to untethering money from precious-metal backing—other than the obvious one of easier seigniorage and control over the business cycle. Part of the challenge of managing a currency is that it must coexist alongside different currencies issued in neighboring countries. Nations that tie their currencies directly to gold are effectively also tying them to each other. For reasons not worth getting into at this point, doing so introduces other forms of rigidity on an economy, and can accelerate crises of confidence that travel across borders.

It's for Your Own Good, I Promise

As confusing as these machinations may sound, they have been discussed and debated by bankers, economists, and politicians for a long time, and the wisdom of our current monetary system has broad support among them. The desire to exert greater control over an economy, and the growing belief that a new class of technocrats can do so effectively, has brought us to the current state of money backed by a promise. That's the headline explanation, anyway. The ease with which seigniorage can now be exercised is also a factor, as the human temptation to free ride is ever present, even for people with a PhD. Although every national currency has taken its own unique path to arrive at this point, most of the world's important ones have arrived, nevertheless. Some central banks still keep deposits of gold (along with those of other fiat currencies) to instill confidence, but it's a far cry from any kind of true backing.

The capacity for central banks to create new money out of thin air represents a radical alteration of the trust framework surrounding a currency. Unlike the Roman emperors who tried to conceal their debasement, central banks today do so transparently, going as far as to announce their plans for monetary expansion in press conferences. They give their actions fancy names like *open-market operations* and *quantitative easing,* and often claim that any radical expansion of the money supply is temporary, but the aim is the same cashing in on user trust that has been practiced for millennia. Ironically, an activity that at certain points in history was thought of as a crime against society, punishable by upheaval and revolution, is now celebrated as being the cure for a growing list of society's problems. The mythology of money, which used to mostly change as a consequence of economic activity, is increasingly manipulated to achieve political outcomes, the proverbial monetary tail wagging the economic dog.

Thus money—and its value—is constantly being tweaked by committee members appointed by politicians. Central banks in most countries are designed to be independent, but the politicians reserve the right to fire the bankers, and nobody wants to upset their boss. To look good, the central bankers have evolved the tools of money manipulation, and now offer to use them to manage everything from a pandemic to climate change. Although their work is quantitative in nature, and the contemporary central banker resembles more a mathematician than a master of the mint, the primary asset in their hands remains our trust. Trust in the stability of money, but also consistent economic growth.

Defenders of this setup argue that the two functions go hand in hand, and that the most trustworthy kind of money is the kind that comes with a healthy economy and a stable banking system. They point to the radical interventions of most central banks in the aftermath of the Great Financial Crisis or the outset of the COVID-19 pandemic as proof. Although paid for almost entirely with record amounts of newly printed money, the mishmash of monetary programs aimed at banks, businesses, and the financial markets during the pandemic are argued to have forestalled a severe global depression. There is little disagreement in political circles over this accomplishment—a fact that in and of itself should perhaps be cause for concern.

Also of note is the way in which the design of central banking intersects with the rest of the government. When central banks like the Federal

Reserve or the Bank of England print money, they mostly use the extra cash to acquire government bonds. Doing so is said to be the safest way of injecting stimulus into the economy but has the added benefit of allowing the government to borrow more than it could otherwise. Whether this is a feature or a bug is also in the eye of the beholder and depends on how governments spend the borrowed money. As with excess printing, excess borrowing is a spigot that's hard to turn off once fully opened.

Viewed through a historical lens, the evolution of central banking requires a tremendous amount of trust and is therefore vulnerable to new free-rider problems. Most central banks used to claim a primary mandate of maintaining price stability—keeping trust in money high and, as a direct result, inflation low. This was particularly true at the turn of the millennium when memories of the inflationary spikes of the 1960s and 1970s, caused in part by the gradual abandonment of any metal standard, were still fresh. But several decades of historically low inflation, combined with financial crises of increasing severity, has led to a form of mission creep.

Whereas central bankers used to worry about prices rising too fast, they now increasingly obsess about prices falling too hard, especially when it comes to things like investible assets. Indeed, one way to understand most of the central banking interventions of the past few decades is to first consult a chart of the S&P 500. Making sure that asset prices don't fall too much is said to prevent catastrophic *deflation*, like the kind that showed up after the Great Depression. But it also has the unintended consequence of raising wealth disparity. Most of the world's assets, including stocks and real estate, are owned by a minority of people. While it's probably true that preventing their values from falling has secondary benefits for all of society, it's definitely true that doing so benefits the people who own them, aka the rich.

Then there is the open question of whether central banks actually know what they are doing. Having good intent is one thing but doing good is another. Since money is only a myth, and impacted by countless intersecting trust frameworks, cause and effect are often not clear, and every action has unintended consequences. Most of that uncertainty is said to be alleviated by complex economic modeling, but numbers in a spreadsheet seldom capture the complexity of human interaction.

Depending on who you ask, government and central bank actions have been either a tragic violation of the trust framework inherent in today's promise-backed fiat money, or a heroic assumption of power. Which side ends up being proven correct is up in the air because, when it comes to the history of money, a few decades is not nearly long enough to conclude anything.

The only certain conclusion that we can make so far is that the current age of central bank activism has had at least one significant unintended consequence: the invention, evolution, and adoption of a new kind of money.

Money as Data

An alternative way of understanding money is to think of it as information. All that really happens when you pay someone a dollar is that the universe now understands you to be a dollar poorer and them a dollar richer. The absolute value of that money, like the final score of a basketball game, is arbitrary. What matters is that there is an accurate way to keep score among economic actors. The world's money is a massive data store of everchanging purchasing power.

With physical money such as coins and bills, the information is implicit, and represented by physical possession. Only the owners of this *token money* know how much they have, and only during a transaction does anyone else need to be the wiser. Token money is a *bearer instrument*, meaning ownership is determined by possession. Payments made with token money are simple, anonymous, and free as they don't require an intermediary. They are also final as soon as the money changes hands.

But token money has drawbacks. It's inconvenient for large transactions, can be easily stolen, and doesn't work from afar. These limitations give rise to the notion of *ledger money,* which is money recorded on a financial register. Ledger money is the most convenient type of money because it fully embraces the informational function. If all that really matters is keeping score, then why not move all money to a scorebook? Users don't have to worry about carrying around coins or bills that deteriorate over time and that can be lost or stolen. With a ledger, you can have a balance inscribed next to your name. When you pay someone, your balance is reduced and their balance is increased. The purchasing power stored by ledger money is explicit and clear for all to see.

Given the historical march toward ever more convenient types of money, it should come as no surprise that the vast majority of money in existence today is ledger money. Of all of the dollars in existence, only a fraction exists in physical form. The rest live as ledger entries inside the books of financial entities such as banks. Our modern economy and its many conveniences would not be possible without ledger money. Imagine if every Uber ride involved a physical payment, or if every stock trade required the buyer to mail cash to the seller.

Ledger money deployed at scale can be traced back to at least the time of the Medicis in Europe, and has existed in smaller form for millennia. Its form has been upgraded steadily over the centuries with improved accounting methods and technological advancements. It took a major leap forward fifty years ago when financial institutions switched from physical books to mainframe computers. Electronic databases are great for the informational purposes of money, for there is nothing more durable, portable, divisible, or interchangeable than bits of data. The only catch is that someone needs to maintain all the data.

These advancements in convenience require yet another trade-off in trust. For ledger money to function, powerful intermediaries are needed to keep track of who owns what. Money is made more portable, but transactions are no longer anonymous or irreversible the way they are with token money. Your bank must know who you are to deduct your account and can reverse any transaction—two drawbacks identified by Satoshi

Nakamoto in the Bitcoin white paper. More pressing, however, is that electronic ledger money is terrible when it comes to the most important characteristic of money: scarcity. There is nothing *less* scarce in the universe than bits of data—not even leaves on trees.

That most of the world's money exists on electronic ledgers, and electronic ledgers are so easy to manipulate, should give everyone pause. A simple typo by a bank teller can wipe out your life savings. The collapse of that bank can destroy an entire town, and the failure of one systemically important bank, either due to outright fraud or mundane mismanagement, could threaten the entire global economy. A society that relies on token money is relatively immune to catastrophic failures as there is virtually no event that could impact a substantial portion of coins in circulation instantaneously. A society that relies on ledger money, on the other hand, is a single corporate failure away from disaster. And so, the same factors that make electronic ledger money so convenient also make it fallible. Data that could be easily manipulated for payments on a ledger could also be permanently wiped out.

There have been several technological innovations over the centuries to manage the risks of ledger money. Ancient societies used to carve balances in stone or clay, introducing an effective, albeit clunky, type of scarcity. The double-entry bookkeeping system, an important early attempt at deploying mathematical certainty to help preserve the integrity of ledgers, was introduced during the early Renaissance. Contemporary societies also rely on stringent regulations enforced by governments, a practice that went mainstream after the cascading bank failures of the Great Depression and was tightened again after the 2008 financial crisis. Nevertheless, the skeleton of the current financial system remains fragile. As long as our primary form of money remains bits of data stored inside electronic databases maintained by central authorities then both our shared trust framework and the resulting free-rider incentives remain askance.

If, however, we evolve from proprietary ledgers to public ones, and from central authorities to decentralized consensus then our system of money becomes more resilient. Most people find blockchain, the solution proposed by Satoshi Nakamoto, confusing because they are tethered to an old way of thinking. That confusion is par for the course and was probably common during each of the many transitional periods for money. Just imagine how confused (not to mention distrusting) a merchant would be the first time a customer in the bazaar proposed to pay with a flimsy piece of paper instead of hard metal. An earlier version of the credit card, which required use of a piece of equipment called a knuckle-buster, may have been even more suspect. Yet, society has routinely made the leap to more convenient ways of doing things. Eventually, yesterday's confusing solution becomes today's status quo.

A Database for the Digital Era

Blockchain technology is best viewed through the historical lens of convenience and trust. Analog ledgers, like the kind that used to be written on paper, are useful for tracking balances of money but very inefficient. Electronic databases, like the ones inside most banks, are a lot more efficient, but not necessarily trustworthy. The ease with which entries can be changed makes them risky. Blockchains combine a mishmash of different technologies to form a different kind of electronic ledger, one that is simultaneously efficient and trustworthy.

To understand how they work, it helps to keep in mind the simple idea that a digital ledger invented for a post-internet society is structurally different from the ones erected in the early days of computing, in the same way that the word-processor application in Google Docs is radically different from a typewriter. It also helps to break a blockchain down into several components, each of which comes from a different field of study.

From the field of distributed systems, which predates blockchain by several decades, we get the notion of a distributed ledger. If one ledger is good, then two copies of the same ledger is better, and three copies are even more resilient. In fact, in a world where everyone has ample hard-drive space on their computer and is connected to the internet, everyone can keep their own copy of the ledger.

Centralized ledgers were necessary when there was no internet and only a handful of companies could afford mainframes. But now that everyone has that hardware in their home or even in their pocket, why not have everyone store the record book? Not just a record of their own activity, but a ledger of *all* activity, for every participant, forever. Access to all that data makes auditing the ledger to verify the integrity of a transaction a snap, in the same way that access to public land records provide certainty for real estate purchases. Few practices increase trust more than complete transparency, and few solutions in the world today are more transparent than a global ledger where each user has the option of keeping their own copy.

There are more than ten thousand copies of the Bitcoin ledger around the world—the so-called *nodes* of the network. There is no cap to that number, and anyone can choose to run their own node at any time, becoming yet another maintainer of the database. There are services that will help you run your own node for a small fee, and free software that will allow you to scan the history of transactions inside your node to make sure nobody is cheating. Unlike the ledger inside a bank, the failure of a single node, or even half of them, is far from catastrophic.

Each node contains a history of every single transaction that's ever happened, in order, with a provable timestamp. Cheating, fraud, and even human error are thus made difficult by the fact that every user can track the transaction history of every other user back to the beginning of time. In a traditional payment system, that task can only be done by the operator, at the expense of more fees and less control for users. On the blockchain, everyone does their own due diligence. Each time someone sends you a bitcoin, you can be certain that they own it by looking up the history of how they acquired it. Don't trust, and easily verify.

A system this transparent and public could never work if the ledger stored personally identifiable information such as names and addresses. Privacy and identity entail their own trust frameworks, as we'll see later, and it doesn't make sense to surrender in that realm if the goal is to return power to individuals. Here, blockchain proposes a solution rooted in cryptography. Instead of storing user accounts, the blockchain only stores unnamed addresses. Each address has two components: a monetary balance, and a cryptographic key that unlocks that balance. Whoever possesses the digital key to an address gets to unlock the money inside of it, akin to the physical lockers that used to be common in train stations. Once the funds are accessed, a payment can be made. As with any other financial ledger, blockchain payments are completed by debiting one address and crediting another.

There are already millions of different Bitcoin addresses, each identified by a random-looking string of characters which can be thought of as an account number. Some hold thousands of coins while others hold a tiny fraction of one. Each address is unlockable with a corresponding *private key*, a different random-looking string of characters that can be used to mathematically prove ownership of a particular address. Like a physical key that unlocks a specific lock, each blockchain address can only be unlocked by a corresponding private key. There is no reasonable limit to how many addresses a blockchain can hold, or notably, how many addresses a person can generate.

As we'll see later, the reliance on cryptographic identity has other benefits beyond privacy and decentralization, including universal access. Traditional ledgers that rely on legal identity as established with documents such as passports and driver's licenses are restrictive. They cannot be used by people who lack such documents, such as minorities and immigrants. Cryptographic identity can be stablished by anyone with a smartphone, or even a plastic card.

A distributed ledger, consisting of addresses unlocked with cryptography, is a good start to building a more trustworthy ledger, but still suffers from the fundamental problem of digital data being too easy to manipulate. Just because you and your counterparty both keep your own copies of the ledger doesn't mean that one of you won't try to fudge entries to make you seem richer than you actually are. Put differently, the problem of counterfeit money doesn't go away in a digital framework and in some respects is worsened. Physical counterfeits like fake $100 bills take resources to create and are relatively easy to spot. Digital counterfeits, on the other hand, are a manifestation of the ease of manipulating bits of data. If a ledger only tracks user balances of money, then inventing fake money is as easy as changing a single number.

Centralized ledgers, such as those that dominate the banking system today, solve this problem by making the maintainers of those ledgers liable for fraudulent behavior. Banks, credit card companies, and other financial intermediaries spend an inordinate amount of resources fighting digital counterfeits, and are, in turn, watched closely by auditors and regulators to make sure that they keep clean books. Since the whole point of the blockchain is to move away from intermediaries, an entirely different solution is needed. Here blockchain borrows from work done by two researchers decades prior, and solves the counterfeit problem by making every copy of the ledger immutable. Once a blockchain entry is made, it can never be changed or removed.

When Stuart Haber and Scott Stornetta, the two cryptographers whose work is cited several times in the Bitcoin white paper, set out to develop their innovative solution, they weren't thinking about money. They were thinking about digital documents. It was the early 1990s, and although the internet was relatively new, it already hinted at an electronic future where important documents would exist in digital form only. How, they wondered, would someone authenticate a digital document? Physical documents (just like physical money) are relatively easy to authenticate. An important contract could be torn in half the way people used to do in the Middle Ages or signed and sealed by a notary as we do today. A digital document suffers from the same lack of scarcity and ease of forgery as digital money.

Haber and Stornetta's solution came from the world of hashing, a subset of cryptography where chunks of data are fed through a mathematical function that yields a unique digital fingerprint (in the form of a random-looking string of characters). Hashing has several fascinating properties. It's easy to derive a hash from a document, but practically impossible to reverse engineer a document from its hash, in the same way that it's easy to fingerprint a person, but impossible to figure out their eye color from that fingerprint. Every document has a unique hash, just like a fingerprint, and the odds of two documents yielding the same hash are close to zero.

To understand how powerful hashing can be, it helps to look at a real-world example. If a simple document like a text file containing the phrase "hello world" is sent through a hash function, it would yield an output such as *1e75046a*. A much more complicated text file, such as one containing all 1,200 pages of *War and Peace,* would yield a similarly formatted but entirely different hash, such as *80b61a78*. Regardless of how many times you run either document through the same hash function, you will always get the same string for each one. Although the output for any document cannot be known ahead of time, the same document will always yield the same output. But the real power of hashing—and the reason why it serves as the backbone of blockchain technology—is how sensitive it is to the smallest change. Taking that same epic novel and changing just one word yields an entirely different output, one that looks nothing like its predecessor. In that regard, hashing is even more effective for authentication than taking a fingerprint.

Taking hashes of digital documents to use for authentication at a later date was only half of Haber and Stornetta's solution, and not the clever half. Fingerprints are only useful inside a trustworthy registry (like the ones kept by police departments) so our cryptographers started a company that provided such a service to anyone who wanted to have their documents hashed. Along with storing the individual fingerprint of every document sent their way for future authentication, they took the innovative step of periodically taking all existing hashes—their ever-growing list of digital fingerprints—and hashing them together, a sci-fi-like solution that resulted in one meta fingerprint that almost magically acted as a representative of every other fingerprint that came before it.

To visualize this process, think of a hash function as a blender, used to mash fruits into a smoothie. Just as bananas, kiwis, and strawberries blended together yield a uniquely tasting smoothie, a bunch of words (or MS Word documents) hashed together yield a unique fingerprint. Now, imagine that you make a different smoothie every day, but always include a little bit of yesterday's smoothie with today's ingredients. What you end up with is a concoction that—though perhaps not very palatable—could only result from every single ingredient that you ever used, in the order and quantity that you used them. Any attempt to lie about the historical list of ingredients is thwarted by a sampling of the latest, combined product, making verification easy. A roommate curious as to whether you've ever used jalapenos doesn't have to inspect all of your supermarket receipts and can instead just taste for the presence of heat.

By constantly hashing the newest documents with the digital fingerprints of the previous ones, Haber and Stornetta were able to create an immutable *chain* of every document they had ever processed. At any moment in time, their most recent hash included a tiny but mathematically provable piece of every character inside every document they had ever hashed. Any dishonest claim about a historical document by a client, like someone claiming that they had submitted a bill for $1,000 when it was only for $100, could be detected instantly by checking for its purported fingerprint in the chain—a digital inclusion of a jalapeno.

The problem of authenticating digital documents had seemingly been solved, but the process now offered for a fee by the aptly named Surety, LLC was vulnerable to its own free-rider problem. Despite their innovative technical solution, the company doing all that fingerprinting was a centralized source of risk. What if it went out of business, or worse, was bribed by a client to cheat the results—the digital equivalent of slipping in some jalapenos while nobody was looking.

A fix was found in the notion of consensus, loosely defined as an agreement formed by a group of people over a shared set of facts. There are many different ways to reach consensus, some social and others technological. Bitcoin consensus relies on both, along with a dash of economic incentives, as we'll soon see. But that wasn't an option for Surety, so it went with the next best option. It would be hard for Surety to cheat anyone, including itself, if it somehow regularly announced its most recent, combined hash—the verifiable manifestation of every document it had ever processed—to the public. So the company began publishing it in the *New York Times* classified section on a weekly basis, a practice it has continued for the past twenty-five years. Once a hash has achieved public awareness, in this case by being printed in a popular newspaper, it can no longer be taken back, so the history of digital events it contains becomes immutable.

Every copy of the Bitcoin ledger is rendered immutable using a similar process. Instead of taking digital fingerprints of documents, the Bitcoin blockchain takes digital fingerprints of transactions. Each transaction can be thought of as its own document, in the format of "this address pays some bitcoins to that address." Would-be counterfeiters are now deterred by the fact that altering their own balance inside their copy of the ledger— say by adding an extra zero—would make their most recent hash different from everyone else's, a proverbial altering of the universal smoothie that violates consensus. The name "blockchain" comes from the fact that the Bitcoin network processes transactions in batches called *blocks*. Each batch is hashed into its own block, but each block also contains the hash of the previous block, forming an immutable chain of payments.

The result is a transparent yet immutable ledger, copies of which are maintained by thousands of users all over the world. Notably, none of these characteristics have to yield a new kind of money. Most of the features tied together by Satoshi Nakamoto are as useful for tracking dollars, or even airline miles, as they are for bitcoins. The problems of an easily manipulated electronic ledger, the need for a central authority to prevent that manipulation, and the resulting free-rider issues are universal in the digital era and extend beyond money. One could even argue that at the time of its invention, blockchain was most needed by industries more seriously impacted by the lack of digital scarcity, such as music. Not surprisingly, it is now being applied to those industries as well, in ways that we'll visit later.

THE EVOLUTION OF LEDGERS

	NOTEBOOKS	MAINFRAMES	BLOCKCHAINS
COPIES	ONE	SEVERAL	INFINITE
USER IDENTIFIER	LEGAL IDENTITY	LEGAL IDENTITY	CRYPTOGRAPHIC KEY
METHOD FOR CHANGING EXISTING ENTRIES	RUBBER ERASER	DELETE BUTTON	NONE

Money Is Consensus

The most important, and still biggest application of the blockchain solution remains the invention of a new kind of money: the cryptocurrency. Some Bitcoin enthusiasts argue that doing so was Nakamoto's intention all along, but a careful read of the original document lets us argue otherwise. Nakamoto probably didn't set out to invent a new currency. The inventor probably set out to create a new kind of online network and ended up having to invent a new currency to enable the solution's third, and perhaps most impressive, component: the need to constantly achieve consensus.

A distributed and immutable ledger of every transaction that's ever happened is fine for locking down the history of past transactions but doesn't do much to help resolve the ones that are about to happen. Preserving history once it has been written is easy. It's the writing part that's hard. The blockchain might help you—a node operator—verify that the money someone is sending you actually belongs to them, but how do you know that they aren't simultaneously sending the same money to someone else? Such sleight of hand, which is practically impossible with physical money, is as easy as "copy and paste" with a digital currency. The fraud would eventually be exposed, but not before the perpetrator makes off with whatever good or service you just sold them. Centralized digital payment solutions such as PayPal solve this double-spend problem by monitoring every transaction and undoing the bad ones, usually at their expense. The problem is one of trust, and before Bitcoin, the only viable solution was to surrender agency to a higher power. Preventing double-spends is one reason why payment platforms tend to be centralized. Peer-to-peer electronic cash has no such option.

Nakamoto's solution is as crazy as it is ingenious: new transactions are to be validated by volunteers. These specialized nodes referred to as *miners* constantly collect batches of proposed transactions, validate them to make sure that everyone owns the money they are sending and that no one is double-spending, then broadcast the results to all other nodes. Since the network is decentralized, the miners are anonymous for the simple reason that verifying identity requires a central authority.

Having anonymous volunteers perform the most important task of validating transactions is almost begging them to break the system, particularly on the internet. To prevent miners from running wild and validating their own or other bogus transactions, the Bitcoin network requires them to solve an arbitrary math puzzle first. The puzzle is constantly updated and the first miner to solve the latest version wins the right to process the latest batch of transactions. Solving the puzzle requires that each miner expend resources, primarily in the form of electricity. The winner broadcasts its solution to the puzzle, along with the transactions it has validated, to the rest of the network. If all the other participants confirm that they've done an honest job—a task made easy by the presence of hashes—then that miner is rewarded with a fresh batch of bitcoins created out of thin air, and the network is said to have reached consensus on the latest batch of transactions. Bitcoin miners earn their name from the work they do to unearth new coins.

If there is one idea that captures the ingenuity of the Bitcoin solution, it's this: the security of the network—its trust framework—is directly tied to the value of its coins. There are countless ways to attack the Bitcoin network, and some could be highly profitable, but using the same resources to perform honest work is even more profitable. By requiring miners to spend fiat currency upfront (to pay the electric bill) then rewarding them in bitcoins, Nakamoto invented a positive feedback loop that perpetuates trust. A miner can cheat but doing so hurts the perceived reliability of the network, which in turn drives down the value of the coins that the miner will be paid. In other words, dollars spent to deceive the network will only yield bitcoins diminishing in dollar value. That doesn't mean that it's not profitable for a miner to launch such an attack, but it does mean that it would be *more* profitable for a different miner to forestall that attack, by committing even more resources than the thief to solving the puzzle. This remarkable design feature is often lost on those who complain about the environmental impact of mining. High energy consumption is a feature and not a bug, one that forces those who secure the network to have skin in the game. Decentralized blockchain solutions use incentives in lieu of a central authority to net out honest behavior. The most incentivized miner is the most honest one, in part because the nodes of the network will reject any blocks proposed by dishonest ones, denying them the right to earn new coins.

Every type of currency, as we've seen, derives value from trust—first and foremost in the scarcity of that currency. When that trust is violated, as was done by the Roman emperors of antiquity or Venezuelan dictators of today, the value of the currency plummets. Metal coins derived scarcity from precious metals. Paper money inherited the scarcity of the metal it was originally redeemable for, but slowly evolved to achieve trust from promises. Fiat money, as it increasingly exists on the electronic ledgers of central and commercial banks, inherits that precarious trust. Bitcoin achieves trust from an algorithm.

Bitcoin miners have two sources of income: a small fee users pay for every transaction, and fresh coins minted out of thin air by the network for every new block. The value of the new coins, the so-called block reward, currently dwarfs the value of the transaction fee, making it the main source of miner income. This algorithmic approach to new coin creation is somewhat distinct from the seigniorage practiced by centralized issuers of money, because it takes work. Indeed, Bitcoin's overall process for validating transactions is known as *proof of work*, because miners must prove that they've solved the puzzle before their contribution is accepted. The first and most important consequence of this design is a secure network. In over a decade of operation, the Bitcoin blockchain has not processed a single double-spend.

A secondary, yet also crucial consequence is the notion of an algorithmically controlled money supply. All of the rules of the Bitcoin blockchain are coded into the software used to run nodes or mine transactions, referred to as the *protocol*. Among those rules are the frequency with which new blocks are created, and the number of new coins generated for each one to pay the winning miner. Since those coins are issued by the network, they can be thought of as an increase to base money, akin to new silver coins issued by a Roman mint. But unlike the mint, the Bitcoin network is decentralized, meaning no single user can alter the formula. As a result, and unlike any other currency in history, Bitcoin inflation is fixed and predictable.

Perhaps intentionally, or possibly by accident, Satoshi Nakamoto's quest to eliminate the small free-rider problem of financial intermediaries abusing their clients also solves the larger free-rider problem of the issuers of currency abusing everyone. Regardless of what you think of any other kind of money, the fact remains that since the standardization of coinage thousands of years ago, the creation of new supply has been placed in the hands of a select few, a power as likely to corrupt as any other. Not the hard corruption portrayed in the movies, where cigar-chomping caricatures get together in back rooms to plan a plunder, but the soft kind, a creeping combination of ignorance and arrogance bound to be accelerated by outside events like wars and recessions. The curse of history eventually catches up with every trust framework, but the issuers of currency are uniquely vulnerable to it, as proven by the simple fact that none of the currencies of antiquity are still with us today.

The advent of fiat currency, and the untethering of money from any natural scarcity, only increases the risk of something going wrong, especially now that the occasional spasm of money printing by central banks is viewed as a virtue. How effectively central banks wield that power remains to be seen, but history does not look favorably upon those who violate trust in the scarcity of money, regardless of their intent.

Cryptocurrencies such as Bitcoin present a radically different trust framework. That doesn't mean that this new type of money is bound to gain global adoption, and the first decade of its relatively young history has shown limited traction in that regard. But it does mean that there is now an alternative approach to money. The major leap forward in convenience represented by digitization no longer has to suffer from a major drop in trust. Crypto users can have their scarcity and transact electronically too.

Scarcity is an important milestone in the history of money, but it does not guarantee the success of either Bitcoin or any of the cryptocurrencies that have come after it. Lots of things have been scarce over time, yet the vast majority never became adopted as money. Switching money is costly, so societies don't do it often. More importantly, myths take a long time to form. They usually do so in unpredictable fashion and are identified only after the fact.

While it is historically unlikely for Bitcoin to become widely adopted, the currency has a few things going for it as far as its mythology is concerned. One is the fact that Satoshi Nakamoto has managed to remain anonymous, despite the attention-grabbing success of their creation.

Unlike the coins of the network Nakamoto invented, there is no scarcity of theories of who actually invented Bitcoin and blockchain. None have panned out thus far.

Not knowing Nakamoto's true identity is made even more remarkable by the fact that there are billions of dollars on the line, not just in terms of branding and fame, but also in terms of cold hard bitcoins. The creator is believed to have done a lot of mining when the network was first launched, but virtually none of the bitcoins earned in the process have moved in the decade since, despite the significant rise in their value. The blockchain domain is all about financial incentives, and there are few activities more incentivized than for the inventor of Bitcoin to step in front of the curtain, if for no other reason than to cash in some coins. The fact that it hasn't happened is the stuff of mythology. Every widely adopted belief requires a powerful origins myth, and Bitcoin has a good one.

Then there is the confusing nature of the solution itself. Blockchain technology is not the natural evolution of any one idea, at least not in the way that smartphones were a natural evolution of mobile phones. It's an evolution of several disparate fields mashed into something unique. It was born out of a marriage of technological convenience, but has proven highly effective at its original task, and is now being applied to other activities. That kind of lineage (not to mention ambition) is also the stuff of mythology.

Cryptocoins cause a lot of controversy, which feeds their mythology. An endless stream of prominent intellectuals, economists, politicians, and CEOs have gone out of their way to denounce cryptocurrencies in general and Bitcoin in particular. Their preferred critique, that Bitcoin can't be money, is telling. There are lots of scarce and valuable objects that could fulfill the basic functions of money—from rubies to baseball cards—but neither Warren Buffet nor Nouriel Roubini have opined on those. The intensity of their contempt for Bitcoin betrays fear. Grumpy old men saying that "Bitcoin is not money" sounds a lot like parents who used to exclaim that "rapping is not music" (while forgetting that *their* parents once said the same thing about rock and roll). Yesterday's taboo has a funny way of becoming tomorrow's reality. The louder the criticism, the greater the signal that the thing being critiqued matters.

Above all, there is the decentralized nature of the blockchain solution. The most important things in life, the ones that are the hardest to explain because they are so ingrained in our collective psyche, are all decentralized. That the English language, the Buddhist religion, or the practice of politeness continue to perpetuate themselves despite a lack of any authority proves that when it comes to building trust and bringing people together, decentralized solutions have a lot of staying power. The presence of any central authority—although in some ways helpful—ultimately leads to systematic decline, for the allure of the free-rider temptation is too strong to resist indefinitely. Power corrupts, and centralized power corrupts absolutely.

Back under the Hood

Most of the attention paid to blockchain technology, positive or negative, goes to its outputs, which include Bitcoin, a growing roster of other cryptocurrencies, and newer applications such as digital art. But more interesting for our purposes are the inputs, the unique blend of features borrowed from the worlds of distributed systems, cryptography, and game theory that yield a new kind of online network. The consequences for this new approach to connecting people are profound. The Bitcoin network is technically a payment system but comparing it to other payment systems such as PayPal (a necessary exercise that we'll undertake) doesn't do it justice. A more worthy comparison of how blockchain networks can be used to organize society would be with the likes of Instagram and Uber.

Digital platforms are an important part of our lives. They provide us with information, connect us to our friends, facilitate our professions, and increasingly dictate economic outcomes. Like blockchain, they can be broken into inputs and outputs: what people experience when they use these services versus what happens under the hood. As varied as the out-puts of platforms such as eBay, Twitter, and Spotify might be to their users and customers, they are all built on a similar—and significantly older—architecture, one that predates the internet. This design choice has an important impact on how they work (and increasingly, don't).

So let us table the topic of money and currency for a while. Before we can understand the role that the Bitcoin currency might play in the economy, we need to better appreciate how the design of the Bitcoin plat-form might eventually seep into other applications, starting with every other digital platform on the planet. Hyperbolic as that may sound, it is important to remember that trust is everything, and few developments alter society more than the arrival of a new framework.

2
PLATFORMS

platform *noun*
an economic utility of the people and by the people, but not for the people.
Not yet anyway.

Trust is invaluable. Or at least, it used to be. The existence of a decentralized platform for value transfers—one that uses financial incentives to drive honest behavior—now enables us to put a price on trust. In the case of the Bitcoin platform, it currently stands at hundreds of billions of dollars, calculated by adding up the dollar price of all bitcoins in circulation—its market cap.

The price of Bitcoin has always been volatile, and is driven by multiple factors. But one input matters more than any other: the perceived security of the underlying platform, for security is synonymous with trust in a decentralized setting. Since there is no *Bitcoin Inc.* to hold liable if the network is breached, and no hope of a government bailout should the whole thing come undone, the platform must stand alone. Bitcoin, like every other myth that withstands the test of time, abides by circular logic. Its platform is only secure so long as miners are willing to expend resources to acquire its coins, but the coins are only worth acquiring if the platform remains secure. The blockchain secures the past while financial incentives drive the future. A decentralized platform is a perpetual motion machine of trust, with the coin supplying the magic needed to keep it going.

When Satoshi Nakamoto devised the clever solution of inventing a free-floating currency to incentivize honest behavior, he made a Faustian bargain with the ever-dueling forces of supply and demand. The Bitcoin platform would be secured by the value of the coin, but that value would fluctuate, in the way that all assets do. To give the coin a fighting chance, Nakamoto limited supply with an algorithmic inflation schedule, an economic decision that would greatly impact adoption.

Bitcoin mining is different from other kinds of mining because the amount of effort has no bearing on production. Unlike a physical asset such as gold, where spikes in price lead to greater supply being brought to market, and vice versa, the price of bitcoin has no bearing on production. Bitcoin miners have no power over how many coins are unearthed at any given moment in time. Miners can commit more resources to solving the puzzle—and many regularly do to gain an edge over their competition—but doing so has no bearing on new coin creation. The platform is designed to detect this kind of behavior and, should the aggregate amount of mining activity tick up, will adjust by making the puzzle harder to solve, akin to gold that magically moves further underground if someone brings a bigger bulldozer. While the sum total of resources committed to Bitcoin mining has increased drastically over the years, the rate of new coin creation has instead declined due to pre-programmed halvings of the miner reward every four years. One of the cleverer consequences of Nakamoto's proof-of-work consensus mechanism is that more mining leads to greater security, but not more supply.

Demand is an entirely different animal. The main driver of Bitcoin volatility over time has been speculation, and that speculation is mostly driven by changing perceptions of both trust in the network and the perceived utility of the coin. Those swings, which at times have been vertigo inducing, have continued to settle at higher prices than the previous cycle, allowing us to make two conclusions: (1) trust has steadily grown in this decentralized platform for value transfers; and (2) that trust has steadily diminished in almost everything else on the internet, including the centralized platforms that still power—and in the case of individual users, often disempower—everything else.

Most people who are passionate about the future of Bitcoin are passionate about the coin. Far more important, as far as trust is concerned, is the future of the platform.

A Brief History of Digital

It's not immediately obvious why a word once used to describe a raised surface on top of which passengers would wait for a train would come to describe the digital networks that increasingly dominate our lives. One clue comes from the other meaning of the word *platform*: the official position of a leading figure or group. This definition presumably rose out of the tendency by those who have something important to say to stand on a raised surface to reach a larger audience.

Usage in the digital domain probably came from the fact that the most successful online platforms are two-sided, providing both the speakers and the audience. What draws us to platforms like Twitter and Instagram is not our affinity for the companies that operate them but rather the access they provide to other people, be they family members or influencers.

The same dueling forces that explain the evolution and undulation of money also drive the history of digital platforms, starting with the very first one: the internet itself. The conveniences provided by that meta-platform initially created a vacuum of trust, opening the door to large and centralized operators able to fill it. The only trade-off? The mother of all free-rider problems.

It's no coincidence that many of the most successful companies today are the operators of digital platforms, as the online economy lends itself easily to two-sided economic interaction. However, as far as business models are concerned, the Googles and Facebooks of the world are a historical aberration. Successful companies used to sell their own product or service; an industrial model of production as likely to be used by a shoemaker as a software company. That model changed due to the great innovation, but also significant limitations, of the internet.

Originally invented to bring together the countless smaller networks that predated it, the so-called "network of networks" that emerged in the 1960s and 1970s was simplistic by design. All it did was create a set of standards by which different networks could communicate and route packets of data to each other. What those bits of data represented, or who sent them, was left to users to worry about.

In computer science, a protocol is defined as the rules and standards by which a network operates. The core protocols of the internet, most of which still comprise the underbelly of the digital domain, treat all data the same. They cannot distinguish between a billion-dollar transaction or a meaningless message, and have no way of knowing the actual identity of the sender. Every device that is connected to the net is assigned a serial number and given permission to start communicating with every other device. This simplicity was crucial to adoption but wasn't necessarily intentional. There were other, more sophisticated protocols also floating around back then, some of which may have been a better foundation for today's more complicated online ecosystem.[9][10] The simpler solution won out as it was easier to implement and appealed to the lowest common denominator.

Like the blockchain platforms that would come decades later, participation in the original internet was open to everyone. Unlike a blockchain platform, though, there was no mechanism for driving honest behavior or building consensus. Anyone could say anything, and seemingly everyone did. The aptly named Simple Mail Transfer Protocol (SMTP) allowed anyone to use a pseudonymous email address, filling inboxes with messages as likely to originate from a friend as from a spammer. Websites enabled by the Hypertext Transfer Protocol were also anonymous, making them untrustworthy and chaotic, a problem exacerbated by the slowness of reputable pre-web content creators such as newspapers to go online. The early web was a veritable Wild West of random sites and questionable content which made it both alluring for early adopters and untrustworthy for those wishing to do business. Despite multiple attempts to corral all that information by aggregators such as Yahoo and search engines such as Excite, separating signal from noise remained a challenge, so trust remained low. Then came Google.

Search engines existed for years before the launch of Google, but they weren't always accurate and had a hard time keeping up with the exponential growth of new sites. The more-well-funded projects deployed an army of humans to manually scour the web and rank each individual site. Other services deployed bots that crawled around and built databases based on nothing more than keywords. One solution put users at the mercy of subjective opinion while the other was eminently gameable by crafty content creators. Neither was very effective for users looking for specific and credible results. As late as November of 1997, three of the four most popular search engines wouldn't return themselves in the results if someone searched for their name.[11] Trust, as far as content curation was concerned, was in low supply.

Google changed everything by introducing a new approach to parsing websites. Instead of taking a site's own word on its content or credibility, the company's innovative PageRank algorithm relied on everyone else's word. By ranking search results based on how many sites linked to a particular one, and giving added weight to links from already-popular sites, Google turned the World Wide Web into a popularity contest.

Despite the negative connotation of that concept, the offline world has long operated as a popularity contest, because popularity is a loose approximation of trust. There are too many ideas, people, companies, products, and services for each of us to rate on the merits, so we often take a cognitive shortcut by relying on the opinions of others. We are more likely to try a popular restaurant or listen to a popular song because, all else being equal, they are more likely to be good than a randomly selected joint or jam. The early internet challenged this approach because it was too hard to tell who was who. Google helped clean things up by importing a familiar offline solution.

The Google PageRank algorithm was the first successful and scalable attempt to introduce the notion of consensus to the internet, albeit in a centralized fashion. Trust, as we've seen in the realm of money, has a winner-take-all tendency. Just as a trusted coin minted by a powerful emperor is likely to take over commerce, a trusted algorithm managed by a sophisticated corporation was likely to take over search, which it did, driving most of the competition out of business and the parent company to great success.

Other platforms did the same for commerce and identity. Shopping platforms such as eBay created more-trustworthy online marketplaces than random websites from who-knows-where. Amazon, which began as a centralized retailer, would diversify into a platform. Social media services such as Facebook and LinkedIn solved the anonymity problem by introducing a mechanism for users to establish an online identity, complete with the offline notion of reputation as derived from "who you know." Other platforms tackled niche areas such as travel, classified ads, and—in the case of Wikipedia—knowledge itself. A second wave of platforms that appeared after the proliferation of smartphones would tackle distinctively offline services such as cab rides.

In each area, the most successful solution was the one that provided the most appealing community to both producer and consumer—including a mechanism for building trust. Doing so created a virtuous cycle of adoption, as both sides wanted to be on the platform that provided the best of the other. This phenomenon is captured by the now almost clichéd notion of Metcalfe's Law, summarized as the value of a network growing disproportionately to the number of users. Put simply, a social media platform that has double the number of users is more than twice as valuable. The winner-take-all tendency is therefore turbocharged, enabling a handful of platforms to dominate. But the more dominant the platform, the greater the free-rider temptation of the centralized authority that controls it.

Free Riding as a Service

Google had no business model at inception. The word "profit" only appears twice in the original research paper published by then-PhD candidates Lawrence Page and Sergei Brin, and in a negative context, inside a paragraph describing the "serious problem" of for-profit services that help people manipulate search engines. The irony of that critique, given today's massive search engine optimization industry built almost entirely atop Google, is only surpassed by the fact that the paper ends with an entire appendix criticizing advertising as a business model for search. Titled "Advertising and Mixed Motives," it states in no uncertain terms:

> The goals of the advertising business model do not always correspond to providing quality search to users.

The appendix includes the example of a Google search for "cellular phone," which back in 1998 returned a study on the dangers of using a phone while driving, as opposed to an ad. A search engine funded by advertising is concluded to be "inherently biased towards the advertisers and away from the needs of the consumers."[12]

The same search replicated on Google today yields dozens of ads for smartphones (some of which are manufactured by the company itself). Google earns over $100 billion a year from advertising, making it the biggest advertising company in the world, and propelling its formerly skeptical co-founders toward the top of the *Forbes* billionaires list. The curse of history, incarnate.

By offering a superior search engine, Google turned itself into *the* digital platform of the World Wide Web, connecting site creators who increasingly optimized their content creation to the Google algorithm to be visible to users who trust the results. All of this activity provided Google with user data it could collect, package, and sell. The better its search engine, the more people rely on it, so the more data Google collects. The company subsequently developed and introduced other services from email to navigation. Each new service proved popular, further enhancing the network effect. All have been free, thus baiting users so that Google can collect even more data. Google has acquired shadow profiles of billions of people it in turn sells to advertisers and data brokers. Cleaning up the internet turned out to be one dirty business.

There is no notion of seigniorage when it comes to a digital platform, but monetization of user data has similarities. Just as with money, the provider of trust can monetize its position, but only at the risk of losing credibility. Like with money, the decline in trust can be measured by inflation, which in this case shows up as an overall decline in the quality of content. The well-documented proliferation of bots, fake users, and click fraud on the producer side of the web, as well as the popularity of ad blockers on the user side, are evidence that content inflation is already here.[13] [14] It's still early, but the Google empire, like the Roman one, now faces a steady decline in trust.

Like most free riders, Google didn't plan to end up here. There was a time when the company's original motto of "don't be evil" was more of an ethos and less of a punch line, and it wasn't that long ago. Page and Brin were genuine in their attempt to make the web a friendlier place. As were other entrepreneurs who followed in their footsteps, including Mark Zuckerberg—arguably the poster child of the free-rider problem run amok. Like Google, Facebook was originally invented to solve an important problem. As stated by the CEO himself in his first public letter to investors: "Facebook was not originally created to be a company. It was built to accomplish a social mission—to make the world more open and connected."[15] The billions of users who participate in its various platforms today prove it has succeeded at that mission. The billions of dollars the parent company makes in advertising proves it has indulged in its option to free ride. The road to platform hell is paved with good intentions.

The inherent tension between what is good for the operator of a platform versus what is good for its users goes to the heart of what is unsavory about the digital experience today. Most users would prefer not to be treated as digital chattel with their virtual lives productized and sold to the highest bidder. But from a purely business point of view, there is nothing wrong with how Google and Facebook operate. Both companies have an obligation to their shareholders to increase profits, and the best way to fulfill that obligation is to constantly improve their product. The problem is that us users—the people who make their platforms valuable in the first place—are that product. Platform companies pay lip service to the importance of user privacy, but privacy is not what their customers, the advertisers that drive their revenues, want, and as the old saying goes, the customer is always right.

The separation of the user, operator, and shareholder into three distinct groups is the Unholy Trinity of every centralized platform. What is good for the owners inevitably comes at the expense of users, with management perpetually stuck between the two. Tempting as it might be to blame the executives of these companies for putting the needs of shareholders ahead of those of users, one could argue that they are simply doing their job.

The Bad Economics of the Gig Economy

Monetization is even more problematic for sharing-economy platforms such as Uber and Lyft that cannot hide their business model behind a veil of free-ness. Rideshare companies generate revenues for their shareholders by taking a cut of every trip. Most deliberately operate at a loss at the outset, subsidizing every ride to spur adoption and build out their network effect. These losses can be sustained for only so long, so every rideshare platform must eventually flip the switch and monetize their service, either by charging riders more or paying drivers less, and sometimes both.

Since prices can only be raised so much until rideshare is no longer competitive with traditional taxis, these platforms are forced to contemplate paying their drivers less in the future. Uber admitted as much in its regulatory filings to go public, where it cited growing driver dissatisfaction in the face of diminishing financial incentives as a significant risk factor.[16] Like all centralized platforms, the profitability of those who own the network must eventually come at the expense of those who make it valuable. From each according to his ability to each according to his equity stake.

A skeptic (or Marxist) could argue that this is no different from traditional companies that maximize shareholder value by keeping employee compensation low. But the employees of a company are very different from the service providers of a platform. Employees enjoy legal protections, receive benefits, and don't have to invest their own capital to do their job. Rideshare drivers have little legal protection, get no benefits, and must use their own car. They also face constant pressure from open-ended competition, even from within the same platform. A programmer who works at *Uber Inc.* has far more job security than a cab driver who uses the Uber app.

Defenders of this model point to the greater flexibility afforded to gig-economy workers, likening their ability to set their own hours or switch platforms to the virtues of being an entrepreneur. But the freedoms enjoyed by entrepreneurs are no panacea and involve a great deal of uncertainty and risk. Entrepreneurs go down that road due to the possibility of an asymmetric payoff: more risk today in exchange for the possibility of a lot more wealth tomorrow. Uber drivers only participate in the first half of that equation. They take on plenty of risk—as either the platform, or their efforts within it, could fail—but their potential upside is limited. The whole point of a centrally owned platform is to capture the excess value created by others and channel it to shareholders. Despite the crucial sweat equity gig-economy workers contribute to the success of a platform, be it Uber or Etsy, excess value accrues to shareholders while power remains with the operator. Risk, without reward.

The very notion of economic incentives that builds trust in a decentralized platform such as Bitcoin undermines it in a centralized setting. That's why rideshare has a lot of turnover, and those who remain are increasingly disgruntled.[17] The drivers do most of the work and take a lot of the risk, only to watch the shares that they don't own appreciate. There is a reason why thousands of Uber drivers around the world staged a strike around the time of the company's initial public offering. That both Uber and Lyft tried to blunt some of that dissatisfaction by allocating a trivial amount of equity to a handful of drivers shows that even they recognize the problem. But the incongruity persists. For every Uber press release about how much management cares about drivers, there is an equal and opposite promise to shareholders to raise the aptly named "take rate"—the percentage of driver income the company keeps for itself.

A TALE OF TWO PLATFORMS

	TYPE	PRODUCER	USER	CONTROL	VALUE CAPTURE
BITCOIN	DE-CENTRALIZED	MINERS	COIN OWNERS	PRODUCERS & USERS	PRODUCERS & USERS
UBER	CENTRALIZED	DRIVERS	PASSENGERS	MANAGEMENT	SHARE-HOLDERS

Hail, Digital Caesar!

To be fair, this critique somewhat belittles the importance of the founders of a digital platform. The biggest risk of all is taken by those who set out to create a platform in the first place, investing time and talent in a new idea whose success is far from a given. When Lyft was first launched, and had neither users nor drivers, it was the app that was the special thing, as without it the platform wouldn't have attracted much of either. For this the founders of the company (and their investors) deserved a significant equity stake. But by the time Lyft went public years later, it was no longer the app that was the special thing, but rather the army of users and drivers who made the Lyft platform valuable. The company itself seemingly agreed with this assessment when it decided to begin its official pitch to potential investors with the impressive stats on how many drivers and users relied on the platform.[18]

Also included in the Lyft investment pitch was the striking fact that—even after going public—Lyft's two co-founders would retain half of the voting shares. Thirty million riders and two million drivers under the thumb of just two managers. Concentration of power is a common practice in tech companies as shareholders want founders to have enough control to execute their vision. But this approach is dangerous in a platform setting, as it introduces even more asymmetry in the Unholy Trinity. Not only do the individuals who make the platform valuable in the first place not get any equity in the network effects they help create, they also have no say over how the platform evolves.

Facebook may have billions of users, but only one person has the final say on important decisions, as Mark Zuckerberg owns a majority of the company's voting stock. Google also has billions of users, not to mention one hundred thousand employees, but Page and Brin rule supreme. For all the talk about openness, meritocracy, and inclusion that Silicon Valley is known for, its platform darlings are all structured as—and increasingly act like—dictatorships.

Money is not the only thing that matters in the digital economy. Governance, culture, and an openness to dissent are also important. The deteriorating reputation of most platform companies is also a consequence of their corporate structures, where the livelihoods of so many are at the mercy of so few. The cognitive dissonance between what these companies are and what they pretend to be is most on display whenever they report earnings to shareholders. Here is a typical example from a Facebook quarterly update:

> "We had a good quarter and a strong end to the year as our community and business continue to grow," said Mark Zuckerberg, Facebook founder and CEO. "We remain focused on building services that help people stay connected to those they care about." [19]

So far so good. But then the same report details a financial metric known as "Family Average Revenues Per Person" (FARPP). Like other overbearing institutions throughout history, Facebook is prone to the occasional doublespeak that borders on propaganda. The "family" referred to in this metric is not yours, but rather the creepy surveillance machine built to follow and monetize your digital existence, more *cosa nostra* than our thing. When critics describe the business model of these companies as surveillance capitalism, they aren't far off. Metrics like FARPP seem straight out of an East German spy novel.

That said, it's still an impressive number. Facebook and Google are among the most profitable companies in history, and their dominance feels insurmountable. Lots of people complain about how they operate, but lots more continue to use them. The winner-take-all tendency makes it difficult for newer platforms to compete, and the vast profits of the incumbents allows them to acquire the few that do. Not that it would change much, as the perverse incentive structure of centralized platforms virtually guarantees that every upstart will eventually behave like today's incumbents. A general sense of futility has set in.

Some critics have shifted their focus to the political sphere, hoping that new laws, regulations, and antitrust measures can deliver what competition cannot. But it is far from a given that these interventions will have the desired effect, given how other highly regulated industries with bad incentive structures still manage to perennially disappoint. Good regulations can't fix bad business models, and new rules often bring new barriers to entry for would-be competitors, making the incumbents even more entrenched. Thankfully, there is a better way.

A Flattened Hierarchy

Like the previously mentioned services, Bitcoin is also a platform. It can't handle activities like rideshare or social media, but its architecture points the way to a more decentralized and egalitarian approach to online interaction. Most people consider its greatest success to be the value of its coins, but even more impressive might be the simple fact that it works.

The Bitcoin platform has no shareholders. It does not have a board of directors, steering committee, or corporate charter. There is no CEO. There was once a founder, who briefly acted as a leader, but nobody knew who this person actually was, and even their online alter ego disappeared long ago. The platform does not abide by national laws or regulations, as there is nobody for a government to punish. There is no individual, group, or corporation in charge. And yet, it works.

The Bitcoin platform has no business model. There are transaction fees to discourage spam transactions meant to clog the network and new coins are paid out to miners to incentivize honest behavior, but individuals in either camp have little control over the process. Fees are determined by demand and the miner reward was hardcoded into the protocol long ago. Even those who have made a lot of money from the platform's success have surprisingly little say in how it should evolve. And yet, it works.

The Bitcoin platform has no clear separation of owners, users, and operators. Miners, who are the closest thing to operators given the crucial role they play in securing the network, are also users, because they get paid in bitcoins. Users, who use the platform to save or make payments, are also owners, because owning the coin is the closest thing to having equity in the platform. Mining and using are both done pseudonymously, so anyone can do either at any time, coming and going as they please. And yet, it works.

The Bitcoin platform is one of the most targeted corners of the online economy, as the value of its coins combined with the openness of the platform practically begs every would-be thief, hacker, or saboteur to take their best shot. Where operators of centralized platforms cite security as a reason they should have asymmetric power, Bitcoin takes the opposite approach, allowing anyone to play any role, akin to a wealthy city that invites its crooks to become cops. And yet, somehow, miraculously, it works.

DIFFERENT PLATFORM DESIGNS

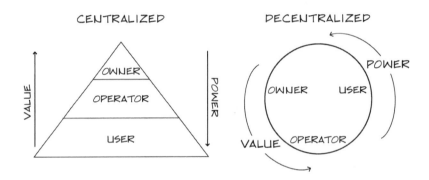

The Bitcoin platform is no panacea. It has many limitations and drawbacks, some of which might very well prevent it from ever being more than a niche payment platform. But its success points the way to a new model of digital trust—one that replaces a shareholder-owned platform maintained by a corporate authority with a public blockchain maintained by a diffuse community. Trust that has traditionally come from opacity and power can now come from transparency and code. The decentralized approach works, leading us to wonder what else we can do with it.

The answer—for the Bitcoin platform at least—is very little. Certainly not web search, social media, or rideshare. Like the original protocols of the web, the Bitcoin network is minimalist by design, only allowing users to own and transact coins. Also like the original protocols of the web, simplicity limits functionality, creating a desire for a more sophisticated solution, one that could handle any kind of digital interaction that requires a strong dose of trust. Ambitious as that may sound, there is no technological reason why the solution crafted by Satoshi Nakamoto couldn't be expanded in scope. To get there, however, the blockchain solution needed an upgrade.

The second generation of decentralized platforms that came after Bitcoin—best represented by the Ethereum platform that was launched in 2015—introduced two additional features: tokens and smart contracts. A token is any arbitrary container of value whose ownership is tracked by the ledger. A smart contract is a conditional transaction whose conditions are also validated by miners. Put simply, tokens let platform users own and transact other things beyond the native coin, and smart contracts let them introduce rules as to how and when those things are transacted. What these things actually represent is up to the users. Since both features are executed by miners guided by a consensus mechanism, they are trustless. Users can expect reliable outcomes without having to trust an authority, or each other.

Tokens and contracts have been staples of the offline economy for a long time. Any store of value, such as a dollars, gift cards, or frequent-flyer miles can be considered a token. The trading and usage of most tokens is ruled by conditions, such as when miles expire. What changes when moved onto a blockchain is that ownership is now tracked on the ledger and conditions are validated by consensus. Trust, which was previously provided by a central authority of some sort, is now provided by a decentralized network, resulting in a profoundly different user experience—as anyone who has ever accumulated airline miles can attest.

Airline miles can be thought of as a sort of corporate currency. Although not as widely accepted as dollars—and certainly not as valuable as bitcoins—miles perform some of the functions of money, and fit most of the characteristics, with the exception of scarcity. Airline reward programs are practically designed with free-rider exploitation in mind and are so lucrative that it's not unheard of for an airline to earn greater profit from its miles program than from flying airplanes.[20] Users of miles are forever at the mercy of the company, as the company decides when and how to issue rewards, who owns how many, and how and when they can be redeemed. Like most traditional tokens, all of this happens inside the black hole of a proprietary database. Anything from a deliberate rule change to an accident of accounting can wipe out a user's purchasing power and send them to customer-service hell.

Blockchain tokens eliminate many of these risks. Since the ledger is ruled by transparency and code, mistakes are never made, as proven by the fact that the Bitcoin blockchain has never made a mistake—despite having processed over 500 million transactions. A blockchain always yields the correct user balance, in the same way that a calculator always returns the correct sum. The Ethereum platform expands this functionality to an infinite variety of tokens—hundreds of thousands of which have already been created by countless users (including for use in loyalty programs).

Blockchain platforms also don't discriminate. They can't because the miners who validate every transaction have no idea who anyone is. Each user is represented by a cryptographic key that looks like a random string of characters. Unlike a centrally controlled database where a company or even a sole disgruntled employee can target a specific user, Ethereum miners have no such power. Nor can they prevent anyone from using the platform. One of the more nefarious abuses of power by a central authority is to deny or revoke access to certain users. Decentralized platforms have no such ability, which is why they are said to be censorship resistant.

As pedestrian as it may sound, the ability to track discrete containers of value in a trustless, errorless, and censorship-resistant fashion is reason enough to re-architect a substantial portion of the economy. Most economic interactions depend on the tracking and trading of some kind of store of value, be it fiat money, securities, land titles, checks, in-game currency, loyalty points, or financial derivatives. Most of that tracking today is done on centralized databases built with outdated technology and seemingly held together by some combination of manual processing and duct tape.

The flaws of our current infrastructure are so ubiquitous and entrenched that we take them for granted, accepting it as normal that a check can take a week to clear, a stock trade can take days to settle, and that a credit card company can't tell us our exact rewards balance until the end of the month. And those are the more luxurious problems, suffered by the wealthy and privileged. In the developing world, it's not unheard of for a corrupt politician to deprive someone of their assets with a phone call. The more centralized the tracking system, the easier it is to abuse. Less odious but more likely are the mistakes, accidents, and system failures that routinely deprive people of their valuables and conspire, albeit unintentionally, to keep the poor and powerless where they are, sometimes by doing nothing more than denying them access.

All these issues are problems of centralization and localization. All can be solved by moving value transfers onto a trustless, errorless, and censorship-resistant digital platform, one that is universally accessible to anyone who can hold a private key—which is everyone.

If This Happens, Then Do That

Simply enabling users to send tokens back and forth is not enough. Most transactions are more complicated than "I transfer this asset to you" and come with certain conditions. The term *smart contract* is something of a misnomer, as it implies that only complicated agreements qualify. In practice, a smart contract is nothing more than one or more set of conditions to a transaction written down in the format of "if this happens, then do that." If it's the first day of the month, then make an interest payment. If a seller transfers ownership of a deed, then the buyer pays them money. If a passenger has a certain number of miles, then they qualify for an upgrade. Smart contracts enable the kinds of rules that we all agree should be followed to be enforced in trustless fashion.

To fully appreciate the leap forward that smart contracts represent, it helps to revisit the limitations of the dumb variety, summarized as problems of interpretation and enforcement. As clever as tearing an indenture in half to prove authenticity was in the Middle Ages, doing so did little to guarantee an outcome. Just because two people agree on what a contract says doesn't mean they also agree on what it means. Agreements written in natural language are open to interpretation so they must be written in exquisite detail to cover all possible outcomes. But the longer the contract, the more loopholes signatories may find, so language must be added to address them, leading to a sort of language inflation that frustrates everyone other than the attorneys who are paid by the hour to write them.

It would be one thing if this cumbersome method of trust building only applied to high-value transfers, but some version of it afflicts every corner of modern life. For proof, look no further than a typical user agreement for a frequent-flyer program, a pseudocontract whose length seemingly grows equal and opposite to the available legroom in coach. The longer the agreement, the easier it is to bury something in the fine print.

Interpretation is only half the problem. The other half is the need to defer to third-party authorities such as regulators, courts, and arbitrators to settle disputes. Just because the language of an agreement is clear doesn't mean that violations won't occur. Since traditional contracts exist outside the system whose operation they guide, enforcement can only happen after the fact. There is nothing to prevent an airline from violating its own terms and alter user balances inside its proprietary database. Victims of this type of abuse can appeal to the authorities but doing so can be more expensive than the value at stake, creating a perverse incentive for those in charge of proprietary systems to regularly push the boundary of what they can get away with.

There are existing solutions to the challenges of interpretation and enforcement, but the costs of using them makes them mostly useful for certain kinds of situations, and by certain kinds of people. When it comes to traditional contracts, justice is a luxury mostly afforded to the affluent—the greatest protections for those who need them least. Throw in the obvious free-rider risks of any central enforcement mechanism and you end up with a sort of soft corruption that permeates even the most just societies.

Trust should not be a luxury, and thanks to smart contracts executed blindly by consensus, it no longer has to be. The interpretation problem is eliminated by the fact that smart contracts are written in a programming language and not a natural one. There are no loopholes in code, just bugs that can be detected ahead of time and eliminated before the contract is submitted to the ledger. Enforcement is also predictable, as miners execute the code the same way that a smartphone executes an app. The process is open and transparent, and anyone looking to subject themselves to the parameters of a smart contract can inspect its code beforehand. Once executed, enforcement happens in real time and with every transaction. A smart contract is the only type of contract that is guaranteed to satisfy those who agree to its terms.

Not every kind of legal arrangement could be turned into a smart contract. Some laws are intentionally written to be open to interpretation, particularly when it comes to serious crimes. But those kinds of laws have little impact on our day-to-day lives. More relevant are the mundane financial agreements that underpin the economy, a good portion of which can be turned into smart contracts to reduce conflict. The challenge is expressing those agreements as code, something that most people can't do. Thankfully, the openness of any decentralized and censorship-resistant platform means they won't have to.

Smart contracts can be designed to be public, so one person's coding effort could serve an unlimited number of users. Since most economic interaction already operates on some kind of a standard, a knowledgeable programmer could easily create smart contracts that replicate existing activities, like betting on sports. Blockchain platforms allow contracts to also hold tokens, providing a crucial escrow capability.

As with a casino, two people taking the opposite sides of a bet can send their money (in the form of a token) to the betting contract to hold until an outcome is determined. Unlike a casino, the smart contract is not a candidate for free-rider exploitation. Nor can it abscond with the money, lose it, be bribed, or go out of business. It helps that the smart contract doesn't need to earn a profit. It's just a snippet of code, after all, and one person's code could be used by countless other users, forever. Not only are smart contracts fairer than their off-chain counterparts, they can also be more economical.

Gambling is not an important activity, but settling financial outcomes based on future events is common in the business world. Today, that type of activity is handled by central authorities running opaque and proprietary systems. Participation is neither trustless, errorless, or censorship resistant—and never will be, either because the operator is incapable of offering those features, or more likely, doesn't want to. The lack of those features is why we need authorities in the first place, and necessity is the mother of all profit margins, from the national stock exchange to the neighborhood bookie. So long as trust is important, someone gets to charge a vig to provide it.

We have not yet learned enough to see how a decentralized platform could someday take on the likes of Uber, but we will get there eventually. For now it's important to recognize the utility of blockchain components like tokens and smart contracts in architecting decentralized solutions. Like metal and glass, they can be combined in different ways to yield an infinite variety of designs, including one that tackles rideshare. After all, other than the cab rides provided by its drivers, Uber is nothing more than an app, one that uses an algorithm to coordinate cab rides and trigger payments. Today, all of that activity is controlled by a corporation, one whose plan to free ride is actively discussed in every earnings report.

A platform like Ethereum changes that formula. The programming language that its miners process is Turing-complete, meaning that even the most complex software instructions, including the ones needed to coordinate cabs, could be written into a smart contract. This feature, combined with its token functionality, means that any activity could theoretically be run on top of it, in the form of a decentralized application, or dApp. It's still early, and there are many challenges to executing nonfinancial interactions in a decentralized matter, but also a major benefit: trust.

Trust that used to come from an intermediary can now be built directly. Promises that are turned into code, validated by consensus, and resolved via tokens are a lot harder to break. Since there is nobody in charge, there is less opportunity for free-rider exploitation. The mechanics of the blockchain solution might be complicated, but the output is simple: predictability and fairness, the digital equivalent of Lady Justice.

It Don't Come Easy

There are trade-offs to the decentralized approach, however. All else being equal, a decentralized platform is less efficient than a centralized one. Building consensus across a global network of anonymous nodes and miners takes time, and the financial incentives used to motivate good behavior cost money. A centralized payment provider just needs one database and one operator—a single node and no consensus, to put it in blockchain terms. The Ethereum platform has thousands of nodes and needs to reach consensus across all of them. Decentralized platforms are harder to scale than centralized ones, and require a different mindset, particularly when it comes to transaction fees.

Centralized platforms could process transactions for free if they wanted to, as fees have nothing to do with protecting a closed database. Security is a lot easier to achieve when someone powerful is clearly in charge. Blockchain platforms don't have these luxuries on account of their openness and censorship resistance. Thieves and hackers can try all sorts of attacks to cause mayhem, and keep trying forever. One defense is to charge a fee for every smart contract call or token transfer, introducing a cost to every attempted attack. Transaction fees, along with the mining reward, are crucial to the security of any decentralized system. Without them, the perpetual motion machine of trust may grind to a halt.

Those fees may limit the types of business models that could be executed atop a decentralized network, or at least alter how they are executed. Uber doesn't charge people every time they check the cost of a ride, it doesn't have to do. If a particular user abuses that ability, then the operator can kick them out. Censorship-resistant blockchain platforms and the decentralized applications built on top of them don't have that option. If they didn't charge a fee for every on-chain activity—the kind that requires the participation of a miner—then an attacker could take up all available resources with endless (and pointless) contract calls. This means that every smart contract execution must entail a fee, requiring a different approach by programmers. All code that is executed within consensus must be lean, and less important activities that don't require a lot of trust are best executed off-chain.

Then there are the delays.

Building consensus requires financial incentives and takes time. How quickly a decentralized platform processes transactions is dependent on several factors and can vary from a few seconds to an hour. All else being equal, a distributed ledger will update more slowly than a centralized one, leading to possible transaction queues. Like most queues, wait times fluctuate based on demand and can be frustrating for users in a rush. Unlike most queues, blockchain platforms don't operate on a first come, first serve basis. They allow users to sort themselves based on the fees they are willing to pay. Those willing to pay more get priority treatment, creating an experience like traffic congestion pricing.

Critics of decentralization often use the capacity constraints and costs to argue that blockchain platforms will never gain mass adoption. On an apples-to-apples basis, they have a point. While a centralized payment platform such as Visa or a cloud computing solution like Amazon Web Services can handle tens of thousands of transactions, or operations, per second, Bitcoin and Ethereum can barely handle twenty. If a blockchain was "just another" digital platform, then the scaling issue would be fatal.

But it's not. The first iteration of any new solution will always be less efficient than the latest iteration of the old. Even the vaunted credit card network, whose impressive transaction capacity is often cited in favor of centralization, began as a slower and more expensive payment solution over the one it hoped to replace. The earliest cards required merchants to first make a phone call, then to take a physical imprint of the card. For this privilege they paid a 7 percent fee. A stark contrast to cash, which was not only familiar, but also fast and free. Early credit cards were so inefficient that even the founder of Diners Club, the first mass-market credit card, once predicted his creation would eventually "disappear like the zoot suit."[21] Today, credit cards are wildly popular, partly because their under-lying infrastructure has dramatically improved, and mostly because they offer features that cash never could.

If every technology was judged by its initial performance, then nothing new would ever be built. Everyone would still be using landlines because the earliest cell phones had limited range, dropped calls often, and were big and bulky. Thankfully, the entrepreneur's imagination is not as lim-ited as the critics', and users care as much about the long-term potential of a new solution as they do about its present utility.

Blockchain platforms are on their way to realizing that potential. Newer platforms offer much higher throughput and faster processing times than Bitcoin or Ethereum, and the latter is set to undergo a major upgrade in its consensus mechanism. Most platforms are also developing support-ing infrastructure that would allow the less trust-sensitive interactions to happen on a sort of ancillary network. More importantly, and regardless of their scaling issues, decentralized platforms promise a better vision of tomorrow, one that is trustless, democratic, and far more economical.

That last feature might seem contradictory, as most legacy platforms appear to be free. But as the saying goes, nothing in this world is free but the grace of God—not the posting of an Instagram story and certainly not the swiping of a credit card. We pay for these platform-based services one way or another. The proof lies in the quarterly earnings reports of the likes of Facebook and Visa. Their profits are somebody else's cost, and judging by their impressive earnings growth over the years, that cost has gone up substantially. To be fair, neither company is doing anything it wasn't invented to do. Management's primary responsibility is to shareholders, and their profits must ultimately come at the expense of users. Until now.

A decentralized platform will likely never be as efficient as its centralized counterpart, but it will always be more trustworthy. What users lose in terms of fees or processing time they gain in network equity and control. Blockchain platforms can't exploit their users to the benefit of their owners because their users *are* their owners. Fees can only increase with demand, and greater demand means greater network effects. Whatever users lose in terms of transaction fees they gain back in terms of equity. If Ethereum transaction fees are high, then the Ethereum platform must be popular, and if the platform is popular, then the coin will appreciate—a previously implicit relationship that was recently made explicit by a network upgrade that burns some of the ETH—the native coin of the Ethereum blockchain—that users pay in transaction fees in every block. This is in stark contrast to a network such as Visa, where the fees paid by merchants (and ultimately customers) only benefit shareholders.

Just as importantly, governance decisions on how to change and improve the platform are also made via the same slow, inefficient, and expensive consensus mechanism. Critics of decentralization claim this as yet another drawback, arguing that important decisions are more easily made under a centralized hierarchy. But theirs is a historically ignorant argument. Preferring a centralized solution over a decentralized one because of more efficient governance is akin to preferring a dictatorship over a democracy because things get done faster. True, and disastrous. What the users of a decentralized platform give up in terms of the pace of change (some of which they may not even want or like) they gain back in terms of control.

Decentralized governance is indeed a messy process. Both the Bitcoin and Ethereum communities have at times stumbled in the face of seemingly trivial questions, like how big a block should be, or how to deal with a hacked smart contract. Since there is nobody in charge, such decisions are made behaviorally. The exact procedure varies from platform to platform but is best understood as participants—be they users, miners, or dApp developers—voting with their feet. Once a change has been proposed and propagated throughout the community, everyone involved acts out their preference. Users submit transactions according to either the old way or the new, and miners process those transactions according to their preference. The solution with the greatest participation wins out. Some platforms formalize this process with literal on-chain voting, with every token owner getting a say. Smart contracts tally up the results and alter the platform accordingly. Either way, the process is slow during the best of times and can feel ineffective during a crisis. But in the long run, all the messy sausage making is more of a feature than a bug. A platform that is difficult to upgrade is also difficult to co-opt or subvert.

The Innovators (Lack of) Dilemma

Ironically, the inefficiencies of governing a decentralized platform, and the resulting inability to make major changes, make it more attractive to founders who want to build on top of it. This is important because entrepreneurs are crucial to the long-term success of any digital ecosystem, regardless of its design. Successful platforms have to be two-sided, because users only show up if there is something useful and interesting in it for them. This is why young platforms go out of their way to woo the best talent, be they app developers or content producers. In a centralized setting, this relationship is one of convenience. Thanks to the misaligned incentives of the Unholy Trinity, it's only a matter of time until the opera-tors turn on the people who helped make that platform appealing in the first place.

Case in point: Google search used to send users looking for directions to outside sites like Yahoo and MapQuest. Now it sends them to Google Maps. If there is money to be made from providing directions, why give away the opportunity? In the beginning, Google needed those outside sites to make its search engine popular. But once the platform became domi-nant, it started directing users to its own monolithic properties—trading variety for expediency, not to mention profit. For all the talk of innovation that emanates from Silicon Valley, the dirty little secret of its corporate-run platforms is that they've all turned heel at some point, morphing from innovation sponsors into innovation killers. Doing so is a predictable con-sequence of a governance model that puts shareholder value ahead of plat-form utility.

Twitter reached a similar inflection point when it eliminated an appli-cation programming interface (API) that was crucial for third-party applications designed to distribute its content in unique ways. Tellingly, the change was made at a time when the company was looking to ramp up its advertising strategy. That these outside services had been crucial to Twitter's early success was not in dispute, and it acknowledged as much in an internal memo:

> 3rd party clients have had a notable impact on the Twitter service and the products we build. Independent developers built the first Twitter client for Mac and the first native app for iPhone. These clients pio-neered product features we all know and love about Twitter. . . . We deeply respect the time, energy, and passion they've put into building amazing things using Twitter.[22]

The company expressed its respect for these independent develop-ers by cutting them out. Its new API rendered their apps both limited in functionality and expensive to run, forcing their users to switch to the platform's native apps.

Like countless other authoritarian rulers, Twitter Inc. explained this strong-arm tactic as being for the good of the people, stating in a blog post that "we feel the best Twitter experience we can provide today is through our owned and operated Twitter for iOS and Android apps."[23] Left unsaid in that post was the fact that those apps were already available, and users had been free to use them all along. The change was designed to deprive users of choice, like a supermarket that decides to sell only one brand of cereal, its own. The trending #BreakingMyTwitter hashtag that became popular in the aftermath showed that users liked having choices, but the rule change was forced on the community anyway. Competition is supposed to be a virtue in the tech industry but gets in the way of seigniorage on a tech platform. Just as an emperor must control the issuance of money inside his domain to remain powerful, a centralized platform must control the earning of profit inside theirs.

As destructive as this kind of headline change can be, arguably even more insidious are the countless micro-censorships, de-platformings, and algorithm changes that occur on a regular basis inside every centralized platform. The road to platform hell is littered with the skeletons of apps that have been kicked off the iTunes or Android stores for no apparent reason, and social media influencers whose viewership abruptly collapsed due to a seemingly arbitrary tweak of a recommendation algorithm. The more successful a business built atop a centralized platform becomes, the more vulnerable it is to changes decreed from above.

And so, the celebrated fast and efficient governance of centralized platforms morphs into a liability in the long run, and the tortoise wins over the hare yet again. A blockchain protocol that can't be easily changed is more inviting to those hoping to build on top of it, because it provides predictability and control. What's more, the same censorship resistance that assures continuity of access for users also applies to developers. No one inside the Ethereum community has the power to deny dApp developers access (in the way that iTunes does) or deprive content creators of their audience (in the way that YouTube, Twitter, and Facebook do). There is still some platform risk, as blockchain networks do change their rules from time to time. But their changes are transparent and implemented with network utility in mind, and app developers who may be adversely impacted are given the opportunity to vote against them. The basic notion of building trust by aligning incentives doesn't just apply to the miners participating in consensus. It also applies to the entrepreneurs who build on top of it—with data acting as the great equalizer.

Data

Every platform is a wellspring of valuable data, regardless of its architecture. Centralized platforms allow the operator to horde most of that data, giving it a distinct advantage over everyone else. Regardless of how much lip service companies like Uber and Facebook pay to the concepts of openness and transparency, they operate giant black boxes, the true contents of which are as much a mystery to their users as they are to service providers and regulators. An Uber driver only knows about his or her own activity, while the Uber corporation knows every driver's and rider's activity. What chance does anyone stand against such asymmetry? Maintaining a monopoly on data is fundamental to the economic success of every centralized platform—so much so that established platforms brag about it in their earnings reports. Such a monopoly further poisons the relationship between the owners of the platform and those building on top of it.

Case in point: Amazon has been accused of using sales data on its third-party vendors to create competing products to sell under its own brand.[24] The company denies that it would ever do such a thing, in the same way that Facebook has claimed to care about user privacy. Not capitalizing on all that data to design superior products would hurt the retail giant's earnings, and management has a more clearly (and legally) defined obligation to shareholders than it does to vendors. Even if Amazon is not abusing its position today, the temptation to do so grows alongside its platform and the copious amounts of data it generates. The business arc of every centralized platform is long, but it bends toward free riding. The final, data-driven betrayal of all the people and businesses that make a platform a success is so likely that it's cliché: information is power, and power corrupts. That's why decentralized platforms share all of their data with everyone.

Spend a few minutes browsing one of the countless free websites that display on-chain data for platforms such as Bitcoin and Ethereum and you'll discover a startling truth: all the data generated by either is open for anyone to see. Every token transaction, every bit of smart contract code, and all governance decisions are public information, from the latest block all the way back to the very first. This form of radical transparency is a necessary condition of decentralization, as consensus wouldn't work without it. The easiest way for participants in a crypto transaction to know they haven't been cheated is to inspect the ledger. When there is no authority in charge, the data can't be horded.

Radical transparency also fuels greater innovation. While corporate operators such as Facebook do share some of their data with third-party developers, the pickings are usually slim and always curated. Developers only get to see what the operator wants them to see, and there is the ever-present danger of access being pulled. Decentralized platforms, on the other hand, share all their data with everyone and have no mechanism to stop sharing, giving developers both a literal and a metaphorical license to plan for the long term. Remarkably, this transparency is achieved without compromising user privacy.

Blockchain transactions are always pseudonymous, as every user is only known by a random-looking string of characters, and access is only granted to whoever happens to have the private key for that address. While the platform is an open spigot of data, it never reveals too much about any particular user. Centralized platforms such as Google and Facebook claim to offer something similar, but history (and Cambridge Analytica) prove otherwise. Entrusting personal data to companies whose business model revolves around data monetization was always going to end badly.

Decentralized platforms have no such profit motive, so they are free to offer real privacy. Bitcoin and Ethereum don't need to spy on their users to thrive. If anything, they benefit from offering the opposite. As the rest of the internet is increasingly surveilled by for-profit companies and anti-freedom governments, platforms that don't have sensitive data to surrender in the first place become increasingly appealing to those hoping to preserve their digital dignity.

Critics of decentralization—particularly those in government—are critical of such privacy-enhancing features. They argue that the dangers of having a single corporation keep tabs on a billion people are offset by the fact that cops and government officials now have a powerful surveillance tool at their disposal. Anonymous interaction and digital payments, on the other hand, are bound to lead to an increase in tax evasion, money laundering, and theft.

Of all the critiques lobbed at platforms such as Bitcoin, the one about criminal usage is usually the loudest. It's also the most ignorant. Cash is even more anonymous than crypto and has been society's primary—if not *only*—payment solution for millennia. Civilization didn't crumble and criminality didn't runneth over. Just because a payment method is natively anonymous doesn't mean that there is no way to catch the bad guys. Doing so just requires different police work. One could even argue that an overall migration from physical cash to digital crypto would make law enforcement easier, as a blockchain-based transaction—however anonymous it may be—is easier to track than a duffel bag of cash. The best way to solve a crime is to follow the money, and few tools make doing so easier than a transparent ledger made immutable with cryptography.

Perhaps more importantly, the most useful things in life—things like arithmetic, the English language, and smartphones—are always going to be used by criminals. The notion that they should therefore be restricted to the general population is the last refuge of dangerous dictators and lazy law enforcement. It's also a cliché. Every new technology goes through a phase of being feared as a criminal enabler, partly because criminals are good early adopters, and mostly because humans tend to fear the unknown. As a rule, the more transformative a technology ends up being, the more it was feared in its infancy.

Case in point, wireless technology used to be so strongly associated with criminal activity that the *New York Times* ran a story in 1988 titled "Schools Responding to Beeper, Tool of Today's Drug Dealer, by Banning It." It's safe to assume that the vast majority of beeper owners were doing nothing wrong in 1988 but it was the criminal usage that got the headline treatment, as it tapped into a general anxiety over technological change. Today, everyone walks around with a far more sophisticated wireless device in their pocket. Wireless communication is too ubiquitous to be considered dangerous, not to mention a great tool for law enforcement. There's no reason why decentralized platforms can't complete the same journey, provided they grow enough to matter.

Network Effects

Of all the arguments made against decentralization, the most valid is the dearth of adoption so far, at least on a relative basis and as measured by number of users. As a platform, Bitcoin is only a few years younger than Facebook or Twitter, but its growth curve barely registers against theirs. As far as network effects are concerned, the corporate-owned platforms have crushed their decentralized counterparts, and there's seemingly no end to their dominance in sight. Indeed, despite the reputational damage that Facebook has suffered in recent years, its primary platform still boasts over a billion users. Bitcoin, Ethereum, and every other decentralized platform put together—to put it kindly—have not.

A lead that big is believed to be insurmountable because network effects are said to be self-perpetuating. Users can't leave a platform that has reached a certain critical mass because the switching costs are too high. In other words, it doesn't matter how much anyone dislikes Facebook. No one can leave it for a decentralized alternative because everyone is on it. This is a compelling theory, and one reason why the company is so brazen with its seigniorage strategy. If only it were true.

The short history of the internet is filled with digital platforms that have gone from dominant to nonexistent. Some were so popular in their heyday that the act of using them became a verb—back when teenagers IM'd their friends and businesspeople BBM'd each other via Blackberry Messenger. At their respective peaks, AOL accounted for half of all instant-messaging users in the United States and Blackberry for half of all smartphone sales. Both services are no more, consigned to the digital graveyard with other fallen angels such as MySpace, Friendster, and Vine. Tellingly, AOL Instant Messenger peaked when Facebook launched to the public, and Blackberry sales began their descent once the iPhone was introduced. The switching costs for the millions of users who depended on both turned out to not be very high after all—particularly when presented with a better solution. Of all the wonky narratives that dominate Silicon Valley today, network effects and Metcalfe's Law might be the most overrated and least understood. To see how, we have to go back to the source.

Credit for the first known illustration of the idea of network effects (but not the term itself) goes to Theodore Newton Vail, president of AT&T for two long stints during the heyday of telephony from 1885 to 1889 and again from 1907 to 1919. The US telephone industry had exploded in size in the years leading up to his second run, thanks to the thousands of smaller networks that had popped up after the 1894 expiration of the original Bell patent.[25] Vail set out to acquire many of those smaller systems to integrate into AT&T, and explained his thinking in the company's 1908 annual letter to shareholders:

"A telephone—without a connection at the other end of the line— is not even a toy or a scientific instrument. It is one of the most useless things in the world. Its value depends on the connection with the other telephone—and increases with the number of connections."

True enough. But an important fact lost on those who regurgitate the same argument in defense of digital platforms today is that Vail was referring to a *physical* network. Physical networks, such as the original telephone network, have tremendous staying power because they are costly to build, difficult to run, and cumbersome to leave. A telephone company such as AT&T had to first invest significant capital in building core infrastructure, then invest even more in expanding its network house by house—or, to put it in networking terms—node by node. Every new user that AT&T wanted to acquire required new wires, new poles, and new in-home infrastructure. The company would also need a healthy operating budget to maintain the equipment, for all its users, ad infinitum. To put it in economic terms, both the initial and operating costs of running a physical network are high—so high that it's extraordinarily difficult for anyone to compete with the first one. In other words, being AT&T required a lot of capital and manpower, and *beating* AT&T required even more. Even if the effort was undertaken by a competitor, it's not clear how they would entice users to switch, as switching physical networks is cumbersome for users.

Vail's vision proved prescient, as the continental network that he built went on to dominate for the better part of a century until it was broken up by the US government. What made his company so successful wasn't that "its network had the most users." It was successful because a competing network would be expensive to build and—given the simplicity of landline service—difficult to distinguish. Startups going after incumbents need to compete on either price or service, but the cost structure of physical networks makes it difficult to do either, which is why most physical networks, including electric utilities and railroads, eventually become monopolies.

The same can be said for the protocol-based network that Robert Metcalfe, co-inventor of Ethernet, helped launch in the 1970s. Metcalfe's Law—summarized as a network with twice as many users being four times as valuable—is a favorite among armchair academics and platform investors. But it's more of a concept than it is a law, and there are obvious instances when adding more users decreases the value of a network, such as when fake and spam accounts inevitably proliferate on centralized social media (a problem we'll visit later). Nevertheless, the ubiquity of the Ethernet communication standard, which exists thanks in part to Metcalf's ability to convince competing corporations to adopt it, is powerful evidence of the staying power of certain kinds of networks.

Although not as unassailable as a physical network, communication and media protocols such as Ethernet, VHS, and fax, have also proven resilient once they go mainstream. Once again, the winner-take-all tendency is more about cost and cumbersomeness than it is about utility. It is expensive to rewire an entire office building for a different networking standard after the first one has been installed. It is also expensive for hardware manufacturers to make devices to accommodate multiple standards. These switching costs give the first widely adopted protocol a lot of staying power, and lead to a more boring kind of winner-take-all tendency, one based on the simple question of whether the existing standard is good enough for users not to switch. The higher the switching costs, the lower that bar.

Software-based networks, such as the centralized platforms that dominate today, have none of these constraints. The fixed costs of coding a new app are relatively low, and the marginal costs of acquiring additional users are close to zero. Users, for their part, can try any new solution, or use multiple ones simultaneously, with little effort. It's a lot easier to switch from Skype to WhatsApp, or use both, than it was to get telephone service from both AT&T and a competitor. Just as importantly, the perceived value of these services, combined with the low barriers to entry, guarantees that there will always be something new to try. Software changes the competitive landscape of building a network, making it easier for newer entrants to compete on price or service, and for users to switch based on either, or both. Just because a particular platform seems to have "taken it all" today doesn't mean they won't be forced to give it back tomorrow. Easy come, easy go.

And so, the tech industry's favorite maxim that "software is eating the world" ends up devouring its second favorite—that successful digital platforms, like diamonds, are forever. Shareholders in a company like Facebook might disagree, or counter that even if software does make competition more likely, the company could remain on top by using its financial prowess to buy its challengers. Indeed, Facebook's timely purchases of Instagram and WhatsApp show that there is something to be said for this strategy. Even if users switch from the company's older platforms to its acquired ones, the profits (and power) remain within the same entity.

There are several problems with this argument. The first is that it's only a matter of time until a competitor refuses to be bought. The desire to become the next great free rider is strong, and Mark Zuckerberg isn't the last T-shirt-clad youngster with dreams of avarice. There are many reasons why a startup might decide not to sell itself to Facebook, including knowledge of Facebook's own journey to the top. Here's a summary, as recalled by Zuckerberg himself:

> "And like Yahoo came in with this big offer for a billion dollars, which is, like, was going to, like, fulfill everyone's financial dreams for the company. And I was like, 'I don't really think we should do this.' And everyone was like 'What?' [laughter] And at the time, we had 10 million people using Facebook, and MySpace had 100 million people, and it was growing faster. And if you believe all the arguments about network effects, there's no chance that we should've been able to compete." [26]

It took Facebook only a handful of years after rejecting multiple buyout offers from Yahoo and the parent company of MySpace to dominate both in terms of users and market cap, something that could not have happened if the winner-take-all tendency was absolute. When it comes to a software-based network, the most appealing product wins, no matter how entrenched the incumbent. What's more, the next generation of digital platforms offer new features that today's incumbents simply cannot. It's not clear if Mr. Zuckerberg still believes in the fallibility of network effects, or if he thinks he'll just keep buying the competition, but it also doesn't matter. You can't buy a blockchain.

Putting It All Together

To be clear, neither Bitcoin, Ethereum, nor any other decentralized solution is mature enough to take on the likes of Facebook. No network exists in a vacuum, and decentralized platforms require a lot of supporting infrastructure to be viable—things like wallets, nodes, smart contracts, and dApps. It must all be developed voluntarily and self-funded. Some protocols have small foundations that give grants to developers, but the amount of money involved is usually a fraction of the R&D budget inside a big corporation. Not that more money from a single source would necessarily be helpful. The best decentralized solutions grow organically over time, like a biological ecosystem that reaches equilibrium through years of trial and error. Progress is slow and uneven, and embarrassing setbacks are a given. But as with nature itself, this is more of a feature than a bug. An equilibrium that takes a long time to establish is more likely to last. As is a new way of building trust.

Bitcoin and Ethereum are software-based networks. But they are also protocols, and—due to their complicated consensus mechanisms—somewhat physical in nature. Building a clone of either network is virtually free, but securing that new network is prohibitively expensive. A blockchain that manages to muster up 50 percent of the mining power of Bitcoin is still only half as secure. Its coin would be less valuable, so it would have a harder time attracting additional miners. The same goes for Ethereum. Both blockchains have seen their fair share of competition in recent years, with some of these newer protocols—having learned from the flaws of the first two—offering arguably superior features. But none have managed to come close to the top two in terms of adoption, because they aren't nearly as secure.

The newest entrants to the 150-year-old world of electronic networking have similar cost structures to the original telephone and telegraph networks of old. They will be difficult to supplant once they go mainstream, because the switching costs for their users—who are also their owners—will be high. Participating in another decentralized network will require first purchasing its coin, so there is a cost of capital to using multiple blockchains, boosting the winner-take-all tendency of whichever happens to go mainstream first.

This presupposes a significantly higher level of adoption for any of these platforms than what is realistic today. Some critics claim that blockchain is a solution looking for a problem, and that decentralization is more appealing in theory than in practice. Judging strictly by the numbers, they have a point. Platform users need to be offered more than a history lesson to switch. They need to be offered a killer app.

For Bitcoin, that's increasingly looking to be as a digital store of value, money that is harder to inflate than fiat currency but easier to store and transact than gold. For anyone concerned with the extent to which governments are abusing their free-rider privileges, there is now a clear alternative, one that comes with its own payment network. Anyone not concerned may want to pull up a chart of the trillions of dollars, euros, pounds, and yen that have been printed since the start of the COVID-19 pandemic, then recall the economic maxim that there is no such thing as a free lunch. All that printing and borrowing is bound to have unintended consequences, and to erode trust in fiat money. The killer application of the Bitcoin blockchain is money that can be stored locally, transferred globally, and used without fear of devaluation or censorship.

Secondary blockchain platforms such as Ethereum also enable a scarce kind of digital money, but their value proposition is more tied to the activities performed on top of them. The sky is the limit on what those activities could be, and everything from basic banking to sophisticated gaming is already available. But ironically, the first killer application built atop these token and smart-contract enabled platforms is something simpler: Satoshi Nakamoto's original vision of peer-to-peer electronic cash. But not, as is the case with Bitcoin, for payments made in crypto, but rather payments made in fiat currency. Indeed, beyond the transfer of a new kind of money, the most popular application for blockchain platforms is the transfer of the old kind.

3
PAYMENTS

payment noun

a highly profitable industry that will soon collect more in taxes than the IRS, unless re-architected.

If money is a myth, then the simple act of a payment is how it perpetuates itself. Historians may disagree on what existed before money, but they generally agree that the need to transfer value, its medium-of-exchange function, was why it was invented. Most of the characteristics of money revolve around payments, as that which is portable, fungible, and divisible is easy to pass around. The history of the clever ways people have managed to do that is as varied and interesting as the history of money itself. From clay tablets with graphic etchings to digital tablets with graphic interfaces, humans have been iterating on payment methods for thousands of years.

Payments are the most important activity that nobody ever thinks about. Virtually every type of economic interaction requires a payment, from earning a salary to buying groceries to trading stocks. A payment is what Abraham had to make to buy a burial plot for his wife, what Jesus instructed his followers to make when taxes were due, and what too many borrowers couldn't make during the 2008 financial crisis.

Most of the convenience upgrades that have defined the evolution of money throughout the ages have revolved around the ease of making a payment, sometimes to the detriment of the overall trust framework. There's a natural tension between the scarcity of money and the ease with which it can be paid to someone else. Giant stones, like the kind used on the Micronesian island of Yap until the last century, were quite scarce, but so hard to transfer that some of the stones were never moved, even after being used in a payment. Gold coins were also unruly because gold is a heavy metal. Paper is a lot easier to pass around, but also easier to devalue. Ledger entries are easier still, on both counts.

The simplest kinds of payments are made with token money. Transferring a coin or paper bill is free, instant, and private: I give you a $20 bill, and you consider yourself paid. There are no fees involved and nobody other than the two of us needs to know that the transaction took place. But token money is cumbersome for large sums, expensive to transfer across long distances, and useless online. Ledger money is more practical, at least for the kinds of transactions that increasingly matter, but requires an intermediary. This important need for a third party is the opening salvo of the Bitcoin white paper and the rest of the document's introduction is an exploration of the drawbacks of payments made via centralized ledgers—and notably not a critique of fiat currency.

Payments traveling through an intermediary are no longer irreversible because the intermediary can be asked to mediate disputes—a fact that anyone who has ever contested a credit card charge is familiar with. The intermediary is happy to provide this service but needs to be compensated for it. To be effective, it also needs the power to keep out the kinds of clients it doesn't want, making the system censorable.

The consequences of these additional costs and restrictions are profound, especially when measured in aggregate. Every other industry must now be designed around the availability (or lack thereof) of electronic payments. The impact is everywhere once you know what to look for. Gas stations with different prices for cash or credit. Coffee shops with minimums for card purchases. Restaurants with discounts for paying with cash. Direct deposits that take days to arrive. Wire transfers that get lost in the opacity of the banking system. Unbanked workers who pay high fees to cash a check, and migrants who pay even more to send money home.

Arguably even more profound are the things we can't see and the industries that don't exist. The *lack* of cheap and universally available micropayments is one reason why so much of the internet is either being consumed by surveillance capitalism or disappearing behind paywalls. Content creators wouldn't have to resort to creepy ads or monthly charges if they could just charge for every article, or even every word. Alas, charging a few cents a word is not viable when every payment costs ten cents.

Standing firmly on the other side of this increasingly worrisome economic divide is a rapidly growing electronic payments industry. One critique of the original Bitcoin paper is the way in which the role of the intermediary is presented as a reluctant one. Today we know that the opposite is true. Case in point: Visa, the world's biggest payment company, is also one the biggest financial companies by market cap. It is more valuable than most banks, despite providing fewer services and having a fraction of the employees. Owning a proprietary and popular payment platform is one of the most profitable businesses on earth.

Those profits are everybody else's expense. If the current pace of digitization continues and cash wanes further, the payments expense will eventually become a de facto tax on every single economic interaction. Imagine a world where a handful of companies get to charge a fee for every single paycheck, purchase, or trade. These companies will also get to veto the types of economic activity that they don't like, as PayPal once did when it threatened to kick out bookstores that sold certain kinds of books, or various banks tried to do to OnlyFans if it continued to allow adult content.[27] Then there is the data collection angle. If you thought the surveillance capitalism of companies like Facebook and Twitter was creepy, consider all the sensitive information that credit card companies collect. Unlike social media platforms, payment providers know your real name and address.

As with any other kind of centralized platform, the Unholy Trinity—the separation of user, operator, and owner in any network interaction—leads to bad outcomes. Unlike platforms designed for social media or rideshare, payment platforms such as credit card networks or mobile pay solutions are increasingly impossible to avoid, especially in the aftermath of a global pandemic that turned even the simplest economic interactions into remote ones. Given the current pace of digitization, it's only a matter of time until physical cash disappears from the economy, turning today's centralized payment providers into our new economic overlords. Never has the economic vitality of so many driven the profit margins of so few. Thankfully, now there's a blockchain for that.

The Architecture of Payment Systems

All the world's centralized payment systems are built on top of the banking system. This symbiotic relationship is no accident, as it was the facilitation of payments (and not lending) that drove the rise of the earliest banks, particularly in the thriving cities of northern Italy during the Medieval period, where the Catholic Church's laws against usury restricted banking as we know it today. While lending and borrowing was not allowed, there was still a need for someone willing to accept deposits as merchants preferred the relative safety of storing their coins at a centralized location, particularly when traveling for business. Doing so also allowed them to make payments by simply ordering the bank that held their coins to transfer ownership to a different client. The bank could resolve the transaction with a simple ledger entry, saving both parties the trouble of having to deal with coins—the aforementioned convenience of ledger money in action.

The need for this kind of payment service was accentuated by the proliferation of different coins issued by the sovereigns of neighboring cities. By accepting deposits in multiple currencies and keeping up with the prevailing exchange rates, the early bankers also played the role of money changer, offering the convenience of currency exchange and payment in a single transaction.[28]

As with any kind of ledger money, using the bank as an intermediary required a great deal of trust. Depositors had to trust that it would keep accurate books, not cheat them, and stay in business. Merchants were willing to take that risk because carrying cash had its own risks, and, with a bank they could take advantage of the intermediary's payment services. If a merchant had a good relationship with a banker, he could enjoy additional services, such as a temporary loan to make an immediate payment—a popular service still provided by many payment providers today.

From the bankers' point of view, offering payment services was a good way to increase deposits, some of which could be invested in income-producing activity or secretly loaned out during the Medieval period. So long as the bank kept sufficient reserves to meet withdrawal requests, it could scale up its business, accepting more deposits in a greater variety of currencies to facilitate a larger volume of payments. Scale is very important to any payment provider, then and now. The more depositors a bank or money changer had, the more likely it was to be called upon to make a payment. The larger the deposits, the larger the transaction size that could be accommodated.

The earliest payment providers enjoyed their own network effects, leading to the dominance of a few money changers or banks in most cities, often run by powerful families. Trust being paramount to this arrangement, an established family with deep roots in a community and its own business interests was less likely to cheat its depositors. But so long as there was more than one bank, there was friction. Merchants who kept all their money at one bank occasionally needed to make a payment to the clients of a different bank. This request could not be met with a simple ledger entry.

The two banks involved could have resolved the request by exchanging coins, but that was both risky and inefficient. A more effective solution was for them to keep accounts with each other. Instead of a payment being resolved with a debit and a credit inside the books of a single bank, it could now cascade as a series of ledger entries involving both banks. In other words, if Gennaro, a merchant who had an account with Bank A, wanted to make a payment to Paolo, a merchant whose deposits were with Bank B, the transaction would be completed by Bank A first debiting Gennaro's account and crediting Bank B's, then instructing Bank B to credit Paolo in its own books. Such a system of *nostro* and *vostro* accounts (Latin for "ours" and "yours") could turn a group of banks into a single payment network.

But implementing such a network using bilateral relationships was very expensive in terms of capital. Since every bank had to keep some money on deposit with every other bank, the cost of participation grew proportionally to the number of banks. A more efficient solution was for all the banks in a region to keep nostro accounts with a single correspondent bank, one that specialized in facilitating bank-to-bank payments. Now, a single account was all any bank needed to resolve payments to many other banks. The correspondent bank could also facilitate currency exchange, doing for merchant banks what merchant banks did for their clients. Centuries later, these dynamics still play an important role in the design of our banking system.

Correspondent banking results in a hub-and-spoke architecture for a payment network and is most efficient if the system is highly centralized. Having too many correspondent banks leads to fragmentation where certain payments become either impossible to make or require multiple *hops* to arrive at a destination. Correspondent banking is a lot like a telephone network and has its own network effects. The winner-take-all tendency drives centralization, and just a few correspondent banks end up moving massive amounts of money.

But now we have a new problem. So long as there is more than one correspondent bank in any economy, then the correspondent banks need to create a way to make payments to each other. Enter the central bank, the only bank big enough to serve as a bridge between the mighty correspondent banks. The presence of a central bank turns an otherwise siloed group of payment systems into a unified network. Indeed, some of the earliest central banks in Europe were originally founded as payment institutions that facilitated bank-to-bank transfers.[29]

THE EVOLUTION OF PAYMENTS

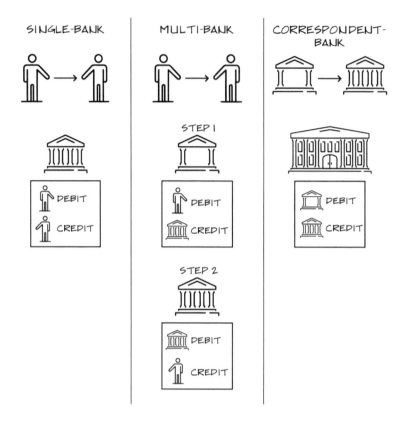

From Payments to Lending

Once Europe entered the industrial era, its centers of finance moved from papist Italy north to cities such as London and Amsterdam. There, the payments industry was able to flourish, as it was free to combine the movement of money with credit, creating a more sophisticated banking system. Manufacturers could now take out loans to build new factories, then pay down the debt with incoming payments from customers. Importers could close deals with a letter of credit that promised exporters a payment directly from their bank, and sellers could factor their accounts receivable for immediate cash. Anyone who had a good relationship with their bank could rely on overdraft protection. Credit is a sort of lubricant in the movement of money. It enables and accelerates the completion of all sorts of payments that may otherwise take too long or not happen.

The economic benefits of combining payments and lending made commercial banking a vital industry and, as a direct consequence, further diminished the use of token money in business transactions. The ascent of ledger-based payments also played a part in the evolution of money. It's no coincidence that the rise of commercial banking as we know it coincided with the transition to fiat currency, as a central bank that doesn't have to back its money with anything can more easily accommodate its movement. It can play the part of payment intermediary during the best of times and lender of last resort during the worst. Even central banks that were not originally created with a payment function in mind, such as the Bank of England, were eventually drawn into facilitating the activity.[30]

Central banks are the most important hub in most payment systems for two reasons. The first is the obvious fact that they are less likely to fail than any private institution. If many commercial banks are to keep deposits with a single entity, better that it be the safest one around, lest the entire network be compromised by a single failure. Secondly, if every commercial bank is required to keep some of its capital with a central bank for safekeeping anyway, then why not use a portion of that money to settle payments? Central bank reserve accounts are the ultimate nostro accounts, allowing commercial banks to kill two birds with one capital efficient stone. Even banks that don't keep reserves with a particular central bank (for the simple reason that they are based in a different country) could benefit from this arrangement by establishing a nostro account with a correspondent bank that does.

And so, the conveniences of ledger money, combined with the overall desire to move funds not just within ledgers but across them, leads to yet another pyramid-shaped hierarchy of trust. The payments pyramid can span countries, even continents, and is one of the most important hierarchies in the world today. Central banks play the role of the most trusted agents, and correspondent banks build bridges beyond borders and across currencies. Like most hierarchies, most of the action takes place at the bottom in the form of the low-value payments we make on a daily basis. The top is reserved for a lower quantity of high-value transfers, the kind large corporations and financial institutions make to each other.

THE PAYMENTS PYRAMID

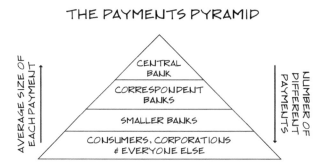

This hierarchy has turned out to be the most efficient way to resolve payments in a modern economy—but only if efficiency is measured in terms of cost of capital. Efficiency in terms of speed, expense, and access for the underprivileged and unbanked is a different matter.

Money Movement Like Molasses

Before leaving the Renaissance era, we must pay homage to one of the most famous banks in history, the one operated by the Medici's of Florence. Although the *Banco dei Medici* did not invent many of the banking innovations that contributed to its ascent—things like double-entry bookkeeping and letters of credit—it did perfect an important payments innovation: the use of different branches for the same bank.[31]

One way for a bank to move money across borders and in different currencies is by opening multiple branches in different regions. Each branch can operate as an autonomous unit, taking deposits, issuing loans, and facilitating payments in the local currency. But as an added benefit, client payments could now be facilitated via branch-to-branch transfers, as coordinated by the parent company. Money movement still happens via cascading ledger entries, but coordinating the communication and controls needed to do this effectively is easier inside the same bank. The Medici's were the preferred bank for the Vatican, a coveted position won in part by having many international branches, enabling them to efficiently handle payments having to do with the collection of tithes and taxes from abroad. One of their branches even traveled with the Pope wherever he went.[32] None of this would have been possible without regular, efficient, and secure communications among its branches. Even then, no payment could ever be faster than the messenger who carried its instructions.

One critique against the hub-and-spoke model of payments is the delay between when a payment is initiated and when it's completed. All of that debiting and crediting across the books of different banks takes time. Most banks don't operate around the clock, so nights, weekends, and holidays are also problematic. Add to the limited time window the need for constant communication and coordination among the parties involved, and what you end up with is a slow, clunky, and error-prone process.

Secure communication is at the heart of resolving payments via ledger money. Token money, by virtue of being peer-to-peer, has no such need. Payers hand money to payees and the transaction is completed. Payments made through the banking system, on the other hand, are a massive coordination problem, particularly when multiple ledgers are involved. They require constant communication. For each payment, the initiating bank must first identify the optimal route (through its own branches, to another bank, or through a correspondent) then communicate the necessary instructions to everyone involved. If the preferred route is not an option—perhaps because a nostro account along the way is insufficiently funded—then a new route must be established and communicated.

Other considerations, such as whether the proposed payment is legal, also play a role. This complicated process of setting up a payment and making sure it can go through is known as clearing and it relies heavily on communication. The actual movement of money is known as settlement, and the natural delay between these two steps has been the bane of the banking industry, not to mention its clients, for centuries.

That industry might look like it has evolved a great deal in recent years—upgrading to electronic messaging and computerized ledgers— but certain processes have not changed in decades. Settling a payment is still a game of monetary hot potato across opaque systems that are not very good at talking to each other. Not that the industry hasn't tried. In fact, most of the payments innovations of the last century have focused on how banks and payment providers coordinate their efforts. Case in point: the bank check.

Checks as we understand them today are the descendants of a Renaissance-era payment instrument known as the bill of exchange, a complicated device that was part loan, part payment, and part foreign exchange transaction. Its complexity was part of its appeal, as it allowed a secret loan to be embedded inside a payment at a place and time when lending was restricted. Modern checks are a lot simpler, and are nothing more than a communication device, instructing the bank of the check writer to make a payment to the beneficiary. Processing them, on the other hand, has never been simple.

If the recipient has an account at the same bank, the request can be fulfilled with a book entry. But what if the recipient deposits the check at a different bank? Not only do the two banks need to coordinate the movement of money, but they also need to coordinate the movement of the check, because the issuing bank needs to confirm its authenticity. As cumbersome as this process sounds, it formed the backbone of payments in the West throughout the industrial era, starting in eighteenth-century London, where an army of "walking clerks" crisscrossed the city daily, presenting deposited checks to other banks for authentication. Seeing how they were already there, they'd also collect the resulting payment in cash.

Being a walking clerk was both dangerous and tiring, as these payments were settled with coins.

Eventually the clerks realized that it would make more sense for them to all meet at the same location each day and come with checks to cash and cash to pay. This being England, a pub in the City's famed Lombard Street was chosen as the unofficial home for interbank check clearing.[33] It's hard to know exactly how much money was exchanged (or how many pints were drunk) during this period, but the numbers would have been substantial given the thriving nature of London banking at that time.

The practice was eventually moved to its own office down the block, henceforth known as "The Bankers Clearing House." There, each bank had its own desk, and each desk would have a small inbox. Clerks from opposing banks would show up throughout the day and deposit checks to be cashed into each other's inboxes. At the end of business, all the amounts owed would be added, and the banks that owed money would pay an inspector whose job it was to first verify the math and then pay the other banks.

Clearing all the checks within a community of banks at once opened the door to one of the most important innovations in the history of payments: the practice of *netting*. Two banks that need to redeem multiple checks from each other don't have to exchange cash for every single one. They could instead calculate the net payment that would result from all the checks within a fixed period and settle them in a single transaction. The process could be expanded to include multiple banks, so just a few payments are all it takes to settle countless checks. Not only does bilateral and multilateral netting reduce the operational complexity of check clearing among a community of banks, but it also reduces the cost of capital for the entire network, for the simple reason that most of the payments cancel each other out. Members of a clearinghouse can therefore settle a substantial volume of payments with a relatively small amount of cash. On the busiest clearing day of 1839, the members of the Bankers Clearing

House were able to settle six million pounds worth of checks with less than a tenth of that amount actually changing hands.[34]

There was one catch, however. For these efficiencies to be realized, payments had to be batched, introducing a delay. The longer the batching period, the more checks could be processed at once, a more efficient process—for the bankers. Clients, on the other hand, had to wait for the cycle to end before they could get paid. Batching pits client interest against that of their bank.

Both netting and batch processing as coordinated by a clearinghouse remain cornerstones of the payments industry today. The one thing that has changed is that banks no longer settle with each other using cash. English banks now settle via their reserve accounts at the Bank of England, eliminating the need for token money in interbank settlement altogether, and proving once again that when it comes to the medium-of-exchange function of money, convenience usually wins out. Virtually all the interbank clearing systems throughout the world work on the same model as the English one, although different communities arrived there at different times on account of regional differences.

The first clearinghouse in New York, for example, had to contend with the presence of a greater number of banks than in London, so it invented a special piece of furniture. The clerks who showed up at the New York Clearing House in the mid-1800s were greeted by a 70-foot-long oval table that was hollow on the inside. Each bank would have one clerk seated on the inside of the table and another standing on the outside, facing each other. The outside clerks would then rotate, spending a few minutes exchanging checks and calculating balances with the seated clerks from every other bank.[35]

Since central banking came relatively late to the United States, American clearinghouses had to use cash (or in some cases, a correspondent bank) for final settlement until the twentieth century. Tellingly, the New York Clearing House acted like a private central bank, and at various times throughout its history maintained its own reserves, issued its own paper currency, and stepped in as lender of last resort.[36] Those functions, along with the mundane but important task of facilitating final settlement for payments, were eventually taken over by the Federal Reserve.

The fact that the void of a proper central bank was once filled by a private institution shows us that payment systems left to their own devices prefer to be organized around a powerful central authority. The reason, as always, is trust. Commercial banks are suspicious of each other and would rather avoid having too much on deposit with another private institution, one that can fail. Using a central bank is both safer and more efficient, in the same way that having a single issuer of a currency, one that standardizes coinage, is also preferred. Here the proponents of decentralization often confuse cause and effect. Neither the merchants of antiquity nor the banks of the nineteenth century were forced to trust an authority. They could have kept on weighing their lumps of gold or settling via walking clerks. That they chose to put their trust in a central authority teaches us an important lesson about the benefits of trading many small risks for a single big one.

Messaging for Dollars

Check usage grew significantly in America in the decades after the Second World War, so much so that back offices started having a hard time keeping up. In the 1960s, banks began incorporating computers to scan and sort every check, effectively turning their payment instructions into electronic messages. But now that paper checks were nothing more than a roundabout way of exchanging electronic data, why not eliminate the paper part altogether? Thus, the creation of the first Automated Clearing House (ACH) systems in the United Kingdom and the United States in the 1970s.

ACH payments allow either the sender or the recipient of a payment to send instructions directly to a bank, and for banks to forward those instructions to a clearinghouse. They are ideal for bulk and recurring payments like payroll and government benefits. Settlement still happens through the payments pyramid, and the need for netting and batching require a built-in delay before settlement. This makes ACH unsuitable for activities that require instant settlement, like paying a restaurant bill before leaving.

Most check and ACH payments are resolved via the payments pyramid, so neither approach is very useful for cross-border payments, as most pyramids are confined to a single country and currency. A small commercial bank in England is unable to settle a payment to a small commercial bank in the United States via either the Bank of England or the Federal Reserve, so it must rely on a correspondent bank. Indeed, most cross-border payments are routed through a handful of correspondent banks that are large enough to keep reserves at multiple central banks. These banks are a vital part of global commerce and move trillions of dollars (not to mention euros, pounds, and many other currencies) of money every day. Most of these payments are wire transfers communicated via SWIFT (the Society for Worldwide Interbank Financial Telecommunication), an organization with a name as long and complicated as the payments it facilitates.

Unlike a clearinghouse or correspondent bank, SWIFT is nothing but a communication system. It was founded in the 1970s by a consortium of banks to standardize payment instructions and build a secure network through which those instructions could be sent. SWIFT is not responsible for clearing or settlement, but its messaging and coordination service is so important that even a short disruption can impact global commerce. Most people only interact with the SWIFT system when sending large-value and cross-border payments. Mundane payments are made with a combination of plastic and mobile wallets.

Card-based payments are the Dr. Jekyll and Mr. Hyde of the payment universe. On the surface, they are the essence of simplicity. The customer swipes a piece of plastic (or increasingly, uses their smartphone) and voila, the merchant is paid—seemingly instantaneously and with even less hassle than cash. But it is all an illusion. What happens behind the scenes of every card payment is a complex Rube Goldberg money machine that can require the participation of over half a dozen banks, payment processors, gateways, clearinghouses, and network providers, over the span of several days. A visual graphic of how the system works is as confusing to a lay person as the engineering schematic of a Swiss watch, and in many ways, just as expensive.

SIMPLIFIED SCHEMATIC OF CREDIT CARD PROCESSING

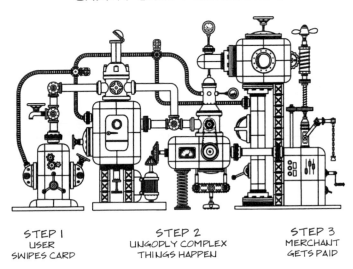

STEP 1
USER
SWIPES CARD

STEP 2
UNGODLY COMPLEX
THINGS HAPPEN

STEP 3
MERCHANT
GETS PAID

The complexity of debit and credit card transactions is a byproduct of the ambitiousness of their networks, attempting to enable pseudoinstant payments between an unlimited number of users and merchants. Card payments are ideal for financial interactions that used to be settled with cash, like buying a cup of coffee. But unlike cash, the shop owner is not paid right away. What networks such as Visa and Mastercard provide is an assurance that the money will arrive eventually. Put differently, they provide trust, for which they charge a fee. Debit cards use money that is already in a person's account to finalize the transaction while credit cards involve a loan. Even though the latter is a more complex interaction, it was invented first.

Appropriately, the first known reference to a credit card comes from a science fiction novel. Originally published in 1888, Edward Bellamy's best-selling *Looking Backward* presents a utopian-socialist vision of America circa the year 2000, one where token money has been abolished. A consumer needing to purchase goods would instead use:

> " . . . a credit card issued him with which he procures at the public storehouses, found in every community, whatever he desires whenever he desires it."

Bellamy might have gotten the idea for such a card from the nineteenth-century practice of individual businesses extending their customers credit, sometimes represented by a metal card. The first successful attempt at offering a card that could be used at multiple merchants, and the solution often credited for launching America's obsession with plastic, was the Diners Club Card, supposedly invented by a businessman in New York who was embarrassed to find himself unable to pay for a business lunch.[37]

Like any other network solution, a credit card is only appealing to users if it's accepted by many merchants, but merchants are unlikely to adopt a card that doesn't have a lot of users. One solution to this chicken-and-egg problem is for the card's issuer to give cards to random people. As crazy as that approach sounds, it's exactly what Bank of America did in 1958 to jumpstart its BankAmericard product, mailing out sixty thousand already-activated cards to the residents of Fresno, California (an early precursor to the practice of *token airdrops* in the crypto community).[38] The gimmick worked—despite a significant amount of fraud, abuse, and political backlash—and the idea of a generally accepted payment solution that incorporated credit provided by a bank was born.

Banking regulations prevented Bank of America from issuing cards outside California, so it licensed the concept to other banks, thus laying the foundation for a card network, one where merchants who agreed to accept a card issued by one bank would be obligated to accept similar cards issued by others. Processing the resulting transactions was a herculean task, so Bank of America eventually handed the operation to a bank-owned consortium, one that would eventually be named Visa.[39] Other networks followed suit.

Modern Payments That Aren't So Modern

The brilliance of this approach to payments was its network optionality. By virtue of being open to an unlimited number of banks, merchants, and users, card networks were able to achieve significant network effects. Like the original telephone network, card networks had a physical quality to them that made switching costs high and new competition unlikely.

Credit card usage really came into its own toward the end of the twentieth century, thanks to the emergence of e-commerce. The payment method's ability to offer remote payment (in a way that cash could not) and pseudo-instant settlement (in a way that checks and ACH could not) proved desirable to early adopters of online shopping. Debit cards were also used, but credit was especially popular due to the built-in consumer protection of it technically being the bank's money, and not the consumer's, that is sent to the merchant. This buffer made it easier for consumers to protest a charge if there was a problem. Credit card–issuing banks are glad to offer dispute resolution because doing so makes their product more desirable, and they can pass most of the cost on to merchants.

Both Mastercard and Visa put an exclamation mark on their importance to the digital economy by going public in 2006 and 2008, respectively. Visa's initial public offering got a lot of attention on Wall Street as it was then the biggest IPO in US history—a fact probably not lost on anyone about to publish a seminal white paper on the possibility of peer-to-peer electronic cash, the kind that didn't require a centralized operator. Visa and Mastercard are now more valuable than most of the banks and merchants whose payments they intermediate, proving once again that when it comes to a centralized platform, the bulk of the value eventually accrues to its owners, not its users.

Card networks are not the only game in town when it comes to instant electronic payments, as smartphone-based and digitally native payment solutions increasingly proliferate. But most of these services are communication systems in disguise and built using a model invented 150 years ago.

Case in point: Western Union, the American company now only known as a niche payment provider, was once the largest telecommunication company in the world, operating a telegram network that spanned from the Atlantic to the Pacific (and even to Russia by way of Alaska). Tellingly, Western Union launched its money transmitter service in 1871—just ten years after completing its first transcontinental link—and much earlier than its other innovations such as the Telex, fax, and Candygram.[40] The basic design of its payment service was no different than the one operated by the Medicis centuries earlier. Senders would deposit cash at one branch and provide instructions for someone else to claim it at another. Western Union's main innovation was to use electronic messaging to deliver those instructions, an innovation that was quickly adopted by the banking industry itself. Telegrams are no longer used in payments, but their legacy lives on in the name we give to the fastest kind of bank-to-bank payment: the wire transfer.

Almost a century and a half later, a similar innovation was introduced by PayPal, this time using email. Now, instead of a telegram kicking off the payment process, a digital message could be used. Final settlement would still have to go through the banking system, as users had to first fund their account and merchants would need to eventually cash out. But the experience at the point of the sale could now be digitized, eliminating the need for mailed checks. That upgrade—as incremental as it may have been—was enough to drive usership from 12,000 accounts to 2.7 million in a single year.[41] Like most payment solutions that came before it, PayPal was just another ledger processing debits and credits on behalf of its users.

But unlike every other solution, its platform embraced the efficiency of digitization from the get-go. Merchants were again forced to pay for the privilege, but the added efficiency was clearly worth the cost.

PayPal is now one of the largest financial companies in the world, the most valuable of a class of e-money providers that claim to be on the cutting edge of digital payments. If we judge these services by outward appearance and ease of use, then they have a point. But if you look behind the outward user experience and consider the payment experience from start to finish, remarkably little has changed from the era of bank clerks playing musical chairs at a clearinghouse. Money that sits inside the ledgers of financial institutions is moved around in a two-step process requiring painstaking coordination. Most of the innovation has been limited to the domain of messaging and the newer solutions have simply layered complexity on top of the old—shiny new towers built atop an aging foundation.

Any economic interaction is only as fast as its slowest link. Given how undigital most of the banking system remains, most payments are still slow and cumbersome. The movement of money is increasingly the bottleneck for other kinds of digital interaction. Despite all of the upgrades to the payment infrastructure, you can take an Uber from New York to Florida faster than the driver will get paid. International payments are even slower, leading to the sad reality that in some corridors it is both faster and cheaper to FedEx someone a box of cash than it is to send them a wire.

The advent of the web should have had a greater impact on the payments industry because money is nothing more than information. But the core protocols of the internet were not built with payments in mind, so there is no built-in system for moving money like there is for email, photographs, or documents. That task was punted to the banking system which, after a few years of fumbling along, booted it to Silicon Valley. For all of the bells and whistles advertised by the likes of PayPal and Square, they are architecturally not that different from their predecessors. Swiping a credit card in a plastic widget that plugs into a smartphone is certainly an improvement over using carbon paper inside a knuckle-buster, but peer-to-peer electronic cash, it is not.

To make matters worse, the entire system is more complicated and centralized than ever, leading to a dangerous setup where the failure of just one or two players could topple the whole thing. One of the lesser discussed motivations behind the seemingly gratuitous 2008 Wall Street bailouts was the fact that some of the banks embroiled in the mortgage crisis were also major correspondent banks, threatening a scenario where trillions of dollars in daily payment flows could have ground to a halt. The bailouts made those "too big to fail" banks even bigger, so the payments pyramid is now more centralized than ever. Most of the money has no choice but to flow through the narrow connections at the top, and some of it, like an international payment that needs to happen instantly on a weekend, can't flow at all. For all the innovating that PayPal has done in twenty years, it hasn't figured out how to let users send money directly to Venmo, even though it operates both services.

The Payments Tax

The costs of our current system are astronomical and will continue to grow. Digitization may have had a deflationary impact on most industries, but not this one. Annual revenues for the industry surpassed $2 trillion in 2019 and are expected to grow by another 50 percent within the next five years—accelerated by a global pandemic that has turbocharged both the pace of digitation and the aversion to physical cash.[42] These revenues are everybody else's cost. Cash payments are, and always have been, free. If we are to believe the thesis that it's only a matter of time until society becomes cashless—a thesis supported by the growing importance of other digital services in our daily lives—then we are headed for a future where every economic interaction will feed a payment provider, like a mafia don who benefits from every form of economic activity on his turf. When it comes to payments, that turf is the global economy. Any fee that is both universal and unavoidable is a tax, and taxes, as every economist knows, are disruptive.

Some of that disruption is visible to almost everyone on a daily basis, such as at the gas station or deli counter. Corporations also carry the burden as seen in the income statements of the world's biggest companies. Uber's long-running struggle to achieve profitability is hampered by the fact that it spends upwards of $1 billion a year on payments.[43] According to the National Association of Convenience Stores, there have been years where card issuers and the payment networks in the United States have made more money from the business of people paying for gas than gas stations have made selling gas.[44] Unlike many other business expenses, fees on payments grow linearly with revenues, and have little regard for an industry's profitability or profit margin.

A 2 percent swipe fee on credit card purchases is a major headache for a retailer whose profit margin is less than 5 percent. Most retailers don't charge different prices for cash versus credit, in part because doing so was not allowed by the major card networks for most of their history. Nor can a retailer refuse to accept one kind of card over another, as both Visa and Mastercard dictate that a merchant that wants to accept one of their cards must accept all of them, regardless of their fees.

Such rules create a perverse incentive structure where the banks that issue the cards are motivated to offer their users ever higher cash-back rewards, then pass the expense onto merchants. There is a reason why the biggest credit card issuers have entered a "rewards war" in recent years, and it's not because of how much they like their customers. The resulting swipe fees ultimately get baked into the prices of goods and services that merchants sell, leading to a sad reality where the poorer consumers who pay with cash are effectively subsidizing the richer ones who pay with a platinum rewards card. Not only is the payments tax pervasive, it's also regressive.

The price inequities of the current payment setup are so bad that they've been the subjects of legislation, antitrust investigations, and class action lawsuits for years. Swipe fees have been capped by some governments, but the solid profitability of almost every centralized payment provider is proof that the tax is alive and well. Free riding always finds a way, particularly for the owners of centralized platforms.

Even more nefarious are the disruptions that we can't see, like the countless business models that don't exist on account of the limitations of our payment infrastructure. The internet has led to the unbundling of many services, enabling music lovers who used to have to buy an entire album to now download their favorite song from iTunes or stream it on Spotify. But Spotify can't charge per listen, nor can it pay its artists per stream, because the cost of each payment would be too high. Micropayments are the Waterloo of the digital revolution.

Last, but certainly not least, is the human toll. Despite the costs and delays that are inherent to our current payment system, virtually everyone who relies on it does so voluntarily, because the alternative of using cash is increasingly not an option. The greatest victims of the current setup are therefore those who cannot participate. According to the World Bank, there are currently 1.7 billion adults around the world who don't have a bank account.[45] That is more than one-seventh of the world's population. These are the people locked out of a payment system built atop the banking system, second-class citizens who don't get to participate in the digital revolution and who—by virtue of being forced to the fringes of the pyramid—pay exorbitant fees just to get by. For proof, look no further than the fee chart at a check cashing outfit or remittance service. A migrant worker who has to use both services to send money home will probably pay a far higher percentage of the amount being sent than a millionaire buying a house.

Some of these shortcomings have been addressed by new laws, regulations, and government-run real-time payment networks. But the solution to bad infrastructure isn't a law that caps how much money someone can make from it. It's better technology. A decentralized network for value transfers that can handle tokens and smart contracts has many different applications. One application is the invention of a new kind of money. Another application is a more efficient method to move around the old kind. Ironically, and despite the protestations of the crypto industry's truest believers, the first killer application for blockchain technology might very well be the US dollar.

Stablecoins

One of the challenges of using bitcoins as a store of value or medium of exchange is acquiring some in the first place. The Bitcoin blockchain is great for transferring value within the platform but has nothing to say about how new users join. Other than mining, which is too technical for most people, the only other option is to buy existing coins from someone else. In the early days of Bitcoin, when each coin wasn't worth more than a few cents, such transactions were coordinated informally through friends or on online message boards. But the cryptocurrency world has grown a great deal since then, as has the price of the coin. Most of the buying and selling today is done on specialized exchanges.

Crypto exchanges are services that exist at the nexus of the old and the new, connecting the existing, centralized financial system with the decentralized blockchain one. On the surface, they look no different than any other financial exchange, providing order books for bids and offers and facilitating a trade whenever there's a match. But underneath the hood, a crypto exchange interacts with both the existing payment infrastructure and the blockchain one, allowing buyers to deposit fiat currency to acquire crypto, and for sellers to do the opposite.

Censorship resistance—as understood within the crypto community—is a cryptocurrency's inability to discriminate against one user versus another (or keep anyone out) as the blockchain only sees numbers and algorithms, not corporations or people. The legacy financial system is built on the opposite principle, treating discrimination as a feature and not a bug, partly to manage costs and mostly due to regulatory constraints. High processing costs make poorer users undesirable, and laws that require payment providers to collect personal data on every user (referred to as "know your client," or KYC) lock out those lacking a proper legal identity, such as migrants and undocumented workers.

KYC requirements, along with anti-money laundering (AML) compliance, are core components of the legacy payment system. They stem from a unique regulatory framework for the financial industry, one built on a presumption of guilt for every would-be participant. Unlike almost every other industry, banks and payment providers are mandated to assume that every client or corporation has bad intent, then work their way backward—with devastating social consequences, as we'll see later. This framework makes payment providers risk-averse and reluctant to serve some industries. Companies deemed to be doing something "high risk," like managing a casino, selling medicinal marijuana, or streaming adult entertainment, are often forced to pay much higher fees for vanilla payment services or simply denied access.

Crypto exchanges have historically been seen as the highest of the high risk, with some having a hard time just opening a bank account, never mind using one to send and receive payments on behalf of their clients. Unbeknownst to the payment providers and regulators who created this situation, this deliberate act of censorship helped sow the seeds for a revolution in payments, because crypto companies barred from using bank-based infrastructure to move fiat money were left with no choice but to build blockchain-based ones.

Fiat currency on the blockchain is colloquially referred to as a stablecoin—an homage to the relative stability of a currency such as the US dollar compared to the likes of Bitcoin. Stablecoins can be issued by anyone, in any currency, on any blockchain that can process tokens. There are several methods for creating one, but the simplest and most popular is for a company to deposit cash inside the banking system, then issue a right to claim that money as a token on a blockchain. So long as users are confident about the eventual redeemability of each token, then its value should be the same as the money backing it. In the meantime, the tokens can be swapped between users, turning the underlying blockchain into a de facto payment rail.

USD Tether, the first commercially successful stablecoin, was launched in 2014 using a bootstrapped token platform built on top of the Bitcoin blockchain. It quickly gained adoption among crypto exchanges that welcomed an alternative to the legacy payment system. The fact that it was accepted at multiple exchanges also made Tether useful for active traders wanting to quickly move dollars from one exchange to another to take advantage of price discrepancies. Stablecoins, as these traders realized, moved quickly and seamlessly—in a way that wire transfers or ACH payments did not. As demand for the stablecoin grew, the company that issued it (the sister company of one of the biggest Bitcoin exchanges) kept depositing more cash and issuing more tokens, eventually representing billions of dollars' worth of tokens on the blockchain.

The rapid rise of Tether as a blockchain-enabled fiat payment solution generated a lot of controversy. Using this new technology to move an older kind of money was not satisfying to idealogues on either side of the decentralization divide. Crypto purists were concerned with the need for a cash reserve kept inside the legacy banking system and the tremendous amount of trust placed in the issuing agent. There was no way to be certain that the off-chain reserve was sufficient, and no guarantee that the issuer wouldn't someday stop redemptions. These concerns were somewhat validated by several incidents in Tether's history where the token lost its peg to the dollar due to problems with redemption, rumors of insufficient reserves, or outright malpractice by the issuer. The stablecoin always recovered its peg, however, serving as a reminder that when it comes to money, convenience trumps mistrust.

Crypto skeptics were even less convinced—not just about the viability of Tether, but about the very idea of a stablecoin. Some questioned the stability mechanism, arguing that just because one asset is backed by another doesn't mean that their prices should remain stable. Others argued that the entire exercise was a scam, a crypto wolf in sheep's clothing designed to dupe users into exchanging actual money for a token bound to be worthless. Clueless academics published convoluted research arguing that Tether was being used to manipulate the price of Bitcoin, and low-rent journalists passed on such claims without an ounce of skepticism. A payment device backed by dollars, the experts argued, is not the same as a dollar.

And yet, most of the money in circulation today is *only* moved via proxies, as it has been for hundreds of years. A stablecoin issuer's declaration that each token is worth a dollar is no different than the claims made by banks about checks and the postal service about money orders. Contrary to what the uninformed may think, PayPal doesn't back every user account with a bag of cash stored in a vault somewhere. It backs *all* its accounts with a singular reserve deposited at a commercial bank (and the commercial bank, in turn, partially backs its accounts with a reserve kept at a central bank). Most of the money flowing through the payments pyramid is nothing more than a proxy for deposits kept elsewhere. The basic design of a stablecoin is an ancient idea, an alteration of an existing trust framework in pursuit of greater convenience. The question, as always, is whether the trade-off is worth it.

The answer—as indicated by the parabolic growth of existing stablecoins such as Tether and the newer USDC, attempted adoption by technology companies such as Facebook, and contemplation of the creation of tokenized central bank digital currencies—is a resounding yes. To see why, we must revisit the architectural flaws of the existing system.

A Digitally Native Architecture

Today's payment systems were all designed long before the arrival of the internet. Although most *look* electronic, few take full advantage of digitization. Their underlying mechanisms still follow the same flow as the era of paper ledgers and telegrams, requiring a tremendous amount of manual processing and after-the-fact reconciliation. Most systems can't process payments in real time, and the ones that do seldom operate around the clock. FedEx and UPS have figured out how to make deliveries over the weekend, but SWIFT and ACH have not, despite the fact that the latter are only moving data, and data should be easier to deliver than a desk.

The problem is one of design, not desire. Existing payment providers would like to be better, but they are held back by batch processing, multilateral netting, and incessant messaging. Regardless of how efficient any intermediary may be, its very presence can only slow things down and drive costs up. Re-architecture must therefore begin with an elimination of as many intermediaries as possible, and a flattening of the payments pyramid. Now there is a blockchain for that.

Ethereum users who wish to make a payment can just send a stablecoin. They don't need to get an authorization (as in a card payment) or wait for the next batching cycle (as in an ACH) or send messages (as in a wire). The miners who secure the platform process transactions in real time and around the clock. There are no weekends, bankers' holidays, or scheduled down times. Payments are processed on a first come, first serve basis, and anyone wanting immediate processing can pay more to jump the queue. A stablecoin payment sent on Ethereum can therefore be considered complete almost as soon as it is sent.

If you are taken aback by the simplicity of this solution, recall that money is just information, and a payment is just a transfer of data. A blockchain invented to enable the transfer of cryptocurrencies can also improve the transfer of fiat ones, as all that happens in either scenario is a series of debits and credits inside a shared ledger. Stablecoins turn any blockchain platform into a nonhierarchical fiat payment system, speeding up transfers and reducing fees. A transparent and open architecture means that anyone can use the service, not just those who live in rich countries and have bank accounts. As an added benefit, smart contracts can be used to introduce conditions on how and when each payment is executed, and fiat money can now travel on the same network as countless other assets, thanks to tokenization. As we'll see later, this final feature can transform any market where users trade financial assets against fiat money.

By eliminating the usual intermediaries required to make payments via the banking system, the blockchain approach ironically behaves more like the oldest payment method of all, cash. For all the criticism that payments made with physical money get in the digital era—criticism that was amplified during the pandemic—there are still many benefits. Cash payments are instant, anonymous, universal, and free. They are only problematic in large amounts and across long distances, or if they need to be integrated into some kind of platform.

Stablecoins represent the best of both worlds. They are cash-like in that they can be used by anyone, anywhere to make a fast and anonymous payment, and free of the surveillance capitalism that is slowly ruining everything. But they can also be stored easily, transmitted globally, and integrated into different online platforms—properties usually associated with ledger money. These hybrid benefits are the result of the solution's dual nature: Each stablecoin is a digital token riding a distributed ledger—the latest convenience upgrade in the long-running evolution of money.

Worth noting, however, is that a stablecoin can never be the native coin of a fully decentralized platform. Lest we forget, the independent nature of cryptocurrencies such as Bitcoin and Ether—combined with their algorithmic inflation schedules—is fundamental to the security of their platforms. Miners are incentivized to do honest work with fresh coins minted by the protocol, and those coins are generally expected to appreciate. Stablecoins cannot be minted out of thin air or expected to appreciate. New tokens can only be created after cash is added to the reserve, and each coin will be as volatile as its underlying currency. Stablecoins can only exist on decentralized platforms that are secured by a native cryptocoin, or on a far more centralized kind of blockchain that doesn't require traditional mining.

VERY DIFFERENT FIAT PAYMENT SYSTEMS

	ARCHI-TECTURE	MIDDLE-MEN	SETTLE-MENT	ACCESS	BUSINESS MODEL
TRADI-TIONAL	HIER-ARCHICAL	MANY	DELAYED	BANK CLIENTS, IN CERTAIN COUNTRIES, AT FIXED TIMES	HIGH FEES TO SUSTAIN PROFITS OF PROVIDERS
BLOCK-CHAIN	FLAT	NONE	INSTANT	ANYONE, ANYWHERE, AT ANY TIME	LOW FEES TO SUSTAIN SECURITY OF PLATFORM

Private Blockchains

Here we should pause for a second and learn about a different kind of blockchain, one that was invented after the creation of Bitcoin, to be a more constrained (and more controllable) version of the technology. Just as traditional networks have unique attributes and varying degrees of openness, blockchain networks can also be designed to be either totally open (like the internet) or highly constrained, like a private *intranet* for the employees of a single company. Put differently, blockchains can be as decentralized or centralized as their creators want them to be.

On one end of the decentralization spectrum are permissionless platforms such as Bitcoin and Ethereum, described that way because anyone is allowed to run a node or participate in mining without having to ask permission from an authority. On the other end are permissioned networks where participation in validation (aka mining) is restricted to certain known entities. Both types of networks use a distributed ledger that is made immutable with cryptography. Both can offer token functionality and smart contracts. Both deploy a consensus mechanism to validate transactions. But in a permissioned setting, mining is restricted to known entities authorized by a gatekeeper.

That distinction significantly changes the nature of the network, for better and for worse. Miners whose identities are known are less likely to behave badly, as they can be kicked out by the authority, have their reputation sullied, or even be sued in court. Consensus is therefore easier to achieve, and the network is easier to secure. Miners don't need to prove honest intent by spending money up front, so the network doesn't have to mint new coins to compensate them.

Unlike their decentralized counterparts, permissioned networks don't need a native coin at all, as much of the security is provided by the central authority. Since there is nothing to mine, those who participate in consensus are referred to as validators, not miners. Given their more simplified form of consensus, permissioned networks offer nominal electrical usage, faster transaction processing, and higher overall throughput.

The trade-off to these benefits is the re-emergence of a gatekeeper, one who must be trusted not to abuse the privilege. Such networks are often preferred for enterprise applications in highly regulated industries where anonymity is considered risky. They are a compelling option for stablecoins—which by virtue of the cash reserve held at a centralized institution like a bank—are not as decentralized as a pure cryptocoin anyway.

Other than restricting participation in validation, another way to centralize a blockchain network is by restricting usage, which in this domain is defined by the ability to generate one's own private key and corresponding address. Private blockchains restrict usage to known (and therefore, identified) individuals or companies. Public blockchains (like Bitcoin and Ethereum), on the other hand, let anyone use the network, and to do so pseudonymously. Every permissionless blockchain is practically public by default, because once mining is open to the public then so is usage—miners can process their own transactions. But if running nodes and participating in consensus is restricted by some kind of authority, then that same entity can also restrict usage.

Theoretically speaking, a permissioned blockchain can still remain public, since whoever is in charge can mandate that validators process transactions from anyone, even users who don't want to identify themselves. But given the tenuous history of trust, it's reasonable to assume that on a long enough timeline, every permissioned network will become private, regardless of their original intent. Those who can censor usually do, thanks to powerful forces such as fear, government pressure, or the curse of history.

DIFFERENT TYPES OF BLOCKCHAIN NETWORKS

	OPEN TO ANYONE	RESTRICTED BY GATEKEEPER
TRANSACTION VALIDATION	PERMISSIONLESS BLOCKCHAIN	PERMISSIONED BLOCKCHAIN
USAGE	PUBLIC BLOCKCHAIN	PRIVATE BLOCKCHAIN

A Contrived Controversy

The distinction between the different kinds of blockchain networks is relevant to payments and stablecoins because of a seismic event that took place in 2019 when Facebook (since renamed Meta) and a consortium of other technology companies announced their plans to launch a new blockchain network for payments called Libra (since renamed Diem). Like Bitcoin and Ethereum, Diem was meant to be public from the get-go, so anyone anywhere in the world could use it. But unlike those two platforms, Diem was to be launched as a permissioned network, with only members of the consortium having the right to participate in transaction validation. The original plans called for the network to transition to permissionless consensus after five years.

Despite the affiliation with Facebook, Diem was meant to be operated by a nonprofit association that took its marching orders from the members of the consortium. The platform itself was designed to be a less decentralized version of Ethereum, with greater transaction through-put, and without a native coin. The association would oversee technical development, the permissioning of validators, and the management of the reserves that backed its stablecoins. When originally announced, the association counted among its members many existing payment provid-ers, including PayPal, Visa, and Mastercard.

The announcement was immediately met with a firestorm of contro-versy, only some of which was deserved. Facebook's history of privacy issues made it an untrustworthy leader, and the company didn't help its own cause by initially designing the stablecoin to be a unified basket of dif-ferent currencies, as opposed to stand-alone representations of each one. Even the announcement process was somewhat botched, as it seemed to place shock value ahead of community engagement. That approach might be effective in a tech industry where Mark Zuckerberg's ethos of "move fast and break things" is considered a virtue but was ill-received in this context.

That said, most of the controversy was misinformed and some of it was unfair, a fear-based reaction to something new. People who didn't know much about the well-established practice of using proxies for payments accused the project of trying to invent a corporate currency, and the finan-cial media confused the issue further by failing to distinguish between a pure cryptocurrency and a stablecoin (probably because they themselves didn't know the difference). Existing payment providers argued that their own innovations were better, citing the latest upgrades to SWIFT messag-ing or the ascent of Fintechs like PayPal, ignoring the costs and limita-tions to both.

Not to be outdone, regulators, who couldn't tell the difference between a bitcoin and a bill of exchange, pulled out the usual canards about illicit use, and central bankers reminded everyone that only they had the abil-ity to create a new currency—ten thousand years of monetary history notwithstanding. Some politicians even went as far as to demand that Facebook halt the project altogether.[46] All of this occurred before the association was officially formed or the network launched. The criticism reached a crescendo when the legacy payment providers that had origi-nally signed on abruptly pulled out. Stablecoins, the skeptics declared, were dead.

But something closer to the opposite was true. The outrage over Diem helped legitimize the application of blockchain technology to fiat cur-rency. Before Diem, the primary critique against stablecoins was that they simply wouldn't work. After Diem, the argument shifted to why they shouldn't be allowed—with the implication that they could work. Why else would so many otherwise intelligent people consider them danger-ous? Even the abrupt and vocal departures of PayPal, Visa, and Master-card—supposedly due to a lack of regulatory clarity—carried this subtext. A decentralized payment network that is bound to fail should be a wel-come development to the biggest beneficiaries of the old way of doing things. One that has a chance of success is an existential threat.

New Plumbing

One way to appreciate the disruptive threat of blockchain technology to the world of payments is to think of money as water, and the networks and platforms through which money moves as plumbing. Today, pipes such as VisaNet and PayPal are highly profitable because they are often the only ones around. Other companies have no choice but to use them, allowing the owners of those pipes to charge hefty fees. Competition is unlikely because new pipes are expensive to build and difficult to maintain. At least, they used to be. Now, there's a blockchain for that.

More decentralized networks such as Ethereum introduce new pipes that are easier to build, cheaper to run, and more modular in their design. Best of all, they are publicly owned by their users. While Visa and Master-card often tweak their fees to maximize revenues for their shareholders the Ethereum community does everything it can to *reduce* transaction fees, for the simple reason that its owners are also its users. Unlike e-money providers or correspondent banks, stablecoin issuers don't need to make money from payments, and usually have a higher-order service in mind, such as enabling new business models that wouldn't otherwise exist. Even a permissioned network such as Diem was designed to minimize fees because most of the members of the association (which included Uber, Lyft, and Spotify) wanted to reduce their own payment costs.

Platform companies like the ones mentioned often get hit with the payments tax twice: once when they accept a payment from a user and again when they pay their providers. A blockchain network can reduce these costs substantially. It can also streamline their other services, such as rewards. Today, Uber needs to handle payments and rewards on different systems. The token and smart contract functionalities of Ethereum or any other programmable blockchain that has a stablecoin could combine both activities into one. A few lines of code are all it would take to automate the issuance of rewards to anyone who pays with a stablecoin—on the same platform, within the same wallet— a better user experience for both the company and its customers than the fragmented approach in use today. A universal cloud computer that can execute smart contracts on an infinite variety of value stores is a very powerful thing.

Programmability and interoperability are not features of legacy payment platforms—their pipes are (and always will be) dumb. Without a token transfer functionality ruled by consensus, the best they can offer is a better user interface—a nicer fax machine that still plugs into the same old telephone lines. Nor can the likes of PayPal or Visa help in the movement of anything other than fiat money, even though dollars, Uber Rewards, and countless other stores of value are nothing more than data. Without the benefit of a transparent ledger locked down with cryptography, different stores of value are doomed to live in different networks. Great for the companies that make a living reconciling these siloed systems, bad for everyone else.

To fully appreciate the transformative impact of stablecoins on the payments industry, it helps to revisit another industry built on monopolistic pipes that was eventually disrupted by a decentralized alternative with better features: the telephone industry. There are many similarities between the telecommunication setup of the twentieth century and the payments one of the twenty-first. Both were built to move data—one conversation, the other money. Both were initially dominated by a handful of small players that grew via acquisitions and strong-arm tactics. Both owned exclusive pipes at a time of explosive demand. Both maximized their right to free ride and invited accusations of monopolistic behavior.

As recently as 1997, AT&T's landline business was so profitable that a former executive famously quipped "Long distance is still the most profitable business in America, next to importing illegal cocaine."[47] Then came the internet. Charging high fees to move just one kind of data was no longer compelling now that consumers had access to a decentralized network that could move any kind of data, including voice. Long-distance communication quickly went from cash cow to loss leader, thanks to the spectacular growth of internet-based services such as Skype, WhatsApp, Google Voice, and FaceTime. AT&T was only able to survive by radically evolving its business model. Today, the company offers free voice calls so it can sell data plans.

Blockchain-based payment rails represent a similar leap in functionality—from closed networks that can move only money to open platforms that can move everything. Along with cost and compatibility, these networks are also better for innovation. Proprietary payment networks, like proprietary social media platforms, do not encourage creativity or competition, because their operators control the user experience from start to finish. PayPal can only be accessed via a single, officially sanctioned wallet, in the same way that Twitter can now only be accessed from its own app. Ethereum, on the other hand, can be accessed via hundreds of different wallets built by countless entities that have nothing to do with the people who launched the platform. Some of those wallets offer unique features—like added protections for user keys or the ability to access competing blockchain networks—because their developers don't live in constant fear of being locked out.

Not only does this kind of platform-based competition improve payments, it also enables new business models. Cost isn't the only reason more industries don't experiment with micropayments. There is also the risk of being on the wrong side of the next ad hoc fee change imposed by a centralized operator trying to maximize revenues. Case in point: Visa's latest proposed round of changes to its fee structure has the network charging more for online purchases while reducing fees for in-store payments, a rather convenient change to make in the aftermath of a global pandemic that significantly shifted consumption online. The payments tax: it's everywhere you want to be.

A more decentralized approach to payments diminishes such risks. A shared network is unlikely to increase fees in a way that would harm its own members. Stablecoins on Ethereum are even less likely to go that route, for the simple reason that there are many choices, and users can easily switch with the click of a button. Merchants, for their part, also have greater freedom of choice. Legacy payment providers often go out of their way to shackle merchants with expensive gadgets and gizmos that—while advertised as improving the payments experience— are designed to increase switching costs from one network to another. Blockchain wallets have no such constraint, and the same software used to access one stablecoin can be used to access any other.

Then there are all the new business models that can now be unlocked thanks to the programmability of money, some of which we can't even imagine. Today, conditional payments using fiat currency only exist in limited form via services such as BillPay. They are not Turing-complete, and it wouldn't matter if they were, due to the pitfalls of putting too much trust in centralized intermediaries. PayPal doesn't let you program payments on its platform, and even if it did, it still wouldn't make sense for anyone to rely on that feature too much, as the operator can always alter it or refuse to process the resulting payments.

Stablecoins on a programmable, public, and permissionless blockchain provide users the assurances that they need to innovate, and innovate they have, as we'll see. Many of the financial products that we enjoy today, things like stock options for investors or flood insurance for farmers, are nothing more than conditional payments executed on fiat currency. If Apple stock goes up, then pay the owner of a call option. If it rains too much, then pay the owner of a farm. Stablecoins on a programmable blockchain allow those activities to be taken out of the hands of options exchanges and insurance companies—centralized and seigniorage-seeking intermediaries in their own right—to be handled by smart contracts.

Progress Takes Time

The migration of fiat payments to decentralized platforms won't happen in a straight line, and it won't be easy. Blockchain networks remain in their infancy and have yet to be battle-tested. Networks gain resilience through crises, and the legacy payment platforms have been hardened over decades, dealing with natural disasters, financial crises, and geopolitical events. Stablecoin solutions and the blockchains platforms on which they reside will have to grow through their own trials, some of which may prove fatal.

There is also a capacity issue. Among the technical challenges of decentralization, network throughput is the thorniest. Ethereum as currently designed can only handle a small fraction of the number of transactions needed to become a major payment platform. Permissioned networks can handle more, but still not enough for our dynamic economy. Critics of decentralization often point to the fact that while credit card networks can scale up to tens of thousands of transactions per second, permissioned blockchains will at best reach a few thousand, and Ethereum as originally designed could barely break ten. These numbers don't necessarily represent an apples-to-apples comparison—credit card networks only process messages, not payments—but still point to a significant hurdle. Blockchains will have to get a lot faster to be competitive.

And they will. The same capacity and speed problems existed for every other kind of payment solution when it was first invented. Checks had to be physically delivered by clerks or the postal service then cleared manually. Credit cards had to be authorized over the phone, then settled weeks later inside the banking system. Too many wire transfers are *still* slow, despite the ubiquity of digital messaging. If the first generation of every new solution was expected to live up to the performance of the latest iteration of the old, then nothing new would ever get built. We'd still be riding horses and using landlines, because the first automobiles were not very fast, and the first mobile phones were not very reliable. But technology improves and networks gain throughput.

Stablecoins came into their own in 2020 for several reasons. The onset of the COVID-19 pandemic caused people and companies all over the world to seek out the relative safety of the US dollar, and one place where they found them was on public blockchains such as Ethereum. Indeed, the public and censorship-resistant nature of these platforms made them a haven for people otherwise cut out of the legacy banking system. Also contributing to the surge was the rise of decentralized finance (DeFi) solutions that made it easy for the holders of those coins to swap them for other assets or earn interest, a fascinating corner of the crypto economy that we'll visit.

Most of all, stablecoins grew because moving money via technology created for the digital era is more appealing than through rusty pipes built long ago. So appealing that despite their infancy, blockchain networks already move more dollars than PayPal, Venmo, and every other Western mobile payment provider combined. The leaders of those companies have noticed. Some have deployed their own stablecoin strategies, and most have embraced cryptocurrencies such as Bitcoin, perhaps as a hedge. PayPal might have a lot of success issuing its own stablecoin, but it won't make as much money from it as it does from transaction fees today. It can't, because the whole point of these instruments is to lower fees. To paraphrase Jeff Bezos, the current profit margins of the payments industry are stablecoins' opportunity.

Growing adoption has also caught the attention of government officials. Payments is one of the most regulated industries on earth, so it was only a matter of time until a new way of making them came under scrutiny. Some of their concerns, such as whether the issuers of these tokens are properly backing them, are valid. Other concerns, like whether stablecoins can become a tool for criminals, are not. That issue, also lobbed at pure cryptocurrencies such as Bitcoin and Ether, stems from the permissionless nature of the underlying infrastructure, and the fact that everyone is granted access—a stark departure from our existing payment solutions, all of which are designed to discriminate.

Most industries operate on a presumption of innocence. They accept anyone as a customer unless bad behavior or law enforcement give them a reason not to. Banking and payments operate on the opposite principle: everyone is guilty and denied access until proven innocent. It doesn't matter that most people are not terrorists or money launderers. Laws and regulations force banks and payment providers to assume that they might be.

This presumption of guilt is a minor nuisance for the affluent. It is an existential threat to the underprivileged because many cannot prove their innocence—not because they are criminals, but because they don't have legal status or lack the proper documents. The restrictiveness of this approach, and the onerous requirements it places on the user, is one reason why poor neighborhoods feature more pseudo–financial services like check cashers and pawn shops than banks, even in rich countries. This state of affairs also contributes to the growing wealth gap because those who have the least amount of money are forced to the fringes where they pay the highest fees. It's not that banks and payment providers don't want these people as customers. It's that the need to vet each one makes it either too difficult or too expensive to bother.

Unlike traditional payment providers that rely on legal identity, stablecoins, like Bitcoin, rely on cryptographic identity, which is universal. Not everyone can get a passport, but anyone can generate a private key. Re-architecture of our payment systems can have a profound impact on economic inclusion. The poor, minorities, oppressed women, refugees, and those living in developing nations can enjoy the same payment services as everyone else. Tellingly, that universality gives certain kinds of people agita. A financial system that is as open to undocumented Mexicans as it is to wealthy Americans, they argue, is bound to be overtaken by illicit activity.

The inherent racism and classism of this argument aside, it's based on a fallacy. It would be one thing if our existing infrastructure, for all its exclusionary tendencies, actually prevented crime. Then we could debate whether migrating to a more open system is worth the risks. But the numbers prove otherwise. According to the World Economic Forum, an estimated 2 to 5 percent of global GDP—some two trillion dollars per year—is laundered through our existing payment infrastructure. Only a tiny fraction of that money is ever caught.[48] There is over $27 billion per year in credit card fraud alone and even tightly controlled payment methods like wire transfers are used for sophisticated phishing scams.[49] Physical cash is even worse, as some substantial percentage of all large-value bills are assumed to be involved in something illegal.[50]

Guilty until proven innocent has failed on two fronts: it has kept out too many innocent people while not catching enough criminals. Blockchain infrastructure enables a more effective approach, one that shifts the focus from keeping out bad actors to isolating bad money—*know your token* as opposed to *know your client*. A transparent ledger of every single transaction that happens in real time is a wonderful tool for law enforcement. It allows them to identify funds used in illicit activity and to instruct the issuers of a stablecoin to freeze those tokens or destroy them. Unlike a pure cryptocurrency, a fiat-backed stablecoin can be programmed to allow such protective measures. No wonder then that most of the world's central banks are considering using blockchain technology to digitize their own money, as we'll soon see.

Bringing It All Together

The drive for convenience that has guided the evolution of payments for centuries has reached a significant fork in the road. One path puts a digital mask on the old, analog way of doing things, and asks society to not only surrender agency to a handful of monopolistic overlords, but also to pay for the privilege. The other offers a natively digital alternative, one that returns control to users, includes excluded peoples, and offers unique features such as programmability and real-time settlement. The informational nature of money, brought to life.

The deciding factor, as always, is trust. The owners and operators of today's centralized payment platforms would argue that their approach is the most trustworthy. So did the first generation of telephone executives confronted with the possibility of the internet. We know how that turned out. Satoshi Nakamoto's vision of peer-to-peer electronic cash is finally a reality. Stablecoins may not be a new kind of money, but they are a better way to make payments with the old, and for now, that may just be enough.

4

MARKETS

The myth of money may be the most important trust framework in society, but it's not the only one. Quantitatively speaking, it's not even the biggest. Financial assets such as stocks and bonds may be a distant second when it comes to importance to our day-to-day lives, but their total dollar value dwarfs the number of dollars in circulation, in part because one of the functions of these assets is to multiply the utility of money. The simple act of lending money to the US government, which happens every time somebody purchases a treasury bond, is enough to grow the overall dollar value of the economy. The owners of these bonds consider themselves no less wealthy for the investment, for all they've done is swap one valuable object for another. But the Treasury Department now has more cash than it used to, so money has magically grown.

If that mechanism confuses you, then you are on your way. Part of the charm and utility of money is its ability to defy the laws of nature, multiplying in supply as a result of some activities and collapsing on account of others. Investment products such as stocks and bonds are similarly unnatural, yet important. There is no law of nature that dictates the existence of a corporation named Apple, the total value of which is in the trillions. But there would be serious social and economic consequences should that value suddenly plunge. These constructs were invented long ago to help organize economic activity.

Just as payments extend the medium-of-exchange function of money, investment products help expand the store of value function. Savers planning for the future can stash their cash in a shoebox or deposit their money at a bank. If they are worried about the bank going under or want more interest on their deposits, they can purchase a treasury bond instead—a legal agreement that dictates how they will lend money to the US government today in exchange for the promise of being paid back later, with interest. Part of the appeal of buying into that promise is that owners don't have to wait for the bond to mature to get their money back; they can transfer the right to someone else by selling the bond. Bonds are a standardized way for savers and borrowers to temporarily swap their purchasing power, with the rate of interest acting as the price of delayed gratification.

Those looking for even more upside can purchase stocks instead—legal agreements that dictate the exchange of cash for a piece of a company. Stocks are riskier than bonds but can be a lot more profitable. They can also provide an income stream known as a dividend. Stocks allow investors and entrepreneurs to exchange money today for the possibility of a lot more value tomorrow. As with bonds, they can transform the purchasing power of money, for better or for worse. Trust is important in the success of either product, one reason why they are called securities.

Stocks and bonds, along with other investment products such as investment funds, real estate, and commodities, form the backbone of the financial economy. Their combined value accounts for almost all the value in the world today, and their fluctuations drive and are driven by the machinations of the physical economy. But just as money is only useful to the extent that it can be paid, investment products are only valuable to the extent that they can be bought and sold. This makes the market infrastructure that moves them—the banks, brokers, exchanges, clearinghouses, and custodians that reside in practically every country—a vital part of the global economy. As with payments, most of that infrastructure was designed long before the arrival of the internet and is ripe for a digital makeover.

The Evolution of Markets

Equity and debt have been around for thousands of years. The modern notions of stocks and bonds—as standardized investment products that can be bought and sold in an open market—date back to the Renaissance period in Europe, in cities such as Florence, Amsterdam, and London. The discovery of sea routes across the Atlantic to the Americas and around the horn of Africa to Asia had kicked off a new era of mercantilism and colonialism among the European powers. All that shipbuilding and conquering was expensive. The resulting demand for ever more capital inspired many of the financial innovations that are with us today.

The first properly public company was the Dutch East India Company —a shipping and trading conglomerate believed by many to be the forerunner to the modern transnational corporation. The *Vereenigde Oost Indische Compagnie,* or *VOC,* as it was known locally, financed itself for the better part of two centuries by issuing stocks and bonds traded in places such as the Amsterdam Stock Exchange, an ancestor to the sophisticated financial exchanges of today.

Many of the market-related institutions, products and ideas that are common today—things like the stock exchange, limited liability company, short selling, technical analysis, shareholder activism, and financial derivatives—trace their roots back to the capital markets that surfaced around the VOC in the first half of the seventeenth century.[51]

The rise of the VOC coincided with a period known as the "Dutch Golden Age," a one-hundred-year period when the Low Countries were the dominant centers of trade, culture, and finance in Europe, thanks to their proximity to some of the busiest trade routes of the era. Cities such as Amsterdam were hotbeds for the trading of grains, lumber, and spices, and all the cultural experience in the trading of physical items helped build sophistication in the trading of financial ones. Both activities tend to thrive in places where there is an abundance of capital, a tolerance for speculative zeal, and sufficient trust. Regardless of whether one is speculating in spices or stocks, markets do better when buyers and sellers expect their counterparties to do the right thing, an outcome made more likely by the presence of clear contracts and a reliable legal system. The Dutch Republic had both.

Shares in the VOC were first offered to the public in 1602, and the very first page of the subscription document spelled out each investor's right to transfer ownership to a third party. That clause, and the fact that shares that were initially meant to be liquidated after a fixed period were eventually made permanent, paved the way for the formation of the secondary market, a place where investors could buy and sell stocks or bonds originally issued in the primary market. The majority of trading, as we think of it today, takes place in the secondary market for the simple reason that a security can only be issued once but traded frequently thereafter. Prior to the VOC, most stock offerings could not be traded and had to be held until some future date when the company was liquidated. The presence of the secondary market made owning shares in a company more appealing, as investors could sell them at any time.

With this came some complication in the form of recordkeeping: the issuing company had to keep track of who its shareholders were for a number of reasons including knowing who to distribute profits to in the form of dividends. In the case of the VOC, the first few such dividend payments were paid "in kind" with the spices that the company imported. It needed to know which shareholders had been issued their spices and which had not. Even once the company switched to paying dividends in cash, it had to know who to pay and how much.

The VOC also needed to know who its biggest investors were so it could occasionally put matters up to a vote, not to mention compliance with local law. The company kept an official record of all shareholders inside a master ledger located at the East India House in Amsterdam. Investors who wanted to swap ownership of their shares had to go there during designated hours on specific days to have a clerk record the transaction, and required approval from no less than two officers of the company.

And so, just like the domains of money and payments, a ledger maintained by a central authority was the ultimate source of truth about who owned what. Similar to how payments worked with the early money changers of Northern Italy, each transfer had to be requested in person and entailed a fee. The cumbersomeness of this process—requiring at least five people to be present to be made official—combined with the fact that the company only opened its books periodically, led to the formation of downstream markets where people traded the right to eventually transfer ownership inside the books of the VOC.[52] Thus the creation of the Amsterdam Stock Exchange.

The exchange—which had been ordered to be built by local officials who had grown tired of traders clogging up public spaces—opened its doors in 1611 and was an immediate success. Adoption was swift, and was aided by a government decree that trading in VOC stock could only take place at a specific corner of the building during specific hours—a nod to the importance of concentrated liquidity in capital markets. Other parts of the building were used for the trading of physical commodities and later, bonds, a template for a centralized financial market that would eventually be replicated all over Europe.

Like payments, trading in the securities of the VOC quickly turned into a hierarchy of claims. The most trustworthy, but also most cumbersome (and therefore least frequent) transfers took place at the top of the pyramid, inside the official books of the company. More frequent (and less official) trades happened between counterparties who knew and trusted each other. These informal transactions allowed two people to trade back and forth for a period of time and only report the net transfer of shares to the company.

Even greater efficiency was achieved if the circle of trust was expanded to include more people. If A sold his shares to B, and B promptly sold the same shares to C, then all that needed to be reported to the company was a single transfer from A to C—a type of netting in financial markets known as *ringing*. The arrangement helped save time and capital for everyone involved, but only if nobody balked. The desire for such efficiencies led to the formation of intimate trading clubs all over Amsterdam and the rise of specialized trust intermediaries known as brokers, middlemen who not only provided the latest news on the company and helped traders negotiate price, but who also vouched for the reputations of potential counterparties. The resulting increase in trust must have been well worth whatever fees the brokers charged, as eventually most of the trading at the exchange happened through them.[53]

THE ORIGINAL MARKETS PYRAMID

These practices spread from Amsterdam to London, where a similar market infrastructure arose around the trading in shares of the British East India Company. Many of these transfer mechanisms mirrored the shortcuts deployed by banks to facilitate payments, including a period of coordination known as clearing (traders A, B, and C tabulating their transactions and netting out the ones that cancel each other out and settlement (the final and official transfer of ownership). But stock trading was complicated by the need for two different value stores to move bidirectionally, with securities going one way and the money needed to pay for them going in the other. Batch processing and netting were still useful but required a lot more math. What if the price of a security appreciated from the time A sold to B and later, when B sold to C? B's temporary ownership of the security didn't have to be reported "up" to the registrar, but seeing how he made money on the trade, he still needed to get paid.

The need to include monetary payments into securities settlement alters the trust framework, making the usual shortcuts at the bottom of the pyramid riskier. All it takes is for one trader involved in a complicated transfer to default on the payment and the whole thing falls apart. Such defaults could happen at any time, and not necessarily out of malice. Anyone can miscalculate how much money they have or experience an unexpected loss, and everyone is more likely to suffer from either during a market rout, causing trust to evaporate. Nothing tests the reliability of market infrastructure more than a crash. The never-ending drive for convenience may dictate that the risks introduced by practices such as ringing and netting are still worth the benefit of not having to visit the registrar frequently, but further innovation is needed to preserve trust.

One solution is to limit participation in an exchange to vetted and approved (i.e., trustworthy) participants, a practice that began in the seventeenth century and is still with us today. Another is to build a specialized clearinghouse for securities settlement, one that has strict membership requirements, keeps tabs on the financial well-being of its members and— like the London and New York banker's clearinghouses—is willing to backstop wobbly participants. Laws and regulations that protect market participants also help.

Today, these solutions are standard practice in contemporary financial hubs such as New York, London, and Hong Kong. They arrived unevenly via a process of punctuated equilibrium, where solutions implemented to deal with fallout from the last crisis are proven insufficient by the next one and have to be evolved yet again. Regardless of the innovation, one constraint of the hierarchical approach has been limited access to the top, where the most trustworthy settlement happens. The greater the proportion of people who settle with the official registrar, the more resilient the market. Given that the principal bottleneck is the need to constantly update a centralized ledger, one option is to just get rid of it.

Securities issuers willing to forgo knowing the identities of their investors could just issue certificates. These bearer instruments—named for the fact that whoever physically bears them is the rightful owner— make it a lot easier to transfer ownership. Instead of needing a clerk to update an official ledger (in the presence of two witnesses, no less) trading is now reduced to a single interaction between buyer and seller, and settlement is as easy as handing over a piece of paper—a complex capital market transaction reduced to the simplicity of a swap. As a bonus, investors can now be anonymous, and trading can take place anytime, anywhere. Making dividend or interest payments becomes a bit more complicated now that there is no central record of ownership, but that problem can be solved by attaching redeemable coupons to each certificate (thus the present-day practice of calling bonds that pay periodic interest *coupon bonds*).

The Law of the Land

Even though companies like the VOC issued paper certificates as a receipt of ownership, their internal ledgers were still the golden record of who owned what. The first mass-market bearer securities did not arrive in European markets until a century later in France, as part of the maniacal schemes of John Law, a Scottish gambler turned French central banker who would ultimately go down as one of the most brilliant and reckless economic minds in history—two traits that seem to go hand in hand in the so-called dismal science.

Law was an early advocate of the contemporary belief that money is nothing more than a policy tool of the state, to be poked and prodded to achieve desired outcomes. He rose to prominence in the court of Louis XV, in the early part of the eighteenth century, at a time when the French government was both powerful and broke. A series of costly wars had left the crown in debt, and attempts to raise revenues by increasing seigniorage on the metal coins that were the standard medium of exchange had eroded public trust.

Law's first contribution was to set up a private bank named the *Banque Générale,* a proto central bank modeled on the Bank of England that issued its own shares and used the proceeds to buy up government debt, then issued banknotes backed by metal—a complicated scheme meant to refinance the government and revitalize the economy via the introduction of paper money. To encourage adoption, Law announced that his notes (a bearer instrument in their own right) were redeemable for the promised precious-metal content of government-issued coins, and not their supposed (yet diluted) face value, making his paper money a sort of hedge against further dilution by the crown. The scheme worked, and the notes proved quite popular, aided by a subsequent government decree that they were also legal tender, and to be used in the collection of taxes. Law's bank would eventually be nationalized into the *Bank Royale,* the first official central bank of France.

Law's second major contribution was to convince the crown to let him set up a joint-stock company in the spirit of the VOC, with a monopoly on trading with France's burgeoning colonies in the New World. Officially named the *Compagnie d'Occident* (Company of the West), it would ultimately become known as the Mississippi Company, tribute to the gold and silver it was bound to discover in the Louisiana Territory. Like its English and Dutch counterparts, the company needed to raise capital to finance its ambitious plans and did so by issuing shares to the public.

To drive demand, Law introduced two important innovations. The first was to let investors participating in the initial share offering put down only 10 percent and pay the rest in installments. The second was to make the shares bearer instruments in the form of stock certificates, so trading in the secondary market would be as easy as possible. These innovations helped democratize access to the capital markets, with spectacular, then catastrophic results.

By reducing the minimum capital requirement to purchase its shares, Mississippi was able to attract a larger pool of investors, beyond the wealthy and aristocrats who usually played the stock game. By reducing the friction of trading those shares, it turned many participants into gamblers. Fueled by exaggerated reports of the endless bounty in the Bayou, poor and rich alike flocked to lively Parisian markets where one kind of bearer instrument, paper money, was exchanged for another, stock certificates. Law built on his early success by issuing even more shares in his trading company and using the proceeds to both refinance the French government and acquire other businesses. To ensure that each additional stock offering was met with brisk demand, he instructed his bank to issue more and more paper money, beyond what it could back with gold. Trust earned, then violated.

Tellingly, nobody complained. The public was too preoccupied with the burgeoning stock market bubble and the government was pleased with the resulting economic growth. Booms and manias can have an intoxicating effect on any trust framework, be it a currency or a security. They can numb participants to the potential pitfalls and infuse a sense of invincibility, at least for a while. They can accelerate the onset of the curse and enable fantastical opportunities for authorities to free ride—money inflated to oblivion or companies run into the ground. The actual resilience of any trust framework is often not revealed until the boom turns into a bust, and the hangover sets in.

Today, the misadventures of the Mississippi Company are taught in economics classes as a warning. But back then, John Law was viewed as an economic savior. What the public (not to mention the crown) didn't realize was that most of the gains were temporary, built on ever more risk. Speculators used their existing shares as collateral and borrowed money (often from the Bank Royale) to buy even more. The resulting increase in the share price gave them even more collateral to borrow against, fueling the rally further. During the decisive year of 1719, shares that were originally issued for 500 *livres* appreciated to 10,000, leading to the invention of a new word: *millionaire*.

Although the availability of shares in bearer form did not create the bubble, the ease with which they could be transferred helped move things along. In one telling anecdote, a servant sent by his master to sell some stock was able to take advantage of the price difference between when he was dispatched and when he arrived at the market by pocketing the difference and using the proceeds to acquire his own shares.[54] Trading can happen a lot more seamlessly (not to mention anonymously) when both money and securities exist in bearer form. But there are downsides to such ease of transfer. With no official register of rightful owners, theft became more common. In one famous incident, an affluent broker was lured to a cabaret with the promise of a trade then brutally murdered, for he had a reputation for always carrying his certificates in his coat pocket.[55]

All that action distracted from the troubling fact that—unlike its English and Dutch counterparts—Mississippi was not delivering results. The swampland of the Louisiana territory yielded a lot more disease and death than gold or silver but its failings were glossed over by a combination of company propaganda and money printing—a combination made easier by the fact that by now Law had merged the company into the bank. The rapid increase in the money supply led to a spike in inflation all over Paris and its surrounding provinces but nobody cared because everybody was getting rich.

An Architectural Breakdown

Like most bubbles, the Mississippi one eventually collapsed under its own weight. When share prices started to fall, astute speculators began transferring their wealth to gold and silver as a protective measure, only to be thwarted by a draconian decree (encouraged by Law) that forbade citizens from possessing any precious metals—as if thousands of years of monetary memory could simply be wished away. But trust is not so gullible, and the law only confirmed the growing suspicion that something was amiss. The emperor had revealed himself to have no clothes. Both his money and the stock of his company collapsed in value.

As his final act, Law responded to the growing crisis by resorting to the last refuge of central bankers then and now: printing even more money to prop up the stock market (an activity since rebranded to a more-sophisticated-sounding *quantitative easing*). It didn't work. Rising inflation, combined with a now-collapsing stock market, led to panicked crowds showing up at the branches of the Banque Royale to redeem their money for the metal they had been promised, but it simply wasn't there. Riots ensued, and people were trampled to death on a daily basis. The bubble had burst.

My shares which on Monday I bought
Were worth millions on Tuesday, I thought.
So on Wednesday I chose my abode,
In my carriage on Thursday I rode
To the ballroom on Friday I went
To the workhouse next day I was sent
—ANONYMOUS[56]

Economic historians debate how critical we should be of the tumultuous reign of John Law, but the numbers paint a grim picture. Shares of the Mississippi Company, as well as the banknotes of the Banque Royal, both ended up being about as valuable as the paper they were printed on. Law's personal fortune followed a similar trajectory. Having once been one of the richest men in France, he was forced to flee penniless and in shame, and would die in obscurity less than ten years later. Establishing an important precedent that would be followed by central bankers for generations to come, he never admitted to being wrong.

Nevertheless, the fallout from the bursting bubble would haunt France for decades to come and was worsened by the specific architecture of its financial markets. After firing Law, the government tried to reestablish trust with the public by returning to a metal standard and restructuring its debt, much of which was now owed to the public in the form of bearer bonds issued during the mania. To reward loyalty, the decision was made to prioritize redeeming certificates held by original owners, the people who had paid the full face value. But therein lay the problem, because—like the shares of the Mississippi Company—some of those securities had changed hands many times, and were now held by speculators who had scooped them up at a discount. Had the bond market relied on some kind of centralized ledger, then figuring out the original owners would have been as simple as flipping to the first page. But bearer instruments have no memory. The government had to hire thousands of clerks and notaries to collect as much data as they could from disparate sources and try to reverse engineer the order of ownership. A convenience adopted during the best of times had become a liability during the worst.

Despite these drawbacks, bearer instruments continued to be used throughout the West for another two hundred years, especially in places where the institutions necessary for a ledger-based architecture were lacking. They were particularly popular in the United States after the Civil War, when capital was hard to come by and borrowers like the US government accepted funding however they could get it. Ironically, one of the main drawbacks of bearer instruments for investors—the ease with which they can be damaged, lost, or stolen—can be seen as a benefit for issuers. Securities that have been lost or damaged will never be redeemed.

But the flip side of that (admittedly dubious) benefit is the appeal to criminals for theft, tax evasion, and money laundering. Ledger-based investments, otherwise known as registered securities, might not be great for user privacy, but do make it easier for governments to make sure that people pay their taxes. Whereas unregistered securities leave it up to their owners to report any tax obligation, registered securities shift the onus to their issuers or whoever oversees the ledger. Registration also makes underworld adoption difficult. A $10,000 bond is a lot more convenient to use in a drug deal than duffle bags full of cash, but not if the transfer has to be recorded.

For these reasons, the issuance, trading, and redemption of bearer securities has been either phased out or outlawed in most places—a transformation aided by the simultaneous electronification of financial markets. As with money itself, the drive for digitization meant moving all securities to centralized ledgers, for the simple reason that there was no such thing as digital scarcity, at least not until now.

How to Settle a Stock Trade in Twenty Difficult Steps

To understand the current structure of our capital markets—and why it is overdue for an overhaul—it helps to review the last transformative period on Wall Street, the late 1960s. At that time and on the surface the pulsating heart of Western capitalism, scattered around a stretch of Manhattan's Broadway known as the Canyon of Heroes, was doing extraordinarily well. Wall Street reflected the positive mood of the United States, at least economically. Inflation was tame, unemployment was low, and corporate profits were soaring. The positivity was reflected in rising stock prices at the New York Stock Exchange. Daily trading volume on the NYSE had quadrupled throughout the decade, registering a 33 percent increase in 1967 alone.[57] Shares that were traded in real time at the exchange, using the most sophisticated electronic systems of that era, were then cleared and settled by an army of clerks over the ensuing few days.

But therein lay a problem. For all the technological sophistication that America had developed in building a nuclear arsenal and sending astronauts to space, the one thing it hadn't figured out how to do was settle stock trades efficiently. Whereas trading on the exchange was a symbol of America's industrial and technological might, the subsequent back-office mess that unfolded across downtown Manhattan more resembled the emerging quagmire in the Mekong Delta. Historians, and the professionals who suffered through it, refer to this period as "the Paperwork Crisis."

The problem began with the hybrid nature of American capital markets, which relied on both bearer instruments and ledgers. Thanks to state incorporation laws, ownership of stocks and bonds was determined by certificates. But federal laws enacted in the aftermath of the Great Depression (another bust that had exposed significant flaws in the capital market infrastructure) required that every certificate transfer be handled by regulated entities known as *transfer agents*. Each stock trade required the collection of the relevant certificates from buyers and the distribution of new ones to sellers. Settling the more than ten million shares that were executed on the New York Stock Exchange involved moving a forest of paper.

The process took days to complete—assuming everything went well—which it often didn't. As with the early days of check clearing a century earlier, everything revolved around an army of young men crisscrossing downtown Manhattan with bundles of paper. For each exchange, the broker who represented the seller had to collect their certificates, confirm their authenticity, fill out the proper forms, then have everything delivered to the deposit window of the transfer agent. A single transaction required more than thirty different forms.[58]

Transfer agents didn't have it any easier. Every bundle delivered to their window included a ticket outlining the trade, signed certificates, a guarantee from the broker that the paperwork was authentic, and a power of attorney. The agent had to first confirm that everything was in order and that the securities in question had not been previously reported as lost or stolen. The slightest issue meant that the bundle had to be rejected and sent back, rendering the transaction invalid. Otherwise, the agent would record the transfer in its ledger, destroy the old certificates, then issue new ones. Due to the importance of final settlement, every step of the process had to be reviewed and audited multiple times. If everything checked out, then a new bundle would be sent to the buyer's broker—sometimes only to be turned around and sent back, as the shares had already been resold. Rinse, then repeat.

The manual nature of this process led to mistakes. Stock certificates could easily get misdelivered or lost in the growing mountains of paper in a broker's back office, a physical logjam that the Securities and Exchange Commission once referred to as "a trackless forest."[59] The work was tedious, and the clerks responsible for it were often overworked and underpaid, leading to high turnover. So-called "delivery failures" mounted, adding up to over $4 billion worth of securities by the end of 1968.[60] Such problems had a cascading effect, as buyers whose shares had not been delivered could not collect a dividend or participate in other corporate actions. Even without errors, there were only so many transactions that could be processed on any given day, turning the back office into a bottleneck. The New York Stock Exchange tried to ease the burden by ending trading early on the busiest days, but even that wasn't enough. Eventually the NYSE had no choice but to close on Wednesdays, lest the entire market collapse under an avalanche of paper.

The Paperwork Crisis took a major toll on the finances of New York's brokerage houses. Mounting losses throughout the crisis, combined with a brief bear market at the end of the decade, drove many into liquidation, raising the threat of cascading failures. The government was forced to intervene. Over the ensuing five years, Congress, working in conjunction with state and federal regulators, passed a series of bills that transformed the American capital market infrastructure into the trust framework that exists today.

Back to the Future

The underlying cause of the Paperwork Crisis was the need for physical transfer of certificates. Computer mainframes and electronic communication had increased the speed of trading, but not settlement, which still moved at the speed of paper. Not surprisingly, the biggest reform enacted in the aftermath of the crisis was the elimination of physical delivery. In the ensuing years, most paper certificates were first immobilized, then dematerialized.

Immobilization is the process by which certificates are taken out of the hands of their legal owners and warehoused inside private entities called central securities depositories, or CSDs. These institutions, often affiliated with specific exchanges, hold paper certificates on behalf of their owners and use a ledger to track ownership. They settle trades by simply swapping names inside their books, leaving the certificates alone. Settlement, like trading, now happens inside of a database.

But if all that really matters to determine ownership is an entry inside a ledger, why bother with the pretense of a bearer instrument? So goes the reasoning behind dematerialization, a fancy-sounding term best understood as rewinding the calendar by several hundred years and going back to the way things were done at the East India House. Ownership is once again determined by nothing more than a ledger entry, albeit one preserved by a computer instead of a notebook.

The eternal tension between trust and convenience came to a head yet again, with convenience winning a decisive victory. Both immobilization and dematerialization required the appointment of powerful and opaque central authorities acting as stewards of the financial system. Investors were asked to trust these entities but had no direct way of peeking inside their books. As with all centralized hierarchies, the power assigned to these institutions came at the expense of end users. Investors—who had previously had the option to "opt out" of the Wall Street–centric system by taking their certificates and going their merry way—now had no choice but to play along, surrendering all control of precious assets to government-sanctioned monopolies. The companies that used this infrastructure to raise capital by issuing stocks or bonds also had to play along, and were now one layer removed from their own investors. The reforms enacted in the aftermath of the crisis centralized the American capital market infrastructure to a shocking degree, so much so that today, a single corporation is responsible for virtually all of it. But things didn't have to turn out that way.

The extent to which the new system should be centralized was a controversial topic in the early 1970s, with different stakeholders arguing for different solutions. Immobilization was already understood to lead to severe centralization, because storing all the outstanding certificates in a vault was only efficient so long as there was only one vault. Dematerialization, on the other hand, could be executed across a network of ledgers maintained by different companies.

As is often the case with transformative legislation, each player lobbied for a different design. The New York Stock Exchange, along with its affiliated banks and brokers, argued for the more centralized, and still certificate-based, approach. Despite its inefficiencies, one of the benefits of the old way of doing things—as far as the New York cohort was concerned—was the need for geographic proximity, giving any brokerage house based in Manhattan an edge over one in Milwaukee, for instance. Immobilization helped preserve some of that advantage. More to the point, the NYSE already owned a "Central Certificate Service" and was eager to expand its footprint in settlement.

Smaller and more dispersed financial institutions, on the other hand, argued for the more decentralized approach as enabled by dematerialization. The relatively young National Association of Securities Dealers (NASD) had already broken the Manhattan monopoly on trading with its ultramodern and more decentralized NASDAQ system, and its members argued that they could do the same for settlement. Their proposal called for a national system of interconnected ledgers preserved by different entities, akin to a primitive blockchain.

The more centralized approach won out, as it was believed to be more practical. Eliminating paper certificates required changing the securities laws of all fifty states, a messy process that would take years. Also of concern was the relative newness of computer technology. It was one thing to automate trading using the latest gadgets and gizmos, but final settlement was considered too important to the overall trust framework to hand over to immature tech. So, one by one, the free-floating certificates that had long been both the backbone of American capitalism, and an extension of her ethos of individual liberty, were rounded up and sent to a maximum-security prison, one operated by a private company. Many believed that the sudden elevation of the CSD to the top of the transfer hierarchy would be temporary, and that the eventual elimination of certificates at the state level would ultimately return the markets to a flatter architecture. They were only half right. Stock certificates have gone the way of the dodo bird and are now nothing more than collectors' items. But Wall Street is more centralized than ever.

As we have seen in the domains of money, banking, platforms, and payments, systems that rely on centralized intermediaries to build trust become more centralized as time passes—driven by a combination of economies of scale, network effects, and regulatory moats. Capital markets are no exception, turning their end users—the issuers who raise money via stocks and bonds, and the investors who buy them—into unwitting participants (or victims, depending on one's perspective) of some of the largest monopolies on earth.

The Depository Trust and Clearing Corporation (DTCC), a private for-profit company, is now responsible for tracking ownership of every single public company in America, settling over a trillion dollars of transfers per day. A descendant of the original certificate service operated by the NYSE, it arrived at its current size through a series of mergers and acquisitions, devouring what little competition it once had. Along with settlement, which in of itself is a profitable business, the company offers a host of other services including clearing, corporate action, underwriting, and issuer services. Its press package claims that it delivers "an unmatched suite of services that provide maximum client value," a statement that—unlike most marketing slogans—is guaranteed to be true. When you are a government-sanctioned monopoly, everything that you do is unmatched.

DTCC's biggest defenders are the banks and brokers that participate in its clearing and settlement services, and for good reason. As with the payments industry, the more centralized the hierarchy of value transfers, the greater the efficiencies afforded to its intermediaries. Settlement shortcuts such as ringing and multilateral netting are turbocharged when run by a single company, allowing DTCC to process trillions of dollars' worth of transactions per day with just a few ledger entries. All the company needs to do in order to settle thousands of individual trades is to batch them into chunk transfers among a handful of brokers, custodians, and trustees. All the Apple shares traded in a single day could theoretically be settled with one hundred million going from JPMorgan Chase & Co. to BNY Mellon and fifteen million going from State Street to Citibank.

Further down the hierarchy, these banks and custodians perform the same kind of batch settlement among their biggest clients, some of which are other financial companies. On and on the process goes, with most transfers within any one entity being netted down to virtually nothing— for the simple reason that for every Robinhood client buying a stock on any given day there is likely to be another selling, so Robinhood's overall allocation of shares inside the master ledger need not change.

Netting requires a lot of coordination among the members of the settlement hierarchy so the process takes two business days. When all is said and done, all the stock trades that take place on any given day can be settled with less than 2 percent of the securities moving inside the books of the CSD. DTCC provides a similar clearing service for the payments required to complete those transactions, netting them down to virtually nothing as well, thus keeping the cost of capital for the participating intermediaries low. Securities settlement might be an exclusive country club, but the cost of membership is surprisingly cheap.

THE CURRENT MARKETS PYRAMID IN THE U.S.

Viewed from the top, such a system for clearing and settlement is a marvel of efficiency. DTCC and its affiliates often argue that the settlement system that they operate works very well, which it does, for them. Users, on the other hand, suffer the same kinds of annoying delays and hidden costs that they do with payments. These delays further enslave everyone to a handful of financial powerhouses with a long history of abusing that privilege, as they did in the years leading up to the 2008 financial crisis. Not surprisingly, many of the companies that needed to be bailed out were major players in securities settlement. Their executives brandished this status like a weapon, arguing for billions in taxpayer money, lest the pyramid collapse. They then used that money to buy their competition, making the system even more centralized.

Governments responded to the crisis by creating more regulations. But regulations can make any trust framework more rigid, as the cost of complying with them becomes a moat for incumbents. An older brokerage company with an army of lawyers and compliance professionals (some of whom used to work for a regulator) can more easily accommodate new rules and requirements than a startup. Competition is virtually nonexistent, and the same entities that benefit from this setup today are guaranteed to be there tomorrow, opening the door to all sorts of violations. As stated by no less a central player than the CEO of DTCC, the current system is akin to willingly putting all your eggs in one basket, then trying to watch it closely.[61] How could free riding not occur?

What Stinks about How We Trade Stonks

Being a stockholder is nothing more than a legal claim. In olden times, that claim was sometimes represented by a physical certificate, and transferring it was easy. Parisians who speculated in shares of the Mississippi Company had no need for any intermediaries, as they were free to show up whenever they wanted, swap some paper, then hit the cafe. Bearer instruments have their downsides, but they avoid a complicated process that requires a separation of trading, clearing, and settlement, and eliminate the need for an army of middlemen who periodically need to be bailed out. But that's not the system we have today.

Indeed, things are currently so centralized that American investors no longer own the securities in which they've invested. Technically speaking, a subsidiary of DTCC does. Every share of companies such as Apple, Walmart, and Disney is now registered to a singular (and aptly named) private entity known as Cede and Company. Thousands of public companies, trillions of dollars, one owner. The individuals who think they own their shares are listed as their beneficiaries, thrice removed. Cede only lists the banks and brokers that it serves. It is up to the banks and brokers to track and remember who their clients are. If possession is nine-tenths of the law, then the American public should be concerned about the fact that it doesn't possess any of her public companies.

The flaws of this highly centralized approach were on full display in early 2021 during the meme stock fiasco. A historic rise in heavily shorted stocks such as GameStop, one that pitted a handful of hedge funds against an army of individuals—with the individuals on the winning side, for once—was brought to an abrupt halt when online brokers such as TD Ameritrade and Robinhood pulled the plug, banning their clients from buying any more of the stocks in question. The bans were indirectly decreed from above in the form of massive collateral calls from DTCC on any broker whose clients were actively involved, the financial equivalent of put up or shut up.

Despite the efficiencies of batch processing and netting for financial intermediaries who sit in the middle of the settlement pyramid, the requisite delay in settlement exposes every intermediary to the problems of another. What if a broker fails in the two days it takes the system to settle its clients buy orders, and can't pay for those shares? In theory, such a failure could have a cascading effect throughout the system. Buffering the rest of the community from this kind of risk is one reason why securities clearinghouses were invented in the first place. As far as DTCC was concerned, the capital call was simply a way to protect itself and the rest of the pyramid.

Skeptics, not to mention the people who lost money on the resulting collapse in meme stock prices, were unconvinced. Unlike the hedge funds that were short those stocks, Robinhood's clients were making money, and there's a certain irony to Wall Street stopping an activity because it's *too* profitable. Also troubling was the fact that some of the hedge funds originally caught in the squeeze were fairly prominent. DTCC's mysterious "man behind the curtain" status, and the fact that it is controlled by the biggest banks and brokers (who count said hedge funds as their clients) didn't help. Last but certainly not least was the opacity of the pyramid. No one, not even the most powerful regulators, had a good handle on exactly what was going on. Regardless of anyone's intent, the top and middle of the capital market pyramid had conspired to hurt the people at the bottom, supposedly for their own good. Trust was eroded.

Putting It All Together

Despite playing the role of a public utility, DTCC is a private corporation co-owned by the New York Stock Exchange and the banks and brokers that most benefit from its existence. Most of its profits are cycled back to its owners. The amounts are modest by Wall Street standards, but also misleading. The real benefit of being a DTCC shareholder is the privileges and protections it brings to its members. As the world's largest CSD, the company handles far more than just stocks. It also settles bonds, mutual funds, treasuries, and esoteric instruments like mortgage-backed securities. All told, and despite having only a few thousand employees, the company's virtual vaults hold several times more value than US GDP. Having exclusive access to that warehouse is like being a member of an elite country club at best, or a dangerous cartel at worst. No wonder that despite decades of technological and financial upheaval, including the rise of the internet and the near-collapse of Wall Street, the overall architecture of the American financial system has not changed.

The people who work at these companies are not bad people, and mostly do an honest job. If you press them about it, they too will admit that

putting all your eggs in one basket then watching it very closely is dangerous. In 2012, a superstorm that passed through New York City flooded
parts of downtown Manhattan, including the offices of DTCC. Trillions of dollars' worth of immobilized securities were either damaged or
destroyed and had to be restored or replaced at significant cost. Thanks to
electronic backups and multiple redundancies kept by DTCC and its part-
ners, the financial markets were able to continue uninterrupted, as they
were during the dark days of the financial crisis.

These events nonetheless serve as reminders of some of the most
important lessons that societies have learned (and painfully relearned)
throughout the ages—the need to keep multiple copies of important
records and to keep them physically apart. Transparent records are better
than opaque ones, and immutable agreements that can only be appended
consensually are best. Important processes should be automated and run
around the clock, keeping reconciliation errors and settlement risk to a
minimum. Ask any intelligent and honest Wall Street veteran to sketch
out the optimum capital market infrastructure for the next hundred years
and what they'll describe is a blockchain—in every important way, if not
by name.

Re-Architecture

For good reason, capital markets have historically vacillated between ledgers and tokens. Each approach has its pluses and minuses, as we've seen
with money. Tokens enable direct ownership, privacy, free exchange, and
instant settlement. But they don't travel very well and can be lost or stolen.
Ledgers are better suited for large and long-distance transfers and allow
issuers to track their investors. But they lead to centralization, exclusion,
and higher costs. One approach is user-centric and democratic while the
other is easier to control. Historically, the designers of financial market
infrastructure have had to choose one over the other.

But they no longer have to, because blockchains are shared ledgers
that enable tokens. Case in point: Bitcoin is both the yin and the yang

of financial engineering. Each coin is a token, in the sense that ownership lies with the bearer (of a cryptographic key), and transactions cannot
be censored by a central authority. But the network those tokens reside
in is a ledger, so each coin has a distinct memory. Individuals control
their asset, but any potential counterparty can look up the history of
the coins in question and act accordingly. This duality makes the underlying infrastructure ideal for more traditional investments. Like stablecoins, tokenized securities return ownership of the world's assets back to
the people they were meant to serve, eliminating the need for an opaque,
centralized, costly, and potentially at-risk hierarchy. They also eliminate
the separation of trading from settlement. Unlike the stock and bond certificates of old, tokenized securities allow issuers and regulators to have a
solid grasp of the big picture. Trust, reinvented.

The first security tokens appeared on the Ethereum blockchain in
2016, perhaps inadvertently. The launch of a new smart-contract-enabled
blockchain platform—one that could track the movement of an infinite
number of tokens—had sparked a great deal of entrepreneurial zeal, and
developers from all over were eager to experiment with decentralized
applications. But first, they needed to raise money. Some projects turned
to crowdfunding, instead of venture capital, and turned to their would-
be users for investment. Most dApps eventually issue either a governance
token meant to decentralize control over the project or a utility token
meant to enable usage of its service. Both types of tokens often fluctuate in
value based on the success of the solution they enable, turning them into
a pseudoform of equity. By selling the tokens ahead of time to prospective
users or even speculators, dApp developers were able to forgo the usual
fundraising routes, saving time and money to begin building their solutions right away.

These so-called initial coin offerings (ICOs)—most of which were
modeled on the crowdfunding effort used to build Ethereum itself—were
arguably the first killer application for the platform. Hundreds of millions of dollars were raised long before the arrival of any sort of successful

product or service, leading some blockchain believers to declare the end of the venture-backed startup model as we know it. Why would founders ever go back to the greedy sultans of Silicon Valley, they argued, if they could instead raise money directly from their customers? Time would eventually prove that line of reasoning wildly optimistic (if not outright naive), but not before ICOs had their own impressive bubble. By the time it burst, billions of dollars had been raised by dApp developers all over the world, sometimes with nothing more than a paper and a promise. The early days of the crypto industry had an unfortunate tendency to go from exciting to stupid in the blink of an eye, and the ICO boom of late 2017 and early 2018 was a shining example.

Not all of the bullishness around this new form of funding was misplaced. A decentralized platform with token functionality is especially useful for raising money, particularly for projects whose eventual product will live on the same platform. Before Ethereum, startup founders had no choice but to raise money via bespoke and non-fungible agreements with angel investors or VC funds. Each investor would be issued equity, but the resulting shares would languish in the opaque and illiquid market for private securities for years, creating a vacuum of trust. Founders had to spend a lot of their time managing their cap tables, and investors had no way of knowing what was going on.

Speculative tokens issued on Ethereum, on the other hand, could start trading immediately, utilizing the existing wallet and exchange infrastructure. The total supply and movement of any token was transparent for all to see, and most of the manual work of servicing investors was now handled by smart contracts. Fundraising efforts that used to require a small army of lawyers and reams of paper could now happen with the click of a button. Founders were liberated to focus on building and investors could literally watch.

ICOs were an ideal way of raising money, except for the fact that they were mostly illegal. Raising money to build a business is one of the most regulated activities on earth. Financial authorities such as the Securities and Exchange Commission in the United States enforce strict laws on how one can raise money, who is allowed to invest, and what can or cannot be done with the resulting equity or debt. Many of the ICOs from the bubble era failed to comply with these requirements, triggering a crackdown. The regulators didn't care what anyone called an asset or how they issued it. To them, a utility token issued on Ethereum was just as much a security as vanilla stock issued on the Nasdaq. The crypto industry's fantasy that ICOs would replace IPOs was officially DOA.

The resulting fines and civil charges had a transformative effect on newer projects hoping to raise capital. Many went back to traditional sources such as VC funds. Others conducted ICOs with regional restrictions, blocking participation from the citizens of countries such as the United States. Then the lawyers showed up, proving once again that the more things change, the more they stay the same. The shadiest projects from the bubble era went away, which was a good thing, but so did many honest entrepreneurs who couldn't afford the cost of compliance.

The regulatory crackdown on ICOs inspired some people to shift their focus on using blockchain technology for more traditional securities. If every token was going to be treated as equity or debt from a compliance standpoint, then why not just issue stocks and bonds? These security tokens could be used to fund any kind of project, not just decentralized ones, and could still take advantage of a platform like Ethereum for trading and settlement. Compliance would arguably become easier, as everyone, including the regulators, would enjoy full transparency on the life cycle of each security, and smart contracts could be used to enforce rules.

Crypto purists scoffed at the notion of security tokens, as they violated the ideals of total decentralization. Cryptocurrencies like Bitcoin and Ether were appealing because their supply was controlled by the protocol and their value entirely self-contained. Tokenized bonds or stocks on the other hand were closer to stablecoins, in that they derived their value from activity outside the blockchain. But here, as with stablecoins, their skepticism was pointless. Permissionlessness is a two-way street, and a platform like Ethereum can be used for any application, decentralized or not. Just as dollar-denominated stablecoins could turn a public blockchain into a global payment system, security tokens could turn it into capital market infrastructure. The only question was whether this new way of building trust among investors was better than the old.

The answer is a resounding yes. Decades of immobilization and dematerialization have already turned most equity and debt transfer systems into a network of interconnected ledgers. DTCC may still hold paper certificates in a vault somewhere, but as far as the market is concerned, its databases are the source of truth. Those databases, though, are suboptimal because they outsource the tracking of investors to the databases of the banks, brokers, and custodians that serve as intermediaries. None of these ledgers are particularly good at talking to each other. They require endless rounds of communication and constant manual intervention to stay in sync, and have a shockingly high error rate by blockchain standards. Reconciliation, exception handling, and error resolution are large expense items in the operating budget of most investment banks, and these costs are passed on to customers, one way or the other. (An online broker like Robinhood might be commission-free, but it still has costs, so it "sells" its clients trades to hedge funds to execute, creating a potential conflict of interest.) The front-office traders on Wall Street might get all the attention, but it's the back-office people who do the yeoman's work of keeping the system going, sometimes with seemingly nothing more than a lot of moxie and a bit of duct tape.

These inefficiencies also make the system fragile. One of the enduring lessons of the 2008 financial crisis was that a lack of transparency and delayed settlement make a crisis worse. Not knowing how much exposure you may have to a counterparty—or whether they'll be solvent long enough to pay come settlement day—are terrifying liabilities during a panic, and two business days might as well be two hundred when your own clients come calling for their money. Clearinghouse and CSDs are designed to mitigate these risks, but there too the opacity of the overall system is problematic. What if the central authorities have mismanaged their own finances during boom times, or misallocated some securities? Lack of competition can make any company complacent and lazy. Regulations are supposed to keep everyone on their toes, but if the regulators had a good grasp of the risks, then there wouldn't be a crisis in the first place.

Blockchain networks don't have these problems. Everything that they do is transparent and all their communication is automated. Better yet, their consensus mechanisms ensure that participants agree on every transaction *before* entering it into the shared ledger, a stark contrast to the scenario where pyramid participants process their own transactions, then reconcile them with counterparties at some future date. Blockchain systems also don't make mistakes. Unlike Wall Street, where mistakes happen so often that setting aside funds to cover them is a normal part of budgeting, the Ethereum blockchain has operated for years without making a single error.

A Transformation Four Hundred Years in the Making

Those in charge of the existing system talk openly about its shortcomings and were among the first to recognize the promise of blockchain technology for better settlement. The CEO of DTCC has stated on the record that he believes it's only a matter of time until his systems are disintermediated by some kind of blockchain network.[62] Smart professionals working inside the biggest banks and brokers agree. But nobody is planning their retirement just yet. Change comes slowly to old industries, and there is almost unanimous consensus on Wall Street that it must come from within. There is little concern for the disruptive power of public permissionless networks such as Ethereum, and many of the blockchain solutions for securities trading being worked on by the biggest intermediaries are of the private and permissioned variety. Not only are these limited networks easier to implement, but they have the added benefit of keeping the existing powerhouses relevant. CSDs may have to become experts on running network governance, and brokers may have to learn how to deploy nodes and program smart contracts, but everyone involved will still get to do the thing they were born to do, which is to sit between a buyer and seller—or so they hope. Free riding is a tough habit to give up.

How much any of these intermediaries are actually needed once a market embraces this new way of settling transactions will be answered in time. In the short term, every bank, trust company, custodian, and CSD must play a part. On a long enough timeline however, most will go the way of the walking clerk or ticker tape operator. The fundamental purpose of any financial intermediary is to build trust—a statement as true for the East India House four hundred years ago as it is for the Depository Trust & Clearing Corporation today. Now, there's a blockchain for that. Cryptographic tokens living inside a shared ledger preserved by consensus is the perfect foundation for any capital market, making re-architecture inevitable.

For now, corporate inertia and regulatory roadblocks rule the day, as the involvement of most intermediaries is mandated by law, regardless of the underlying infrastructure. Case in point: security tokens issued on the public Ethereum blockchain still have to designate some kind of off-chain entity as their transfer agent, even though the platform does a better job of tracking who owns what than any company ever could. These outdated requirements have limited tokenization to niche markets where the settlement infrastructure is even worse. As absurd as T+2 settlement days for stocks may seem in the digital era, trillions of dollars in more esoteric products such as mortgage-backed securities take even longer to settle, and rely on an embarrassing combination of phone calls and fax machines.

Most of the permissioned networks currently being deployed take an incremental approach. Instead of using tokens recognized as securities for instant on-chain settlement, they use the blockchain as a shared database of facts to improve the current processes. While these improvements are better than emailing spreadsheets back and forth, they are a far cry from the instant and around-the-clock settlement already enjoyed by security tokens issued on public networks.

Similarly piecemeal progress can be expected with security tokens riding public networks. There the action will be led by crypto-native startups that help issuers tokenize their securities—service providers that have no delusions about their own importance in the markets of tomorrow. Indeed, the contrast between the incumbent banks and brokers embracing private networks, and the tokenization startups going straight to the public ones is both telling and predictable. The startups, most of whom are only a few years old, take a more utilitarian approach, because they understand that it's the platform—and not the companies that serve it—that will capture most of the value. An entire ecosystem of tokenizers is still needed, however, because crypto securities will always be more complicated than pure cryptocurrencies or even stablecoins, and someone will have to act on behalf of the issuers, programming bespoke tokens and managing corporate action like mergers and dividends.

Most of the securities tokenized on public blockchains so far are of the private variety—legal instruments representing things like startup equity, investment funds, or real estate. Despite representing some of the largest capital markets in the world, such illiquid assets presently rely on settlement infrastructure such as manually updated spreadsheets that is so bad it makes the "trackless forests" of the Paperwork Crisis era look downright elegant.

Private securities seldom trade and are often priced at a discount of their book value—telltale signs of a market lacking in trust. Tokenization is a quantum leap in transparency and efficiency. It is also easier to implement for private securities because regulations are light and entrenched incumbents are few. There are many benefits to doing so, starting with smaller investment minimums. Blockchains—unlike every other kind of financial infrastructure—don't care about denominations. Just as a single bitcoin can be broken down into a million tiny fractions, so can the security tokens representing an investment in a single property. A $1 billion skyscraper can be tokenized into a billion $1 tokens, making investment exposure to what used to be a highly exclusive asset class as affordable as a can of Coke.

A Feature-Rich Upgrade

Fractional ownership is the ultimate promise of the modernization of the architecture, and is much needed in a world where limited access to quality investments is a leading driver of economic inequality. As a rule of thumb, the better the performance of a particular asset in the past few decades, the more limited the pool of people who have had an opportunity to own it. Most people can't afford the minimum investment threshold for things like collectible art or private equity, so their returns accrue to the already rich. Tellingly, the exception to this rule is Bitcoin, the rare asset that has both been universally accessible and outperformed most investment benchmarks. The blockchain, it's worth reiterating, doesn't discriminate.

Re-architecture of the capital markets is inevitable and will reach an important inflection point once regulators switch from being cautious skeptics to fierce advocates. Regardless of whether they are public or private, blockchain platforms can do more for investor protection than the thickest manuals or heftiest fines. Unlike traditional securities, where detection and enforcement take place after the fact, security tokens can be programmed to only ever do the right thing. Regulators will be able to run their own nodes and watch everything, but they'll have little to do beyond blessing the code of the smart contracts that will do their bidding.

Other benefits of a systemwide redesign include the compression of trading and settlement into one step, and guaranteed swaps of one kind of value store for another—a security token exchanged for a stablecoin. So-called smart securities will effectively manage themselves. Smart stocks will issue their own dividends using stablecoins and smart bonds will have their waterfall structure programmed into every token. Tokenization will also enable new financial instruments that we can't even imagine today. There is no law of nature that says there are only two kinds of financial instruments and that their names are equity and debt. People have always innovated on ways to enhance the store-of-value function of money, and the only limiting factors have been an absence of trust or a lack of imagination. As we are about to see, when the former is solved, the latter can run wild.

The skeptics, many of whom have enjoyed illustrious careers inside the biggest intermediaries, will push back. They will question new business models, cite the risks of returning to bearer instruments, and wonder whether further democratization of investing is actually a good idea. They will extoll the wonderful efficiencies of batch processing and multilateral netting for intermediaries. They will remind everyone of the historic contribution such players have made to the evolution of capital markets. On this point they'll be correct, except for the fact that the best intermediary is the one you no longer need.

5

FINANCIAL SERVICES

financial services   noun
an industry built on trust that is slowly running out of it.

For all the criticism leveled at the financial services industry, the world as we know it could not function without it. Banks, brokers, exchanges, investment funds, and insurance companies are the neurological system of the broader economy. They coordinate between buyer and seller and facilitate the flow of risk from those who want to protect against it to those who want to take it. The markets that these businesses enable also serve as a useful signaling mechanisms. For instance, rising oil prices tell a producer to pump more while falling foreign exchange rates tell a government to borrow less.

Criticizing the companies that facilitate modern finance is a luxury of the first world. As a rule, the more developed the financial services industry of any country, the wealthier its citizens are, including the poorer ones. There is a reason why the biggest banking hubs exist in the wealthiest countries. For all the grief that financial institutions get, it's the lack of their services that drives economic inequality.

Banks, brokers, exchanges, investment funds, and insurance companies are all institutions of trust. Regardless of the product or service that they offer, the underlying ingredient is the same and always present. You can see it in their names, logos, and architecture. Tall Greek columns, vast marble entryways, and names that combine a dark color with an icon that signifies permanence and solidity, like a stone or a rock. The word *bank* comes from the Italian *banca,* or bench, a reference to the Italian money changers of old, who'd set up shop at the same table at the local *piazza* every day, rain or shine. Exchange rates and the weather fluctuated, but the bankers were always there, ready to serve their clients. (Unless they acted irresponsibly, at which point someone may have broken their bench, rendering them *banca rotta,* or bankrupt.)

Banks and other financial services firms eliminate the need for a double coincidence of want and trust among economic actors. Just because one person wants to borrow money while another wants to lend doesn't mean a loan can happen. Those involved need to trust each other. They also need to agree on the terms of the loan, which can be tricky. Borrowers, such as home buyers seeking a mortgage, often want to borrow for the long term. Savers, on the other hand, would rather not lock up their money for the next thirty years. Financial intermediaries solve this problem by pooling deposits and staggering loans, managing the flow of capital.

Once a bank opens its doors, savers can open savings accounts and borrowers can take out mortgages. Where the money comes from and where it goes is not their concern. Savers trust the bank to vet each borrower and deploy their capital wisely. Borrowers trust the bank to not force them to repay a loan on short notice. This outsourcing of the complicated business of building trust is an important efficiency for the broader economy. It allows most people to learn some other skill while the bankers become experts in property values and credit scores. It also means that the savings of a thousand different depositors can be used to fund a single mortgage, a feat that would be practically impossible without the intermediation of a bank.

Other types of financial firms provide similar benefits. Stock exchanges allow a single seller who owns a lot of stock to simultaneously sell to many buyers without knowing anything about them. Insurance companies use the small premiums collected from all their clients on a regular basis to pay out the occasional large claims filed by a few. Their expertise on evaluating risk helps keep premiums low.

Trust building leads to scale. A bank with a good reputation can attract more savers, allowing it to issue larger loans at lower rates. The more liquidity an exchange offers its buyers and sellers, the more of each group it can attract. The more diversified an insurance company's pool of clients, the less vulnerable it is to any one event, so the lower the premiums it can charge across the board. These efficiencies create their own economies of scale and winner-take-all dynamics. They also drive consolidation. Few industries have more blockbuster mergers than financial services.

Scale leads to convenience. A bank with millions of customers can facilitate payments between them and introduce other services such as investment management. An exchange that has a lot of buyers and sellers can branch into other products, while an insurance company can bundle coverage for home and auto. Consumers and other industries benefit from this consolidation, up to a point.

As we have seen, concentration of services has other, less desirable consequences over the long run, such as free-rider exploits and abuse. A bank that has consolidated its way to being the only player in town can eventually turn on its customers, charging them more for the same services while innovating less. Regulations can help, but only to a point. The more complicated compliance becomes, the harder it will be for a new bank to enter the market, making incumbents even more entrenched. Lack of competition leads to hubris and stasis.

Banks have shareholders, and shareholders want profit growth. The easiest way for a bank to make more money is by taking more risk with client deposits. If the bank is big enough, then a slight increase in leverage—more bang sought for the same buck—might be all that's needed. A bit of risk-taking is only natural during an economic expansion anyway, and nobody need be harmed in the process. More risk leads to greater profits, so shareholders are happy. More profit means bigger bonuses, making the employees happy as well. So begins a virtuous cycle. Ambitious department heads who push for a more aggressive stance are promoted to corner offices while concerned risk officers who oppose it are banished to windowless back rooms. The cycle is then repeated, this time with even more risk, leading to even greater profit. Nobody complains, because as far as the folks in charge are concerned, everyone is winning, no one has been harmed. As with most things, the first few violations of trust are often a victimless crime. It's that last one that damns us all.

The story of a financial services firm becoming so big that it ultimately collapses under the weight of its own hubris is so common throughout history that it could be considered a cliché, were it not so tragic. The economic conditions that drive any bank to grow ultimately lead to its undoing. Yet, the most rational thing for every other bank is to follow in its footsteps. Size is a sort of weapon in financial services, and not just because it leads to greater efficiency. The bigger a firm gets, the more leverage it has over the rest of society. Every good bank executive knows— either consciously or subconsciously—that the government will never let them fail. The social and economic consequences are too dire. The most prudent strategy is to grow. Become too big, so you can be considered too big to fail.

Financial regulators try to prevent this cycle from playing out with restrictions on risk-taking and mandates on keeping a certain portion of customer deposits invested in safe assets—the so-called fractional reserve in fractional-reserve banking. Depositors also have a vested interest in keeping their bank in check. Yet there's only so much that either camp can do from the outside. The heavy doors and thick vaults of the world's financial institutions serve a dual purpose. They keep the bank robbers out, and they keep the information in. No matter how inquisitive the regulator or observant the customer, neither will ever know as much as the banker. This informational asymmetry, combined with its unique economies of scale, make the financial services industry highly cyclical. Few sectors have as many booms and busts. We live with them because we understand that our modern economy cannot function without banks, exchanges, insurance companies, and the like.

Or can it? What the economy truly needs are the trust-building services provided by those institutions, not the firms themselves. No law of nature dictates that banking and financial services must come from opaque, centralized, and hierarchical entities. Their existence was born out of the need for trust among disparate economic actors and the fact that there was no other way to achieve it. Now, there's a blockchain for that. The world is full of would-be lenders, borrowers, buyers, and sellers. All they need is for their assets to be tokenized, for the contracts that rule their interactions to become smart, and for their financial lives to move on-chain.

Crises, Structural and Human

The history and evolution of financial services is already familiar to us from the vantage points of money, payments, and capital markets. But the current state of the industry cannot be fully understood without paying a visit to two important events: the Great Depression of the 1930s and the 2008 financial crisis.

Few periods in modern economic history have been scrutinized as much as the decade preceding World War II, and for good reason. The Great Depression was one of the darkest moments of the industrial era, as measured by metrics like falling GDP and rising unemployment. Historians continue to debate why it was so severe or lasted so long, but the one thing they generally agree on is that it was made worse by one of the most cataclysmic banking crises in modern history, particularly in the United States. The 1920s were in many ways a decade of excess—featuring overinvestment in industrial production and rampant speculation on Wall Street—so some kind of correction was inevitable. But few industries suffered more from the comeuppance that began with the stock market crash on Black Tuesday in October 1929 than American banking.

Banks have always been a sort of magnifying glass on the rest of the economy. The nature of the services they provide means that they tend to do better than the overall economy during the good times but suffer more during the bad. The first half of that equation was true enough during the Roaring Twenties when the bank stocks traded on the New York Stock Exchange significantly outperformed their nonfinancial counterparts.[63] But no recession before or since has seen the devastation that unfolded between the years 1929 and 1934 when nine thousand different banks failed across the United States.[64] Those failures had a cascading effect, first on other banks, then on the overall economy.

The problem was partly structural. Unlike Europe, where large national banks with diversified client bases and loan portfolios were the norm, American banks were legally not allowed to operate across state lines and often served specific communities. This led to a patchwork system of thousands of small banks, some of which had extreme exposure to a single area or industry. A bad crop failure in one state was sometimes all it took to force a particular bank to the brink, as lending to local farmers accounted for a substantial portion of that bank's risk portfolio. Too many small banks with few branches also led to a heavy reliance on correspondent banking, forcing every small bank to keep precious funds on deposit with at least one—if not multiple—big banks.

The funds in those accounts often sat idle and were not as useful as cash kept in a vault if there was a sudden surge in withdrawals, the kind of stampede that can happen if there is some sort of economic shock. Too many small banks trying to meet such redemptions simultaneously could drain the nostro deposits of a correspondent bank, escalating the problem upward the payments hierarchy. The complexities of a system of interconnected ledgers could turn a small crisis into a bigger one, resulting in cascading failures. Overreliance on slow-to-settle payment methods such as checks exacerbated problems.[65] The most important number for the risk officer of any bank is the amount of liquid deposits on hand. But in a world where some portion of those deposits may have already been spoken for by rectangular pieces of paper making their way through the postal system, exact math is hard to come by.

None of these structural problems guarantee a banking crisis, and all were as true during the boom as they were in the bust. Too many small banks and slow settlement times were more like oxygen that kept the fire burning after it was lit. An inferno of such historic magnitude still required fuel, and a spark. Kindling was provided by the irresponsible things many bankers did in the years leading up to the crisis, like lending too much to stock speculators or becoming overexposed to the most illiquid asset on earth: real estate.

One of the most important services that commercial banks provide is the practice of maturity transformation, otherwise known as borrowing short term and lending long term. Although we don't usually think of them as such, banks are among the largest natural *borrowers* in the economy. Every dollar deposited by a consumer or business is technically a loan—cash swapped for a ledger entry with the promise of someday getting it back, possibly with interest. Customer deposits are recorded on a bank's balance sheet as liabilities. On the other side of the ledger are mostly the loans it dishes out using funds borrowed from its depositors. These are a bank's assets.

As a general rule, depositors who lend their money to a bank do so for short periods, and can request their money back at will. After all, what good is a checking account if you can't make a payment when you need to? Depositors pay for these privileges by accepting less interest than they would otherwise, thus why more restricted deposits like CDs pay higher interest. Those who borrow from a bank, on the other hand, like home buyers looking for a mortgage, gladly pay higher interest for long-dated loans that get repaid on a fixed schedule. Maturity transformation is the tricky business of intermediating between these disparate needs, the reward for which is the interest rate differential between what the bank charges borrowers and pays depositors, a difference that could be quite large under certain conditions. As the old joke goes, being a banker is all about practicing the 3-6-3 rule: borrow at 3 percent, lend at 6 percent, and hit the golf tee by 3 p.m.

The derogatory tone of this joke is somewhat unfair, as it assumes that anyone could do it. Bankers need to be experts at deciding which borrowers are creditworthy. They also need to stagger their borrowing and lending so there is always enough money coming in to cover whatever has to go out. Most of all, they need to fulfill their duty as anchors of trust. Loan officers might only ever interact with borrowers, but they actually work on behalf of the depositors, lending out *their* money in a (hopefully) responsible fashion. Too little risk and the depositors won't earn much interest. Too much, and they may not get their money back.

Walking the line between enough and too much is more art than science, particularly so in the 1920s, a decade that would eventually earn the adjective *roaring*. Risk is a relative concept and has different textures throughout the economic cycle. Lending money to stock traders who only put 10 percent down and take the rest on margin—a practice pioneered centuries earlier by the Banque Royale—might seem like a dangerous idea but worked well for everyone during the five-year span leading up to the October crash, when the Dow Jones Industrial Average more than tripled. Any conservative risk officer would have looked foolish for trying to curtail the practice.

Bull markets have a way of loosening standards, and lenders who don't join the party are taking a different kind of risk, that of disappointing their shareholders. Margin lending was big business in the 1920s, particularly for banks in New York, many of whom commingled commercial banking with securities services. In a setup that would foreshadow their "financial supermarket" status a century later, both National City Bank of New York (Citibank) and Chase National (JPMorgan) had securities underwriting and brokerage affiliates. Each affiliate was technically a different company from the bank, but the twin activities of lending and trading were so intertwined that the stock certificate for the brokerage businesses was simply printed on the back of the bank's.[66]

When the stock market crashed on Black Tuesday, the selling was so amplified by margin lending that the losses were translated to the banking sector. Borrowers who couldn't put up additional funds had their shares liquidated, driving prices even lower, and thereby pushing other borrowers into margin calls. The problem was further exacerbated by the now-familiar delays between trading and settlement (for securities) and messaging and settlement for payments. Cash raised by a broker by selling stock did not actually arrive until days later. The resulting liquidity crunch hampered the balance sheets of certain banks.

Then there was the banking system's heavy commitment to real estate, a lumbering asset that unlike stocks could not be unloaded with a call to the exchange. Property bubbles have a long history of causing problems for lenders. Under normal circumstances, real estate is the ideal collateral. Unlike securities (which can be diluted by the issuer) or personal property (which can be stolen) physical property is fixed, unique, and durable— thus the use of the adjective *real* in its name. Real estate also mostly goes up in value, two traits that make it generally safe to lend against. But therein lies the rub because too much borrowing and leverage can turn a real estate boom into a bubble. Manhattan real estate prices climbed by more than 50 percent in the decade leading up to the crash, with the average American household more than tripling their mortgage debt as a percentage of total net worth. All of that was great for the profits of the financial sector. Then came the collapse, and property prices fell by over 70 percent in five years, driving even the most conservative mortgages underwater.[67] American banks foreclosed on a record number of properties during the Depression, but with limited benefit, as the money they were getting back was often a fraction of what they had loaned out. Manhattan prices didn't recover until 1960.

None of these challenges to the basic business of banking need to be catastrophic. Banks that find themselves shorthanded have many tools at their disposal. They can sell off their own assets, raise additional capital from shareholders, or borrow from other banks. Worse comes to worst, they can call for help from a Higher Authority. Not god, but the next best thing in financial services: the central bank. Indeed, a major force in the evolution of central banking over the centuries has been the need to occasionally rescue their more pedestrian, commercial cousins. To stave off a crisis, central banks can provide an emergency loan, usually against valuable but currently illiquid assets, such as a basket of mortgages. But this "lender of last resort" facility is only meant for banks that are having problems of liquidity, not insolvency. In theory, what a central bank doesn't want to do is to send the message that it's willing to bail out reckless bankers.

The First Domino

All these issues—reduced risk standards, too much overlap between commercial banks and their securities counterparts, and overexposure to the real estate market—came to a head for the American banking system in the waning weeks of 1929. But very few commercial banks failed that year, thanks to close attention from state and federal banking authorities and a few heroic measures by the then relatively young Federal Reserve. Clients, for their part, continued to believe in their institutions of trust— at least for a while longer.

But the ongoing deterioration of the economy, combined with even greater declines in the prices of stocks and real estate, would ultimately lead to an avalanche of failures in the ensuing three years, a shattering of the trust framework that would not cease until President Franklin Delano Roosevelt declared a nationwide bank holiday on his second day in office. Today we understand the first major crack to have begun with the gathering of a small crowd outside of an otherwise unremarkable bank branch in the Bronx.

The story of what happened to the aptly named Bank of United States (a publicly traded company that had no affiliation with the US government) was in many ways the story of America in the first few decades of the twentieth century. It was founded by a German immigrant, who in 1913 opened its first branch among the now historic tenement houses of Manhattan's Lower East Side. It catered to immigrants and small businesses.

It grew slowly until it was taken over by the founder's son, an Ivy League graduate, in the late 1920s. It then expanded rapidly via a series of mergers and acquisitions, eventually becoming the third-largest bank in New York by assets and the largest in the country by number of customers. It would fail over the span of two days.[68]

The Bank of United States was a poster child for all that could go wrong with any trusted entity in a prolonged expansion. The company had expanded faster than its own operations or risk officers could keep up with. It had lent aggressively to low-quality real estate projects and tied up depositor funds in its own executives' misadventures in the stock market. It did not have the cleanest books.

State and federal banking regulators were concerned about its health even before the crash and did everything they could to pull it through the immediate aftermath. But falling prices continued to take their toll on the asset side of its ledger, and rising unemployment led to diminishing deposits. By the summer of 1930, the only reasonable path forward was to merge with several other banks, with the blessing of concerned regulators. A tentative deal with three other New York banks was announced in late November.

Opacity is the ultimate kryptonite for any trust framework. When people don't know what is going on and can't verify, they will assume the worst. When it comes to banks, the paramount question is whether they can get their money back. Those who are uncertain will show up and find out. On the morning of Tuesday, December 9, the *New York Times* ran a short article revealing that the proposed merger had been called off on account of irreconcilable differences between the negotiating parties. The next day, rumors of solvency issues drew a crowd to a small branch in the Bronx. Some people withdrew their money, just to be safe. Others followed suit, and the crowd grew bigger. Seeing that more and more people were taking out their money, less concerned depositors decided to line up as well, sometimes only to chat with a banker. The police were called in to control the crowd, one that would ultimately grow to over twenty thousand people. Crowds also began to show up at some of the bank's other branches, in far-flung locations like Brooklyn. Everyone who wanted to withdraw their money did, but the public's anxiety grew. The run was on, and spreading, alongside ever more terrifying rumors.

Bank runs are a lot like stampedes: once they get going, it doesn't matter if there is any actual danger. At a certain point, *not running* is the most dangerous thing to do. Later that evening, the New York Police Department announced that it would post two officers outside of each branch the next morning to prevent "undue excitement." But the issue turned out to be moot. At an emergency late-night meeting featuring the bank's executives, state and federal authorities and other leaders from New York's financial community, the decision was made to forestall the inevitable and shut it down.[69]

The collapse of the Bank of United States was not the first major bank failure in the aftermath of the crash, but it was the loudest. The proximity to the country's financial capital, combined with round-the-clock coverage in newspapers like the *New York Times*, spread doubt throughout the land. Doubt in a financial system is contagious. If *that* bank could fail, some depositors must have wondered, why can't mine? There is no financial cost for withdrawing one's money out of fear—only an inconvenience—and the customers who showed up first in the Bronx turned out to be the smartest. Not surprisingly, bank failures accelerated in the early 1930s, with each collapse making the next one that much more likely. The people's trust had been violated, and society as a whole would pay a price.

Ironically, when all was said and done, customers of the Bank of United States still recovered 80 percent of their money.[70] Bank failures generally don't mean that depositors lose everything unless there is outright fraud. What they do lose is access to their capital (in the short term) and whatever value is irrecoverable from the bank's loan and investment portfolio, a figure that even for a poorly run bank turned out to only be 20 percent. And yet, lack of transparency into its books and growing mistrust of its executives still led to a panic. It did not matter that—as the *New York Times* would report the next day—the run was triggered by a false rumor. Trust in the economic situation was frayed twelve months after the crash, so a rumor was enough to take down one bank, and the failure of that bank was the spark that started an inferno.

Banking regulators would later report that customers of the Bank of United States had withdrawn almost 25 percent of their deposits in the weeks leading up to the run, with almost half of that money being taken out in the final few days. Such numbers would have had a chilling effect on depositors elsewhere, making them more likely to opt for the mattress. Economic historians consider the loss of confidence in the banking system as one important reason for the unique severity of the Great Depression.[71] The problem was even known back then, as stated starkly in a sermon by a New York pastor in the waning days of 1930:

"If bank closings are caused by whispers of false tales, then they are the worst type of traitors the world has ever seen. Beside them Judas was an angel. Such destroyers not only bring runs on banks but they undermine faith, without which neither commerce or happiness is possible."[72]

Rumors and "false tales" thrive in a financial system built on opacity and discretionary control. The problem wasn't that people suddenly stopped believing in the idea of banking, but rather lost faith in *those* banks at *that* particular moment in time. Had there been some way for the depositors to be certain that the bankers hadn't misbehaved, perhaps by directly inspecting their books to make sure—the proverbial "trust, but verify"—then most of the runs may have never happened. But such luxuries do not exist in banking as it has been architected for the past five hundred years. Regulators are supposed to solve this problem with rules and audits, but they have a nasty habit of being behind the curve just when the public needs them most.

The contagion that took down a significant portion of the American banking system ended after the weeklong bank holiday declared by President Roosevelt. Remarkably, the holiday ended with people lining up to redeposit their money at banks across America, newly assured that their funds would be safe. Credit for that shift in psychology goes to FDR's decisiveness (which included his first nationally broadcast "fireside chat") and a transformative piece of legislation passed by Congress called the Emergency Banking Act. The bill paid heed to the fact that the crisis was as much psychological as it was financial and granted extraordinary new powers to the federal government to boost both. It dramatically expanded the Fed's "lender of last resort" functionality and allowed the federal government itself to buy the stocks of ailing banks if need be. It also created new mechanisms for unwinding troubled banks in a manner that would protect depositors. Last, but certainly not least, it granted the president emergency powers to do whatever else needed to be done to end the crisis.

Government to the Rescue

History would later remember the introduction of deposit insurance via the Federal Deposit Insurance Corporation (FDIC) as the turning point of the crisis. But that solution came later and wasn't all that powerful, as it imposed strict limits on how much protection each depositor could obtain. What made the Emergency Banking Act potent was the implication that going forward, *all* deposits in every bank would be guaranteed by the government, one way or another.[73]

The president and his supporters went out of their way to communicate that implication with impressive results. Not only was a substantial portion of the cash that had been withdrawn before the holiday returned, but the stock market—which had also closed during the holiday—surged by 15 percent upon resumption of trading, making March 15, 1933, the single biggest up day in the 130-year history of the Dow Jones Industrial Average. The US government had opened a bazooka of trust on an ailing banking system and confidence had been restored. Not only would the number of bank failures fall dramatically, but the economy itself would begin to recover. History would remember this as the turning point of the Great Depression.

If trust in a financial system is a static measure that can be increased with laws and regulations and then left in an elevated position, then our story would end here, and the American banking system would have been uninteresting ever since. The challenge is that prolonged stability in any trust framework can be self-defeating. The more trusting the beneficiaries of the framework, the greater the free-rider temptations for the people in charge of it. So goes the curse of history, and thus how trusted currencies get diluted by their issuers and popular platforms turn exploitative against their users. In the case of financial intermediaries, an abundance of stability allows bankers to become reckless with depositor capital, again. But now, the depositors don't care.

In economics, moral hazard is defined as "the lack of incentive to avoid risk where there is protection against its consequences," a phenomenon to which anyone who has ever driven a rental car more recklessly than their own can relate. The great banking interventions of the Depression era did not solve the problem of an economic crisis caused by a financial one. The interventions simply delayed the arrival of the next one, and made it bigger.

Depositors who believe that either they or their bank will always get bailed out are less discerning about which bank to use. After all, if every bank that is given a charter by the government is also guaranteed by it—either explicitly via deposit insurance or implicitly via emergency bailouts—then why not just use the most convenient bank? Or the one that pays the highest interest? Indeed, the most prudent course of action might be to actively seek out riskier banks. If things go well, they'll make depositors more money. If they don't, someone else will foot the bill. Heads I win, tails you lose.

The unintended consequences of America's new approach to banking first arose during the savings and loans crisis of the 1980s. S&Ls, also known as thrifts, are limited financial institutions meant to help working-class people save money or buy a house. They grew in popularity in the decades after the Second World War when a growing population, low unemployment, and suburban expansion led to growing demand for savings accounts and mortgages—particularly from institutions that offered better terms than traditional banks.

As with the banking crisis of the 1930s, the collapse of the thrift industry was caused by a nasty combination of a challenging economic period and over-levered balance sheets, particularly as tied to risky real estate. Lack of transparency, poor internal controls, and flat-footed regulators were also a factor. But there was no widespread panic this time around, and no runs, because savers believed that they were protected, either by government-run deposit insurance or some other kind of bailout. They were right. Despite the collapse of over one thousand thrift banks in the span of nine years, depositors hardly lost anything. Taxpayers, on the other hand, lost over $100 billion.[74]

The moral hazard of the Depression-era programs meant to stabilize banking now had a price tag, and a steep one at that. To make matters worse, the cost was socialized across an entire nation. Citizens who had nothing to do with thrifts and never benefited from their existence were nevertheless billed for their folly. This was not supposed to happen. There is a reason why America's primary banking backstop is called the Federal Deposit *Insurance* Corporation. The money needed to rescue failed banks is supposed to come from premiums charged to all banks. But the premiums collected from thousands of thrifts across the span of several decades turned out to be woefully inadequate, covering less than 20 percent of the money spent on the rescue.[75]

The concern that government protections in banking might ultimately encourage reckless behavior is as old as the protections themselves. No lesser an influential figure in enacting them than Franklin

Delano Roosevelt himself expressed his own fears in a newspaper article published less than a year before he signed the FDIC into existence. He predicted that deposit insurance would "lead to laxity in bank management and carelessness on the part of both banker and depositor," eventually causing "an impossible drain on the Federal Treasury." [76] It would take seventy-five years, but history would prove him right.

The Problems Are Not Contained

We are still too close in time to the Great Financial Crisis (GFC) that enveloped the planet in the first decade of the twenty-first century to fully comprehend it. The events and details that explain seminal moments take time to unravel, and it took economists and banking experts decades to decipher what happened in the 1930s. There are, however, some things about the biggest financial crisis in US history that we can be certain of, starting with the fact that it was even more dangerous than the financial crisis of the Great Depression. Banking has always been important to the economy, but the financial sector that tiptoed to the brink in 2008 was more intertwined in the life of the average person than the one in 1931. It was also more complex. Decades of economic growth, wealth creation, and financial innovation had resulted in a lot more saving, borrowing, investing, and every other form of financial interaction facilitated by centralized intermediaries.

Ironically, in the minds of most experts, the financialization of the economy also meant that a crisis of this magnitude should never have happened. The business of banking had matured in the years since the Depression, growing more sophisticated in the postwar years and taking a turn toward the scientific at the turn of the millennium. Unlike the bankers of old, who relied on a little bit of math and a lot of intuition to do their job, modern bankers relied on risk management models developed by Nobel prizewinning economists. The perceived sophistication of the craft was one reason why many countries deregulated their financial sectors in the years leading up to the crisis, a decision that some came to regret. However, the role of deregulation in the financial crisis should not be overstated. The companies that blew up in 2007 and 2008 were among the most regulated in history. Unlike the Bank of United States, which was mostly accountable to a single regulator, companies like Lehman Brothers and Washington Mutual were overseen by an alphabet soup of local and national agencies such as the FDIC, OCC, SEC, NYSDFS, Office of Thrift Supervision, and Federal Reserve.

None of these agencies saw the crisis coming. Few words will live in financial infamy more than the ones from the chairman of the Federal Reserve at the start of the crisis when he reassured Congress that the fall-out from the subprime loan market "seems likely to be contained."[77] It's hard to blame him for his misjudgment when the CEOs of the companies involved also felt that way. The opacity of the traditional banking system makes it tough to regulate, because the regulators have to rely on the companies they supervise to provide the information they need to do their job—like cops without radar guns who have to ask every driver how fast they were going. The public had no clue about what was happening either, but by now it could be fully excused. Decades of depositor protections and bailouts had convinced most people that they didn't have to care about the soundness of their bank.

The financial crisis revolved around (as they often do) the real estate market. Years of appreciating home prices, combined with government incentives, had convinced most people that about the safest thing they could do financially was to buy a house. That perception also made it OK to finance the purchase with a loan, especially at a time of historically low interest rates. But there was only so much depositor capital that any one bank or community lender could lend out. That's where Wall Street stepped in. To keep the mortgages flowing, large investment houses such as Lehman brothers and Merrill Lynch began buying thousands of mortgages from smaller players, bundling them together, and selling them to institutional investors such as pension funds and insurance companies. This process of securitization created a virtuous cycle. The mortgage originators that sold their loans could get fresh capital to lend again, the Wall Street banks that bundled those loans into mortgage-backed securities (MBS) could earn fees, and the investors who bought those securities could enjoy higher returns.

Securitization was believed to make the mortgage market more democratic, bringing cheaper loans and first-time homeownership to a larger pool of people. It was also believed to make the mortgage market more resilient by diversifying exposure. Regardless of the economic situation, any individual homeowner could default on their loan, and house prices in a single market could always fall. Too much exposure to a single property market, like farmland in the Midwest, caused many of the earliest bank failures during the Depression. A security consisting of thousands of mortgages from all over was diversified on both fronts, so a pension fund that had exposure to farmland could be diversified with loans against condos in a big city. If mortgage-backed securities had only included high quality loans to qualified borrowers, then our story would have had a happy ending: more people would have bought a house, pension funds would have made more money, and Wall Street would not have been occupied.

But trust is a seductive creature. It lures people in with the promise of stability, then tempts them to push the envelope. The success of the first few decades of securitization inspired the bankers to innovate. What if not every mortgage in the latest bundle was of the highest quality? So-called *subprime* loans paid more interest. A little bit of subprime in an MBS is like a pinch of salt in a bland dish—enough to make things interesting, but not enough to make anyone sick. And since that's OK, why not slice and dice the resulting security into different tranches and sell the parts to different investors based on their risk profile? Doing so will better serve every client. And now that we've got all of these tranches from different securities lying around, why not repackage some into their own Frankensecurities? Surely somebody has an Excel model that demonstrates the wisdom of doing so. Speaking of which, now that the risk models have confirmed all of this is safe, what if we lever the whole thing up with even more borrowed money? What might happen then?

The answer, at least in the beginning, was a historic bubble in housing and record profits on Wall Street. More risk meant more money for more houses. But things could only be pushed so far. There were only so many qualified mortgage applicants out there and only so many loans for Wall Street to buy. Now it was up to the originators who created these loans to innovate. What if the traditional requirement of a 20 percent down payment was reduced to 10 percent, or even nothing? Since house prices only ever went up, the worst thing that could happen was a foreclosure sale at a profit. And since defaults aren't that big of a deal, why not reduce the minimum income and credit qualifications for borrowers? Now that homeownership was America's favorite pastime, everyone should have a chance to play. While we are at it, let's stop asking borrowers to prove their income. Sure, some people will lie on an application, but that problem, along with the resulting mortgage, will soon be somebody else's.

All of these justifications were used to dial up risk at every level of the securitization process. Nobody complained because everybody was making money. The few observers who questioned the sustainability of the whole thing were brushed aside. The economy was strong, house prices only ever went up, and the bankers knew what they were doing. In other words: trust us.

Nothing that we've learned so far is all that new or unique to this crisis. Asset bubbles driven by too much debt and too little skepticism are an ancient phenomenon, perhaps even a part of the human condition, and prosperity achieved with borrowed money exists on borrowed time. Financial crises are a fact of life, and the American economy had experienced so many in its history that, before the twentieth century, recessions and depressions were often called panics. Technology had come a long way since the adoption of telegram messaging in securities trading during the debt bubble that resulted in the now-forgotten Panic of 1873 and the resulting "Long Depression," but technology cannot solve human nature.

What it can do, however, is make it harder for people to lie to each other, not to mention themselves.

House prices in the United States turned in 2006, and the impact on Wall Street was felt immediately. Mortgage defaults began to creep up and MBS values fell. Those who had purchased these securities with borrowed money were forced to book big losses and a few levered investment funds blew up. A virtuous cycle quickly turned into a vicious one, and the dominos began to fall. but the people who had benefited on the way up refused to give up the dream. Instead, they settled on a new narrative, one that enabled them to keep doing what they were doing: *some* mortgage originators had acted irresponsibly, and a *few* subprime loans had ended up in the wrong securities. House prices would soon rebound, and only a handful of small banks faced any serious risk. The big banks would be fine, because they were protected by a Maginot Line of excess capital. Subprime problems, like a German army amassing in the Rhineland, were contained.

It was a convenient narrative, enabled by an opaque and architecturally haphazard financial system that made it practically impossible to know what was where. If the shareholders, depositors, and regulators that sat outside of this system had some way of verifying what they were told at this early juncture, then the crisis may have never happened. Instead, they had to take everything on faith.

House prices continued to fall in 2007 and the demand for risky mortgage-backed securities fell. Here Wall Street innovated yet again. The risky instruments that couldn't be unloaded by the mortgage departments of firms like Merrill Lynch would be bought by an investment arm of the same bank—an egregious violation of shareholder and depositor trust, not to mention the first commandment of selling toxic substances, which is to never get high on your own supply.[78] A crisis the size of an iceberg was approaching, but the outside world had no idea, in part because the few Cassandras screaming that the big banks were in trouble couldn't prove it. The internal books of the world's centralized intermediaries, like the waters of the North Atlantic, were murky. Not even the leaders of the companies in question had a firm grip on what was happening. Here is Alan Schwartz, the CEO of Bear Stearns, in March of 2008, on a day when his company's stock was trading at $65 a share:

"We don't see any pressure on our liquidity,
   let alone a liquidity crisis"[79]

Bear would be insolvent within the week and sold off to JPMorgan for a symbolic $2 a share (eventually raised to $10). It would have been completely bankrupt had the Federal Reserve not sweetened the deal with $30 billion worth of taxpayer money. Schwartz wasn't the only CEO who proved clueless until the bitter end, as similar assurances were uttered by the heads of other firms right before they collapsed. Historians (and federal prosecutors) would later debate whether these men were intentionally dishonest or just clueless—a distinction that, for our purposes, is almost moot. If the financial well-being of the world's intermediaries is of fundamental importance—so much so that there is no limit to how much money governments will spend to save them—then why risk either?

In the case of Lehman Brothers, the focus would fall on its infamous "repo 105" maneuver, an accounting trick used to make the company's capital position look stronger when it reported earnings. The bank's clients and shareholders may have behaved differently had they known about this lie, or so the latter would claim in a massive class action lawsuit against management.[80] But a centralized financial system doesn't offer that kind of transparency. What it does offer is an army of supposedly independent auditors, every one of which had signed off on the riskiest practices—news that should come as no surprise to anyone who has heard of a company called Enron and its accounting firm Arthur Anderson.

The collapse of Lehman Brothers in September 2008 exposed all of the flaws of an overly complex and opaque financial system built on discretion and good faith. Financial losses traveled up and down the banking pyramid, followed by rumors of even bigger losses and outright terror. The complexity of the pyramid meant that every bank had some exposure to every other bank, but nobody knew how much. The situation was worsened by the now-familiar inefficiencies of the capital market infrastructure. Investors who tried to ascertain the riskiness of their securities discovered that it wasn't clear which mortgages belonged to which bundle, because there was no central register, no verifiable database. If there was ever a market that suffered from a *lack* of a single source of truth, this was it. Those who tried to sell their securities had a hard time doing so at any price, in part because some banks had stopped trading with each other. In a world where every trade still took days to settle, nobody wanted to sell their securities to an institution that might not be around to pay come settlement day.

There was also a lack of knowledge about who owed how much money to whom. Knowing how much exposure any one bank had to the likes of Lehman wasn't enough. Risk managers wanted to know how much exposure every other bank had to Lehman, for fear of widespread contagion. Some companies had insured their exposure to the mortgage market and each other, but there was growing concern that the insurance companies had not set aside enough capital to cover every claim. Insurance is another heavily regulated industry that suffers from a fundamental lack of transparency. The companies in question went out of their way to reassure the public that they had more than enough money. The rushed $150 billion bailout of industry-leader AIG—announced within 24 hours of the collapse of Lehman Brothers—indicated that they did not. Trust was evaporating everywhere.

No one can say for certain why Lehman Brothers was allowed to fail while Bear and AIG were saved. What we do know is that the fear of total contagion after Lehman filed for bankruptcy convinced government officials to spare no (taxpayer) expense to save everybody else. They were egged on by falling stock prices and frightening forecasts (often made by the bankers themselves) of another Great Depression. Whether those predictions were accurate, and whether these firms deserved to get bailed out, was beside the point. Wall Street had unintentionally hijacked the well-being of the economy and gotten its way. Those who had lived by the sword of risk-taking and bravado would not die by it.

Despite the bailouts, the near-collapse of the banking system still took a heavy toll on the rest of the US economy. The stock market lost over half of its value and unemployment jumped to a thirty-year high. Both would take almost a decade to return to pre-crisis levels. Housing prices would take even longer, thanks in part to a record ten million foreclosures, many of which were personal tragedies that ruined the lives of entire families. Wall Street pay, on the other hand, set a new record less than two years after the crisis.[81] Heads I win, tails you lose.

And so, FDR's forgotten prediction about the dangers of government protections for financial intermediaries had come true. Instead of stabilizing the banking system, decades of depositor insurance and banker bailouts had made the system more fragile and opaque. The notion of *too big to fail*—once viewed as something to avoid—was now accepted as a fact of life, thanks in part to shotgun weddings that made the biggest banks even bigger, as either coordinated by the government or mandated by it. The only thing left to do was to prepare for the next go-around, when the bankers would once again push the envelope, the regulators wouldn't know, the depositors wouldn't care, and the taxpayers would pay.

While many governments did introduce stringent regulations after the crisis in the way of increased capital requirements, tightened lending standards, and restrictions on so-called "systemically important financial institutions," they didn't do anything to address the fundamental flaws of centralized intermediaries, for the simple reason that they couldn't. Banking still relied on too much faith and not enough transparency, the same way it had for hundreds of years.

How much confidence government officials had in their response to that crisis became evident at the start of the next one, caused by a global pandemic. This time, the authorities didn't even wait to see who was overextended and might need to be saved. They acted preemptively by unleashing a historic torrent of liquidity. In early 2020, the Federal Reserve pumped more money into the financial system in the span of a few months than it had during the entirety of the previous crisis. Most other central banks followed suit, with little controversy. This time, there was no debate about *whether* and *how much*. Everything from the safest securities to the riskiest junk bonds were backstopped by the government, with vocal promises to do more if necessary. It was the kind of intervention one would expect from government officials who had lost all faith in the underlying financial system.

Defenders of these programs argued that the pandemic was a once-in-a-century crisis warranting a heroic response. As true as that assessment may have been from a biological point of view, financial pandemics seem to hit the banking system every ten years. While the government response to the pandemic also included bailouts for other industries and stimulus checks for individuals, the amount of money targeted toward the financial sector dwarfed those amounts. In one telling example, the Fed's capital commitment to its Wall Street-oriented "repo" program was more than three times what it made available for the Congressionally approved Main Street Lending Program.[82] As usual, the banking sector was spared the important pruning of weak players that every other industry experiences during a recession, almost guaranteeing that the next shock would require exponentially more public resources to preserve the status quo. Placed inside a historical context, any reasonable observer would have to wonder if there isn't a better way.

Now, there is.

DeFi

Most of the risks inherent to any financial transaction are captured by the idea of counterparty risk, a technical term loosely defined as "the people you interact with not doing what they've promised." Counterparty risk exists in all human interaction but is uniquely dangerous in the financial realm because all fates are intertwined. A payment system that fails to deliver someone's paycheck may result in a missed mortgage payment that hurts the value of a security owned by a pension fund, like dominos falling.

One way to diminish counterparty risk is with a contract, one that spells out the terms of the interaction and the punishment for not following through. Few industries rely on contracts more than financial services, and most of the products that we interact with on a regular basis—our bank accounts, mortgages, and investment portfolios—can be thought of as nothing more than contracts that control the movement of money if and when certain conditions are met. One way to think about the banking pyramid is as a series of horizontal and vertical contracts between counterparties meant to hold everyone—from the mighty central bank to a lowly payment provider—accountable.

The current web of contracts is meant to increase trust, which it does, but only until it runs up against a lack of transparency. There's not a lot of visibility beyond our immediate counterparties, in spite of the fact that what happens to *their* counterparties might someday impact us, especially during a crisis. There's also too much discretion. Just because someone has a contractual agreement to do something doesn't mean that they will. Stuff happens, and individuals and corporations can act in unpredictable ways.

That's where the legal system comes in, at least in theory. Counterparties that don't hold up their end of an agreement are subject to financial penalties and criminal prosecution. But history has proven this sort of after-the-fact intervention to be a weak deterrent. Lawsuits are expensive and there's little to be gained by suing a counterparty that owes you money if they've already gone belly-up. Besides, most financial counterparties are corporations with a liability shield that protects their shareholders. Their executives could theoretically be held accountable for misdeeds, but this too is impractical, especially when they can use their ill-gotten gains to hire an army of lawyers. Case in point: despite the shameful actions of many bank executives in the leadup to the 2008 financial crisis, almost nobody went to jail.

A more trustworthy financial system would be perfectly transparent, with every participant having the ability to track their counterparty exposure to every other participant—regardless of how far apart they might be in space or time. It would be direct, replacing reliance on the goodwill of centralized intermediaries with a mechanism through which borrowers and lenders, or buyers and sellers, could directly trust each other. A more trustworthy financial system would be automated. It would enforce the rules of every contractual agreement in real time, as opposed to after the fact via a legal system that takes time and money, and that may not prevail. A more trustworthy financial system would be built on a blockchain platform. It would use smart contracts to process every interaction and tokens to apply its services to an infinite number of value stores. That more trustworthy financial system is already here, and is known as decentralized finance, or DeFi.

DeFi is not so much an industry as it is an ecosystem. It consists of a series of dApps and protocols on public blockchains designed to replicate the services of banks, brokers, exchanges, investment funds, and insurance companies. All use smart contracts to make important decisions and tokens to execute the resulting transaction. There are no bankers, market makers, or insurance adjusters, just open-source code executed within the consensus framework of the underlying platform. DeFi is impersonal, cold, and calculating—by design. Every solution does what it's supposed to in a predictable fashion, like a calculator, regardless of what the user would like the numbers to be. Counterparty risk is therefore diminished. There are no fallible executives pushing the envelope to meet earnings expectations, no banker bros gunning for a bigger bonus.

The first successful DeFi protocol was MakerDAO, a lending facility and stablecoin solution launched on the Ethereum blockchain in 2017 (DAO is the acronym for Decentralized Autonomous Organization). It was created by a group of like-minded developers who understood the benefits of using a global blockchain platform for moving dollars but wanted to build a decentralized stablecoin. Dollar-denominated coins like Tether had been around for a while but suffered from their own form of counterparty risk due to the need for an off-chain cash reserve. What if the issuer lies about the reserve? Or a government confiscates the money? Maker's solution was to replace the backing of off-chain dollars with that of on-chain collateral *valued* in dollars.

The MakerDAO protocol allows owners of assets like Ether to transfer their coins to smart contracts programmed to hold them as collateral, then generate a proportional amount of a dollar-pegged token called Dai. This is a loan, an open-ended credit relationship between the user and the system, with the Dai tokens acting as a digital receipt. To get their collateral back, users repay the loan plus interest. In the meantime, they are free to use their Dai tokens as if they were dollars. Other blockchain users are willing to accept Dai as being pegged to the dollar because they understand each token to be redeemable for at least one dollar worth of collateral. As confusing as this mechanism may sound, it's no different from how most of the money in existence today came about.

The earliest forms of paper money in places like England were nothing more than receipts for gold or silver held by a goldsmith, commercial bank, or (eventually) the central bank. This too was a claim on collateral, a type of money known as representative money, because every note was a loan, denominated in the national currency. That's why people called them banknotes. Trust in the ability to someday redeem each note made the paper useful for commerce. In other words, an English cobbler was willing to accept a 10 pound note for his services because he was confident that he could either redeem it for gold or pay it to someone else. Paper checks issued by a contemporary bank operate on a similar principle, and users can sign them over to someone else, transferring the right to redeem them for cash. The British pound is no longer backed by anything other than a promise, but 10 pound notes still have the phrase "I promise to pay the bearer on demand the sum of ten pounds" next to the Queen's head.

Dai is a more trustworthy banknote. Unlike the metal vaults of a gold-smith or the balance sheet of a bank, the collateral held by the smart con-tracts of MakerDAO is fully transparent and instantly verifiable, as everything is recorded on the blockchain. Dai users don't have to take anyone's word that the currency is fully backed—they can examine the ledger. Indeed, the general public has more information about the finan-cial viability of MakerDAO than the most hard-nosed regulator has about any bank. DeFi users never trust. They verify.

MAKERDAO: THE DECENTRAL BANK

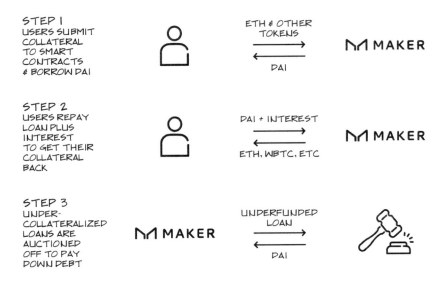

STEP 1
USERS SUBMIT COLLATERAL TO SMART CONTRACTS & BORROW DAI
ETH & OTHER TOKENS
DAI
MM MAKER

STEP 2
USERS REPAY LOAN PLUS INTEREST TO GET THEIR COLLATERAL BACK
DAI + INTEREST
ETH, WBTC, ETC
MM MAKER

STEP 3
UNDER-COLLATERALIZED LOANS ARE AUCTIONED OFF TO PAY DOWN DEBT
MM MAKER
UNDERFUNDED LOAN
DAI

There are some challenges to this mechanism for creating stablecoins, however, starting with the volatility of the collateral. The value of ETH—at times the most popular form of collateral used by Maker—fluctuates wildly. If it falls too much, then the collateral held by the system's digital vaults may not be sufficient to cover the amount of Dai outstanding. To diminish this risk, the protocol requires users to heavily over-collateralize every loan, putting up at least $125 worth of ETH for every 100 Dai they hope to borrow. If ETH falls so much that even that buffer proves inadequate, then the loans below the required threshold are automatically liquidated. Smart contracts auction off the collateral in an open market and use the proceeds to pay down the user's debt, like a margin call triggered by falling stocks.

Part of the charm of the DeFi ecosystem is the ability to revisit first principles, taking financial models that have been around for a long time and augmenting them with a new source of trust.

The model used by Maker—a loan issued against valuable collateral held by a lender with the right to sell it in case of default—is all around us. Variations of it are used in everything from the multitrillion-dollar "repo" market that underlies the banking system to your local pawn shop. For as long as human beings have owned objects of generally accepted value, they've wanted to borrow money against them, either to fund some other economic activity or to place a speculative bet.

Like other credit facilities, Maker charges interest for every loan. Unlike traditional banks (or pawn shops), however, there are no employees to decide what that rate should be. Decentralization becomes tricky when it comes to complex decisions that can't be automated so most DeFi solutions defer to their respective communities. The developers who created MakerDAO included a governance token called MKR in their design. Owners of these tokens (who can be anyone) vote on important decisions such as what types of collateral to accept, minimum collateral ratios, and the interest rate. As a reward for their contribution, MKR token holders get to collect the interest income the system generates, but only if they do a good job. Should anything go wrong with the system, they are financially liable. Not after the fact the way traditionally bankers are liable, but in real time.

The same use of incentives in lieu of a central authority that was pioneered by Satoshi Nakamoto to secure a blockchain is here applied to a dApp built on top of one. Those who participate in governance are effectively the underwriters of the MakerDAO system. When things go well and the system generates income, the money is used to purchase MKR tokens in the open market and burn (destroy) them—the blockchain equivalent of a share buyback. Conversely, should the collateral held by the system ever prove insufficient, then additional MKR tokens are instantly minted and auctioned off to raise money—the DeFi equivalent of a capital raise that dilutes existing shareholders. Those who participate in governance are incentivized to walk a fine line between growing adoption by offering favorable terms and preserving integrity by not taking too much risk. Decentralized finance gives a whole new meaning to the notion of community banking.

Maker has evolved over the years to accept many kinds of collateral and boasts a multibillion-dollar loan portfolio, one that is already bigger than the vast majority of banks in America. Dai has gained adoption as a reliable dollar proxy and is used in everything from remittance payments to crypto trading. Like any experimental solution, progress has been uneven and there have been setbacks, most notably during the pandemic-induced crypto crash of March 2020, when a perfect storm of falling collateral values, spiking transaction fees, and code glitches resulted in a capital shortfall. But the overall architecture of the solution has served the community well, and in doing so has proven the viability of a brand-new way to build trust among financial counterparties. Like the rest of the DeFi ecosystem, it also serves as a powerful reminder of all that is lacking with traditional banking, including its inefficiency and systematic bias.

Traditional banks rely on people to do most of the work, and people are expensive. That's why banks have minimum account balances, or why mortgage originators charge closing costs. The dangerous problem of discretionary control that dooms financial intermediaries in a crisis has a more banal downside in ordinary times: it's expensive to operate. That expense limits what these companies are willing to do and who they are willing to do it for. There's no point in giving someone a $100 loan if it takes $200 to process their application.

Smart contracts have no such constraints. Other than the transaction fees paid to the miners who process every interaction, the marginal cost of each interaction is zero. There are no processing fees or closing costs. This efficiency frees up some DeFi protocols to give out the tiniest of loans, sometimes for only a few dollars. Microlending has a lot of important uses, particularly in the digital domain. It enables brand-new business models and makes the rest of the financial system more efficient. It also onboards the less fortunate among us, the kind of people who've been almost entirely abandoned by the traditional financial system.

Of the many drawbacks of centralized finance, the saddest might be the systematic exclusion of the people who could use its services the most. Cost is only part of the problem. More challenging is the same exclusionary and guilty-until-proven-innocent compliance framework that locks so many out of the existing payment system. DeFi protocols don't discriminate because they can't. Anyone with access to a computer, smartphone, or even a plastic card can generate their own private key, and in the eyes of a smart contract, every user looks like every other. The only thing anyone needs to prove is the fact that they are the rightful owner of the assets they want to utilize. DeFi is also more egalitarian. Censorship resistance in decentralized financial services goes beyond the simple question of whether someone gets access. It also applies to the quality of that access. DeFi is arguably the first banking system in history as willing to give a million-dollar loan to a billionaire in America as a ten-dollar loan to a student in Thailand, and to charge them the same interest rate.

An Open and Fluid Ecosystem

The financial innovations pioneered by the community behind MakerDAO have by now been used by dozens of other DeFi protocols. Money market platforms such as Compound and Aave allow users to save or borrow in a variety of digital assets, with smart contracts facilitating the process from start to finish. Unlike Maker, these protocols allow users to borrow the deposited assets themselves, not just a dollar-pegged claim against them. Also, unlike Maker, Compound and Aave use automated algorithms to determine interest rates, and vary them based on supply and demand. Since there is no corporate entity sitting in the middle, savers will earn more, and borrowers will pay less. All else being equal, a DeFi solution will always be more competitive than a centralized equivalent.

There are even aggregator protocols that constantly move users' deposits back and forth between competing solutions to get the best return. Users who want to maximize their income deposit their tokens with the smart contracts of the aggregator, and those smart contracts in turn deposit their coins in the protocols with the highest returns—like a bank whose only purpose is to shuffle money in and out of other banks. Programmable money residing on a platform that provides full transparency of data and easy movement of capital is a powerful thing. It keeps everyone honest.

In traditional banking, the lack of transparency of who is offering what, combined with high switching costs, protects incumbents. People who deposit money at a bank might not know that another bank offers a higher interest rate. Even if they did—a tall task given the preponderance of limited-time offers, marketing gimmicks, and fine print—it would be impractical to have too many accounts at different banks just to optimize yield. DeFi eliminates that friction. Since the pertinent data is recorded on the ledger, knowing who pays the highest returns is easy, and since identity is defined by a private key, switching is simple as well. Unlike traditional banking, where switching service providers is a time-consuming hassle, DeFi users can switch service providers as easily as iTunes listeners can switch songs.

This unprecedented amount of user freedom keeps the people and communities who conceive of, code, and control any DeFi solution via its governance token honest. Whether it's the return paid to depositors or the rate charged borrowers, a protocol can't arbitrarily change the numbers to something uncompetitive because its users would leave. There is no such thing as predatory lending in DeFi because everything is transparent, and every project is expendable.

Or replicable. Since there are no branches to be operated or licenses to be acquired, and everything is based on open-source code, creating a competitor to any existing protocol is as simple as downloading its code, making a few modifications, and redeploying it on-chain—competition as easy as copy and paste. Some of the most popular DeFi protocols are forks of their predecessors, slight modifications created by developers or community members who believed they could build a better mousetrap. The constant threat of new competition keeps the more established projects accountable to their users and always looking to innovate—a stark contrast to the legacy financial system, where a lifetime of moats provided by hard-to-get banking licenses and expensive infrastructure has made the incumbents hubristic and lazy.

The limitations of traditional banks and payment providers have been known for some time, and entrepreneurs have been trying to disrupt the industry for decades. Until recently, most of that effort came from so-called Fintechs—non-blockchain-based startups such as Revolut, Chime, and Credit Karma. Despite their lofty claims, these companies are not that different from the lumbering incumbents they seek to replace. They take the same business models that have been around for a long time, unbundle them into specific services, and incrementally improve them with tools like cloud computing and AI. They are iterative at best—more DVD disc than streaming video—and still require faith in an opaque intermediary operated by humans. Companies like PayPal and Square might record their balance sheets in the cloud, but that doesn't make them any more transparent, or trustworthy. Like any other centralized intermediary, their revenues come at their users' expense. Compared to the innovations coming out of DeFi, most of their services are rather unimaginative.

The blockchain's ability to diminish counterparty risk by building trust directly between disparate users all over the world, combined with its smart contract and token functionalities, enable revolutionary financial models that have never existed before. One example is Uniswap, a decentralized and noncustodial exchange founded by an unemployed coder that is now one of the largest crypto exchanges in the world, thanks to a novel approach to sourcing liquidity that may soon become the stuff of academic conferences and PhD dissertations.

DIY Financial Services

Cryptocurrency exchanges—services where users trade one coin for another or against fiat currency—have been around for almost as long as cryptocurrencies themselves. Despite the novelty of the assets they handle and the blockchain infrastructure they tap into, most use a custodial model, with the exchange serving as direct counterparty to every client. People who want to use them must first transfer their coins to the exchange, temporarily surrendering possession, in the same way that stock owners surrender ownership to DTCC. The coin balances that these users see in their exchange accounts are not real by blockchain standards, because somebody else controls the private key. Protections such as asset control and censorship resistance no longer apply. The trading that happens at these exchanges has nothing to do with the blockchain either. It takes place in their proprietary systems. Not surprisingly, the mechanics of trading are not that different from how things are done at the 200-year-old New York Stock Exchange. Buyers, sellers, and liquidity providers post bids and offers in a central limit order book, and matches are recorded as trades. But that too is theoretical. Nothing is certain until users withdraw their assets back to their own blockchain address. A lot could go wrong in the interim.

Custodial exchanges were an important driver to the growth of the crypto industry in the early years. Without them, there would not have been a scalable way to onboard millions of new users into the decentralized domain. But they suffer from some of the usual pitfalls of centralized intermediaries. They can lie about their holdings, go out of business, or be shut down by a government. They can also be hacked. The bearer nature of cryptocurrencies makes any exchange that holds a lot of them a massive honeypot for thieves and hackers. The New York Stock Exchange does not need to worry about someone penetrating its servers and stealing peoples' stocks in the way that Coinbase has to for crypto. Almost all the biggest crypto hacks in history have been from exchanges, leaving their users in the lurch.

DeFi solution Uniswap takes a radically different approach to trading, starting with the elimination of a centralized intermediary tasked with holding everyone's coins. Its users interact directly with smart contracts and each other. Crypto owners who'd like to provide liquidity—be they professional market makers or amateurs—submit their holdings to smart contracts that keep them in transparent pools. Submissions are made in pairs that make up a market, like ETH and a dollar stablecoin. Anyone who wants to trade this pair, like someone looking to cash out of ETH for dollars, solicits a quote from the protocol. Smart contracts return a price based on the available liquidity. Should the seller accept that price, then a transaction of ETH being sent to the pool in exchange for dollars is submitted to the miners for processing. Those who funded this pool in the first place collect a small fee.

The first important thing to note about this process is that everyone involved is dealing with verifiable code, not a fallible human. The second thing to note is that there is no need for traders to surrender their assets until the exact moment the trade goes through. This so-called atomic approach to trading significantly reduces counterparty risk. The last thing to note is that every trade is cryptographically guaranteed. Our seller will not have her ETH leave her wallet until the exact moment (or block) when the resulting dollars arrive. If either leg can't happen for any reason, then the entire trade is nullified.

Uniswap's other great innovation is the use of math to determine prices. Traditional markets rely on a chaotic process of liquidity providers posting the prices at which they are willing to engage, and would-be buyers and sellers effectively negotiating simultaneously to get their order filled. There are no guaranteed executions and larger trades often must be broken into multiple chunks executed at different prices. The user experience is terrible. Uniswap (and other protocols that have copied its approach) use a mathematical formula to quote each user a single price for their total order—regardless of size—based on how much available liquidity that trade will consume. Small trades get competitive quotes while larger ones become increasingly expensive. Technically speaking, this approach offers infinite liquidity, but with infinite slippage (the difference between the price a trader was hoping to get and the price they did get). In layman's terms, users usually get more or less the same price they would get from a traditional exchange, but with a friendlier user interface, not to mention instant gratification.

Like the rest of the DeFi ecosystem, automated market makers (AMMs) are far more egalitarian than their legacy counterparts. Trading in traditional markets such as the NASDAQ is dominated by a handful of firms that use their size, licenses, and access to the latest technology to crowd out everyone else. Providing liquidity in traditional markets is a winner-take-all affair. AMMs are different because every liquidity provider that submits assets to a pool is treated the same as every other regardless of whether they submit one coin or one thousand. Everyone earns a proportional share of the pool's profits. There is no edge to be had by a mega player over a minor participant.

To make things even more open, Uniswap issues every user who provides liquidity something called a liquidity-pool share (LP share)—a unique blockchain token that represents their proportional claim to the tokens held within a pool, plus any accrued fees. LP shares can be transferred on the blockchain like any other, so users who commit capital don't have to withdraw their assets to cash out. They can transfer the right to collect those assets to somebody else. They can even post that right as collateral in a protocol such as MakerDAO and borrow against it. The Maker protocol is willing to accept Uniswap LP shares as collateral because the transparency and code of the blockchain guarantee that LP shares can always be redeemed for deposits held at Uniswap.

This unusual ability not just to transfer one's assets, but also to transfer the *right* to collect those assets if they've already been put to work somewhere, is common throughout the DeFi ecosystem. Users who deposit assets into the Aave and Compound money markets get corresponding *a*Tokens and *c*Tokens that can be used in a myriad of activities, including payments—the blockchain equivalent of paying someone by giving them ownership of your checking account, as opposed to writing them a check. There are a few analogues to this phenomenon in traditional markets, such as when investors in a private equity fund sell their share of that fund to someone else. DeFi abstracts this phenomenon to anything, making the first derivative of any financial product as transferable as the product itself.

Along with saving, borrowing, and trading, there are also DeFi protocols for simplified insurance and synthetic assets. Nexus Mutual is a mutual protection solution where members contribute capital to pools that cover events like bad code in the smart contracts of some other decentralized application. Thorny questions such as which smart contracts to cover, coverage limits, and whether an event qualifies for a payout are settled democratically via a governance token. The model is quite similar to traditional mutual insurers, a version of which already exists in almost every country. Not only does running everything on a blockchain make the insurer more trustworthy for its members, it also reduces operating costs. Traditional insurance providers spend a shocking portion of the premiums that they collect on back-office expenses, sometimes up to 35 percent.[83] That's a lot of money that doesn't go back to the members. Automation via smart contracts can do away with a lot of that expense.

Synthetic asset protocols such as Synthetix and UMA allow their users to get financial exposure to almost anything, including off-chain instruments such as the S&P 500 and gold. Structured products that give investors exposure to an asset without owning it are common on Wall Street but suffer from the usual risks of interacting with a trusted intermediary.

DeFi can theoretically offer a better approach though it must first overcome a thorny blockchain-specific data issue known as the oracle problem. Blockchain protocols are great at getting information about everything that happens on the same network but terrible at sourcing data from the outside world.

Oracles are services that collect external information (such as the closing price of the S&P) and transmit it to smart contracts that need the data to determine financial outcomes. Their partial existence outside of a decentralized platform makes them a liability, because the security provided by the platform's consensus mechanism doesn't cover whatever needs to happen off-chain. In other words, the Ethereum platform can only guarantee that the data submitted by an oracle is processed correctly by its smart contracts. What it can't do is guarantee that the data is accurate. Every DeFi solution that relies on outside data has its own variation of the garbage in, garbage out problem. To help mitigate this risk, there are decentralized protocols that specialize in providing reliable oracle services by using financial incentives to reward anonymous users who find and deliver accurate data. Anyone can call upon their services in plug-and-play fashion.

Financial incentives are also used by many of these solutions to encourage usage and adoption. That idea in and of itself is not original to DeFi. When PayPal first launched, it literally paid people to open an account. Further back, American banks used to give away toasters to people who opened a checking account. DeFi protocols go one step further and give away ownership, or the closest thing to it, in a decentralized setting. Many projects have bootstrapped adoption by giving a portion of their governance tokens to anyone who uses their service. Not only does this strategy lead to growth, it also invites the customers of a solution to participate in running it. The giveaways have even inspired their own profit maximization strategy known as yield farming or liquidity mining—loosely defined as the practice of constantly moving one's assets around and doing a lot of saving, trading, and borrowing to maximize earning financial rewards.

This being an open ecosystem, there are aggregator services that farm on users' behalf.

The ultimate value proposition of decentralized finance is captured by the notion of composability—best understood as the ability to use the output of any one solution as the input of another. Since every DeFi protocol is open to the public and censorship resistant, then new solutions can be built on top of existing ones. There is no need to reinvent the wheel. A developer who has a clever idea for a new financial product that starts with borrowing money against ETH doesn't have to build their own lending solution, they can simply call on Maker. If the product also requires the occasional trading of one asset for another, then it can source liquidity from Uniswap. Automated market makers are ideal for integration into other applications because they can guarantee liquidity (albeit at potentially steep prices). Composability enables creativity. Since every solution that is launched today could serve as the foundation for an even more innovative solution to be built tomorrow, then the sky's the limit for what clever people can come up with. The colloquial term for this phenomenon in the crypto community is "money Legos."

MONEY LEGOS

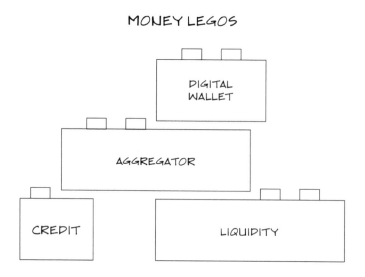

Putting It All Together

The answer to the earlier question of whether there is a better way to build a financial system is a resounding yes. Not only does decentralized finance present a more transparent and trustworthy system, it also enables financial innovation the likes of which has seldom been seen before. While some of its components might seem confusing to those tethered to old ways, future generations will not have this problem. To them, a decentralized financial system built on credit from MakerDAO and liquidity from Uniswap might make more sense than banking and trading as we know them today. The Danish entrepreneur Rune Christensen was only twenty-four when he first conceived of Maker while teaching English in China (Dai is Chinese for "to lend"). Hayden Adams, a formerly unemployed mechanical engineer with little prior coding experience, was around the same age when he unveiled Uniswap. MakerDAO is already bigger than 95 percent of American banks by total assets, and Uniswap offers more unique markets than the New York, Amsterdam, London, and Hong Kong stock exchanges combined. Plenty of people working in the tech or finance sectors talk about changing the world. These kids actually did. Confusion is a necessary condition of comprehending something truly original.

Despite its relative youth, the DeFi ecosystem has already begun to impact the broader financial system. Fiat-backed stablecoins are popular dollar proxies in protocols such as Aave and Uniswap, so much so that the resulting demand for these coins has forced their issuers to find more places to deposit the dollars that back them. Tokenized commodities and real estate have also begun to appear. As different types of stocks and bonds also become tokenized and move onto the blockchain, they too will be integrated into DeFi, enabling more disruption. It's now only a matter of time until we have tokenized treasury bonds that are used in a decentralized repo market.

On a long enough timeline, every kind of financial interaction that can be automated will be, for the same reason that cars will drive themselves.

Code is more reliable than people. But given the importance of trust and stability in financial services, the automation will occur on a public platform, one where users interact directly as ruled by transparent code executed within consensus. There will be less centralized intermediation, more innovation, less free riding, and more trust.

This transition will threaten a lot of institutions, not to mention the people who work for them. Financial services firms have enjoyed a privileged position within society for centuries, for good reason. Without them, every other industry would have been significantly impaired. But the free-rider opportunities enabled by that privilege have been too big to ignore, so those in the middle have indulged. Tempting as it might be to single out specific people or companies, the real culprit is human nature. Thankfully, now there's a blockchain for that.

The skeptics will harp on DeFi being unregulated, and in doing so, reveal their own ignorance. DeFi is the most regulated financial system in the history of the world, because code does not waver. It does not have bad days, ugly divorces, or bonus envy. Code has no ambition. There will be no Repo 105s in this domain. That's not to say that bad programmers (or bad people) won't try to build bad solutions. In fact the censorship-resistant nature of most major platforms almost invites them to try, and some already have. But they haven't gotten very far because the system is too transparent.

In time, the world's financial regulators will probably evolve to inspecting smart contracts and opining on DeFi governance mechanisms. They'll then grab a magazine and put their feet up, for there will be little else to do. Every interaction will unfold in predictable fashion. The ecosystem's transparency, reliability, and innovative new models will attract more and more users. On a long enough timeline, DeFi will lose its decentralized moniker and just be known as finance, because it will be everywhere.

As this transition unfolds, the banks, brokers, exchanges, investment funds, and insurance companies that make up the backbone of the legacy financial system will have to evolve or perish. Lest we forget, financial services exist to empower money and people, not the other way around, and both money and people usually end up where the trust is highest. That's not to say that there won't be a need for these kinds of companies in a more decentralized setting. But it does mean that they'll have to get used to serving the network, as opposed to owning it.

The relationship will be a symbiotic one however, as DeFi will also need these institutions to scale. We are years away from the point when governments issue tokenized bonds or corporations tokenize stocks directly on-chain. Getting those assets into the decentralized finance ecosystem in the interim will require the help of financial institutions willing to act as a bridge. Case in point: stablecoins that derive their value from an off-chain reserve are already one of the most loaned, borrowed, and traded assets within the ecosystem. The rise of DeFi also elevates the importance of off-chain custodians, because tokens are bearer instruments that require the aid of an institution of trust for safekeeping.

The transition to a more decentralized financial system won't happen overnight, as the DeFi ecosystem is still too new and hasn't been battle-tested enough. Some of the problems of traditional finance, like speculative bubbles and crashes, will occur just as often in decentralized finance because these systems and products serve humans, and humans are prone to manias and panics. Some challenges will be amplified. Twenty-four seven markets that allow anyone to attain leverage and play along are great during a bull market, but hellish in a crash, particularly if that crash were to take place on a Sunday night. Everything happens faster in a decentralized setting, for better and worse.

But transparency will make it easier for everyone to make informed decisions, and automation via smart contracts will make it harder for one group to deceive another. The curse of history can never be cured, but it can be abated.

6

MONEY, AGAIN

money   noun

a trust-building mechanism that is always evolving, despite the protestations of those who benefited from the way it used to be.

Is Bitcoin Money?

The answer matters to a lot of people. Those who own it would like to see it grow. Those who don't would like to see it fail. Governments that have enjoyed a monopoly over the issuance of currency for a long time would rather not deal with the threat, and central bankers who until recently were viewed as infallible would rather not deal with the competition. Older people have a hard time accepting anything that's purely digital as having any value, never mind achieving the coveted status of being considered money. Younger people who grew up online don't have this problem.

Whether Bitcoin is money is a difficult question to answer because money is a social construct. Some people argue that Bitcoin can't be money because it doesn't fit the dictionary definition. This is a poor argument, because language, like money, is a made-up thing, a figment of the human imagination that's always in flux. Lots of things that are new don't fit the definition of whatever came before, but that doesn't make them any less legitimate. When rap music first hit the scene, certain critics claimed that it wasn't music. That didn't stop it from taking over the music charts.

Others argue that Bitcoin is not money because it's confusing and difficult to use. They claim that consumers don't want to deal with unfamiliar things like private keys or use bearer instruments that can be lost or stolen. This argument is shortsighted. A key-based financial system is, in many ways, superior to an identity-based one, as it enables instant settlement, universal access, and privacy, features that have been considered essential for money for millennia. Physical representations of the US dollar, or any other currency, can also be lost or stolen. It happens every day.

There are challenges to migrating from the current way of transferring value to a key-based one, but they can be overcome with new tools and better infrastructure. Besides, just because users have the option of taking full ownership of their assets by way of a private key doesn't mean they always have to or want to. Lots of people prefer to employ the services of a trusted custodian to manage their keys for them. What makes Bitcoin and every other type of tokenized asset unique is the ability of self-custody if anyone really wants to. That optionality keeps service providers honest and ensures healthy competition. Unlike traditional financial custodians, crypto custodians don't need the blessing of a government or permission of a DTCC to exist.

Money on the Rise

The most credible argument as to why Bitcoin isn't money is the fact that it has yet to fulfill the three basic functions of money, which are unit of account, medium of exchange, and store of value. Few items are bought or sold for bitcoins, and fewer still are priced in it. Indeed, even the most die-hard believers in the cryptocurrency still think in terms of fiat money, they don't budget their spending in bitcoins or quote their labor in crypto. To the extent that any kind of tokenized asset is used for pure payment activities, it's stablecoins. People who own bitcoins often don't want to spend them, and merchants are sometimes hesitant to accept them. This lack of adoption for everyday use is a favorite gripe of the anti-crypto crowd.

The rebuttal from those who have studied the history of currencies is that it's too soon to tell. Money is a myth, and myths take a long time to form, sometimes decades, often longer. The US dollar was first introduced in 1792, but mostly as a unit of account, with its value derived from silver and gold, and effectively pegged to a then-popular Spanish curren-cy.[84] Foreign currencies would remain popular (and acceptable as legal tender) in America until the 1850s. The first government-issued paper dollars would not appear until the Civil War, and then only briefly. It took the US dollar over 150 years to become a global standard, and only with the aid of an industrial revolution and two World Wars. Bitcoin is twelve years old.

A critic could argue that a comparison to one of the most successful currencies in history is a straw-man argument. Plenty of other fiat curren-cies, issued by the governments of much smaller countries, have managed to achieve widespread medium-of-exchange status in short order, at least within their own borders. True as that may be, those currencies cheated. Their mythology was enforced at the point of a gun (mostly metaphori-cally, but sometimes literally). National currencies like the Mexican peso or Indian rupee achieved widespread use thanks to legal-tender laws that mandated their acceptance in the settlement of debts and contracts, not to mention their governments themselves borrowing, collecting taxes, and paying salaries exclusively in that currency.

Bitcoin has no such advantage. There is no government forcing a bil-lion people to use it (as is the case for the Chinese yuan) or military pro-tecting its purchasing power abroad (as is the case with the US dollar). Bitcoin has had to convert every single user on its merits, selling them on the benefits of digital scarcity or the novelty of the infrastructure. Decen-tralization has its benefits but lacks a proper PR department. What's more, not having a monopoly on a single country or economy in the way that fiat currencies do means that Bitcoin can only succeed on a global scale. With no offense to the peso or the rupee, it's the rare currency that has a fight-ing chance of doing so—because it is decentralized.

Using a fiat currency issued by a single government as the global stan-dard has certain drawbacks, starting with the obvious free-rider exploits enabled by so much global demand. The United States now indulges in those opportunities with gusto, as proven by the Federal Reserve's increasingly profligate ways. Not that far away from the Fed's headquarters in Washington, a different arm of the US government increasingly abuses a different privilege, by using economic sanctions to weaponize the flow of dollars around the world. Other nations have noticed and are slowly responding. The share of US dollars held as foreign exchange reserves by other central banks has been declining in recent years and now sits at a twenty-five-year low, a phenomenon known as de-dollarization.[85] Major governments in Europe and Asia are also looking for ways to break the stranglehold of US sanctions, particularly in cross-border trade that has nothing to do with America.

But switching from the dollar to a different national currency will only transfer these privileges to another entity. One option is for everyone to switch to a basket of fiat currencies but doing so has its own inefficiencies. Something more traditional like gold can also be used, but metals are inconvenient for payments and a substantial portion of the global gold stock is currently held by the US government. Thankfully, now there's a cryptocurrency for that. Bitcoin's limited base supply, decentralized governance, censorship resistance, and around-the-clock liquidity make it an ideal currency for foreign exchange reserves and international trade. In time, it may evolve to become a preferred alternative to the dollar, especially if the United States continues to act like a decadent power. To be clear, no major central bank holds any just yet, and cryptocurrency is almost never used in cross-border trade. El Salvador has made Bitcoin legal tender, and other small nations may follow suit, but being a viable alternative will require participation from larger countries. Getting there will take time. More importantly, it will take *price*.

Ironically, for all the hand-wringing about Bitcoin's price volatility, it has been the cryptocurrency's single greatest selling point because, for over a decade, and despite several bear markets, it has always resolved itself to the upside. Put differently, those who have believed in its monetary prowess have been handsomely rewarded. To them, bitcoin's volatility is a feature, not a bug. Had they held dollars (or any other fiat currency) instead, then they'd be a lot less rich. That wealth creation, along with the titillating prospect of even more to come, has propelled both the coin and the underlying technology forward for over a decade. It has converted skeptics, inspired imitators, funded an entire industry, and made a fool of multiple pundits who have predicted its demise—a fitting start for anything that hopes to succeed as a global myth.

Here people tend to get thrown off by the dollar cost of a single coin. How could a currency where each unit costs tens of thousands of dollars become a global standard? That (admittedly large) number is misleading. What denomination any currency gets broken down into is a question of accounting, not value, in the way that a single $100 bill, 100 $1 bills, and 10,000 pennies represent the same purchasing power. The Bitcoin blockchain accommodates fractional transfers all the way down to one hundred millionth of a single bitcoin (0.00000001), a unit called a *satoshi,* and most transfers are only for a few hundredth of a coin. The decision to quote the dollar price in full coins is a social convention, in the same way that soft drinks are sold in two-liter bottles, not two thousand milliliter ones. If the community wanted to, it could switch to quoting the price of each unit in 1,000th of a coin, a unit known as a *milliBit.* Switching to this denomination would make each unit worth a few dollars, without impacting the value.

Irrespective of what denomination is used, the fact remains that even after years of exponential growth, the total value of all bitcoins in circulation is still a tiny fraction of the total amount of dollars.

This is not an apples-to-apples comparison for several reasons, most of which favor Bitcoin. The US dollar is only a currency, nothing else. Bitcoin is both a currency and a means of capturing the network effects generated by a popular platform. Platforms are currently among the most valuable assets on earth, but most of that value is captured by the shareholders of companies such as Facebook and Visa. Bitcoin is different because the only way to capture the value of the platform is to own the coin. In that sense, it's both a currency and a form of equity, a novel concept in the world of money. Each coin's long-run value proposition is therefore multi-functional: participation and equity in a growing platform today, ownership of a potential global reserve currency tomorrow.

More importantly, cryptocurrencies such as Bitcoin are programmatically scarce, in a way that fiat currencies such as the dollar are not, and never have been. As of mid-2021, there are twenty trillion dollars in circulation, a number that is significantly higher than where it was two years ago. As we have seen, central banks such as the Federal Reserve increasingly respond to economic or financial problems by printing money. Since each intervention reinforces bad behavior and prevents a healthy reset, the next intervention has to be even bigger. This is in stark comparison to Bitcoin, where base inflation programmatically ratchets downward every four years. Indeed, calendar year 2020 was monetarily historic in two ways: on the fiat side, central banks the world over printed a historic amount of money. On the crypto side, the Bitcoin protocol cut the number of new coins created per block in half. When all was said and done, a year that saw the supply of dollars increase by a record 20 percent saw the supply of bitcoins increase by a record-low 2 percent.

Here we should pause for a second to consider the environmental impact of mining, as it is often presented as a negative. Indeed, other than its (highly exaggerated) use in illicit activity, the Bitcoin platform's electrical consumption, which we should admit is significant, is the most popular argument against further adoption. As with other critiques against crypto, there is an obvious double standard. Lots of activities negatively impact the environment, especially when measured in aggregate. Tellingly, none are as controversial. The United States uses more power for air-conditioning than the UK does in total, yet there is no shortage of crypto cryptics waxing poetic from their comfortably cool offices.

Bitcoin's electrical consumption is a feature and not a bug, the natural evolution of the long-running relationship between money and power. Those who have issued the former have often deployed the latter to preserve its purchasing power. Case in point, one of the primary purposes of the US military—a major energy consumer in its own right—is to protect the purchasing power of the dollar. It does this by protecting unsavory regimes that price their exports in dollars and by dropping the occasional bomb.

Bitcoin's clever contribution is to make this previously implicit relationship explicit. People trust its coins *because* they require a lot of power to produce. Human beings don't value things that are easy to make. That's why a handmade automatic Swiss watch costs one thousand times more than a machine-made quartz one, even though the latter is better at telling time.

The complexity and cost of mining provide Bitcoin with a stronger foundation to grow from. They also allow it to become the rare monetary system that doesn't rely on coercion, and is strictly opt-in. With fiat money, even the most pacifist nations force their citizens to use the local currency for certain activities. Bitcoin usage on the other hand is always voluntary, an important feature that allows the network to operate on a presumption of innocence. Anyone concerned about the Environmental, Social and Governance (ESG) impact of mining should consider the social and governance benefits of a monetary system that is universally accessible, fully meritocratic, and not predicated on the threat of violence.

None of this is to say that Bitcoin is guaranteed to someday become a widely accepted form of money—or that its value will continue to appreciate. Most myths die before they achieve escape velocity. But if a currency that comes out of nowhere and has no national backing is to even try, then it must, almost by definition, grow exponentially. Those who focus on the short-term volatility are missing the forest for the trees. Just as any collapsing currency on its way to oblivion has a lot of volatility, so must an ascendant one on its way to becoming some kind of global standard.

Imitation Is the Ultimate Form of Flattery

Anyone who takes a strong stance on the question of whether Bitcoin is money—on either side of the debate—reveals an ignorance of history. The list of items that have qualified as money throughout the ages is as long as the human imagination is broad. Soldiers in World War II POW camps used a combination of cigarettes and receipts for food as their money (in a structure remarkably similar to Dai, except that canned food, instead of ETH, served as the primary collateral). The residents of the Yap island group in the Pacific used a stone form of money until the twentieth century. Some of the stones were so big that nobody ever moved them. Who owned which was preserved by oral tradition, leading to the unusual situation where someone making a payment might do so with a large stone in their neighbor's yard. There was even a family whose immense wealth was tied to a stone that had sunk to the bottom of the ocean generations ago.[86]

The biggest skeptics of whether cryptocurrencies can become a widely accepted form of money tend to be the stewards of the fiat variety: the central bankers who issue them, the commercial bankers who distribute them, and the government officials who wield them. The obvious conflicts of interest aside, their skepticism of any new type of money gaining traction is richly ironic given the recency of the type they control. The US dollar, as a free-floating currency not backed by anything, is only fifty years old. The euro is even younger, having been launched only a decade prior to Bitcoin. Just as London and Paris are practically next to each other when viewed from space, Bitcoin and the US dollar are not that far apart in time. Indeed, the precious-metal-backed forms of money that the dollar and euro recently vanquished predated them by thousands of years. If they can do it, why can't crypto?

And yet, pure cryptocurrencies such as Bitcoin or Ether have been of minimal interest to most of the world's central bankers for most of their history. A 2018 research report put out by the Federal Reserve Bank of St. Louis began with the declaration "Traditionally, currency is produced by a nation's government."[87] The report compared Bitcoin to the Dutch Tulip bubble of the 1600s, quoted a few Wall Street skeptics who had dismissed it using colorful adjectives, and ended with the following comment from Janet Yellen, then the chairwoman of the Federal Reserve.

"Bitcoin at this time plays a very small role in the payment system. It is not a stable source of—store of value, and it doesn't constitute legal tender. It is a highly speculative asset."

Yellen—along with most of the world's other central bankers—changed her tune on the prospect of blockchain-based money shortly thereafter. Not because of any perceived threat from Bitcoin—the 2018 bear market had taken it off most people's radar—but because of the announcement of the Diem (then Libra) stablecoin network by a Facebook-led consortium.

That announcement shook the world of central banking. Seldom had a group of people otherwise known for their mild temperaments been so agitated, and all in response to little more than a press release. Here is Jerome Powell, Yellen's successor at the Fed: "Libra raises serious concerns regarding privacy, money laundering, consumer protection, financial stability."[88] Not to be outdone, Mario Draghi, then president of the European Central Bank, had the following to say:

"These concerns are concerns about cybersecurity, AML/money laundering, terrorism financing, use of these currencies for criminal purposes. All this is linked also to the anonymity, how would this work? At the same time, concerns about privacy. I mentioned cyber risks. Tax evasion, monetary policy transmission, financial stability and the global payment system."[89]

Lions and tigers and stablecoins, oh my! The absurdity of worrying about something being both anonymous and yet somehow *not* private—or the ignorance that central-bank issued cash has always been both—aside, the central banker was obviously worried. Such rambling and at times incoherent concerns were repeated by government officials throughout the West. Within a few months, most sprang into action. If digital currencies were good, and tokenized money was desirable, then it should be the issuer of that money that does the tokenizing, not untrustworthy intermediaries such as Facebook. In other words, if digital currencies like stablecoins were somehow good, then central bank digital currencies (CBDCs) would be even better.

To understand the design and potential impact of central bank digital currencies, we must return to the fundamentals of money, because not all money is created equal, even within the same currency. People who use dollars often think of all the dollars in their possession—the paper bills in their wallet, the balance of their savings account, or the value of their gift cards—as the same. But from an economic point of view, these dollars are more equivalent than they are equal, because they have different levels of counterparty risk.

All fiat money is a promise, and promises can be broken. A $20 gift card from a merchant is a promise for $20 worth of goods or services at some later date. The merchant can renege on that promise or go out of business. A $20 deposit at a commercial bank is a promise to be able to withdraw $20 later, one that is backed by the reserves and investments the bank diverts such deposits into. Commercial banks can't just renege on their promises, but they are nevertheless fallible. They can become insolvent and fail. A $20 bill, on the other hand, is a direct promise from the Fed, and central banks are the closest thing to an infallible bank that there is. They can't be insolvent in the traditional sense because they can always print more money. That printing might diminish the purchasing power of a $20 bill, but it doesn't impact the *creditworthiness* of a $20 bill. Unlike the privately owned Bank of United States, the publicly run Federal Reserve cannot experience a run. Part of the charm of issuing money that is backed by nothing is that nothing is always in abundant supply.

Economists use these criteria to break fiat money down into distinct categories based on counterparty risk. Central bank money, also known as public money, is the safest kind of money. It consists of the physical coins and bills that a central bank puts into circulation and the reserves commercial banks must keep with it. Commercial bank money, also known as private money, is everything else. It consists primarily of the money kept on the internal ledgers of commercial banks, but technically includes everything from money market funds to gift cards. Put together, the different kinds of money in any fiat currency form a hierarchy that looks a lot like the payments pyramid.

THE HIERARCHY OF FIAT MONEY

For centuries, consumers and corporations have used a combination of public money and private money to conduct their affairs, going back and forth between the two for a host of reasons. An individual who buys groceries with cash is paying in public money. The store owner might prefer this kind of payment because it's safe (and free). There is no risk of a check bouncing, credit card transaction being disputed, or bank failing. But too much cash on hand might be dangerous and inefficient. The store might get robbed and the owner has to pay their bills. So, the store owner may periodically deposit some of the cash at the local bank, converting its savings from public money to private money. Having money in the bank makes it easier to pay the bills—by writing a check or making an online payment. A different individual, one who keeps most of her money in a savings account, might visit an ATM to withdraw some pocket money, converting some of her private money into public money.

All these people are constantly calculating the risks and benefits of holding different kinds of money, albeit subconsciously and even if they are unaware of the specific risks. Store owners who frequently deposit their cash at the bank opt for the risk of their bank failing over the hassles of keeping so much cash on hand. In the event of a bank run, the people who line up to take their money out would rather take the opposite risk. Even bank executives grapple with these issues when they decide how much of their deposits they should keep on reserves at the central bank and how much they should lend out. All else being equal, private money pays more interest than public money because it's riskier.

Other than risk, convenience is the other major deciding factor in what kind of money people use. This is especially true in payments because most payments today happen with private money. Only the large financial entities that get to keep reserves at the central bank—the exclusive top of the payments pyramid—get to make electronic payments using public money. Everyone else must use either cash, which is safe but inconvenient, or make payments using private money within the commercial banking system. Even fiat-backed stablecoins fall into this category because each coin is a claim on money held by a commercial bank, not a central one.

Digitization has upset the historic balance between the different kinds of money. Since cash can't be used online, more and more activity—from ordering groceries to taking a cab—now happens exclusively in private money. People who get their paychecks direct deposited into a bank account and pay for everything with a debit or credit card seldom possess public money, making their monetary lives riskier and more laden with fees than that of an earlier generation. Digitization has made everything more expensive thanks to the payments tax, and more surveilled. Not only did older generations use a safer type of money, but they and the businesses that they interacted with paid less fees in aggregate and didn't have to worry about their financial data being hacked or sold. Worse of all, digitization has accelerated economic inequality. Poor people, migrants, and underserved minorities have a hard time getting bank accounts and rely disproportionately on cash. Their inability to access private money means that the digital services that the rest of us take for granted are either unavailable to them or can only be accessed via expensive pseudo-banking products like prepaid debit cards.

These trends—the disappearance of public money from day-to-day living, a growing payment tax, financial surveillance, and economic exclusion—are on an inevitable trajectory unless governments step in and restore the traditional balance between public and private money. The most effective way of doing so is by introducing a central bank digital currency.

Central Banks Go Digital

CBDCs are not a new idea. One could even argue that they've existed for decades in the form of the electronic payment systems operated by central banks to resolve payments between commercial banks. The more contemporary notion of a central bank digital currency looks to upgrade such systems while expanding access. As far as the hierarchy of money is concerned, CBDCs represent a historic third type of public money, a broadly accessible digital version that combines the safety of physical cash with the convenience of instant payments without the fees.

The simplest way for a central bank to offer such a thing is by allowing everyone—not just large financial intermediaries—to open an account with it and use its payment infrastructure. The user experience would be similar to PayPal but the ledger would be maintained by the central bank, thus the money being sent back and forth would be public money. Users would enjoy a safer kind of account and a cheaper kind of digital payment, because unlike PayPal, a central bank can't fail and doesn't need to earn a profit.

This brute-force approach is not very realistic, however, and would have limited utility. Most central-bank-operated payment systems are decades old and not very good by internet standards. They are clunky, unprogrammable, and only available during certain hours. A digital currency that can't be used to pay for gas at night or groceries on Sunday is not very useful. Having been originally designed to serve a limited set of financial intermediaries, these systems could never handle the load required for a national solution and would have to be significantly upgraded before being opened to the public. How a small and reclusive institution would handle an endless stream of user complaints, forgotten passwords, and other customer-service issues is a whole other matter.

A more sensible approach would be for the central bank to deploy some kind of blockchain network and issue a digital currency on top of it, a so-called tokenized CBDC. Unlike stablecoins, these would not be fiat-backed tokens, but rather fiat money itself. Like cash, each token would be backed by the full faith and credit of the government. Users—be they individuals, corporations, or financial institutions—would store their digital money in some kind of wallet and use a private key to initiate payments. A distributed ledger made immutable with cryptography would record every transfer.

By virtue of riding a blockchain network, payments using pure digital cash could now happen instantly and around the clock, to anyone, anywhere. Society would no longer have to rely on an army of intermediaries to move money across a clunky network of centralized ledgers, every one of which has its own counterparty risk. Double-spending would be prevented by a combination of transparency and a consensus mechanism. The network could be designed to handle smart contracts, ushering in the era of programmable cash—a true first in the history of money. Tokenized CBDCs could also enable micropayments and be integrated into the internet of things in ways that accounts can't. The network itself would not be very decentralized, however. CBDCs are a government-run utility, and governments like to be in charge. While a central bank might ask for assistance from banks and payment providers in setting up and operating its network or helping users store and protect their tokens, it would retain control.

And so, the now-familiar debate between accounts and tokens that is raging in the world of private payments is creeping into the public variety. The central bankers and economists researching potential designs sometimes present the two approaches as equally viable, but that's a little like saying that the next hit album is as likely to be consumed on compact disc as it is via streaming. Using accounts to move money is an ancient practice that has outlived its usefulness. Accounts cannot be programmed with smart contracts. They can't be integrated into objects like self-driving cars, their content cannot be elegantly swapped for other assets, and accounts can't have DeFi. They are also not private, because each one must be tied to a specific individual or institution. Having a private corporation such as PayPal know about some payments is one thing. Having the government know about all payments is another, far more disturbing, thing, especially in Western countries where Orwellian surveillance is frowned upon.

Worst of all, accounts do nothing for the unbanked. A central bank digital currency that requires the same "know-your-client" standards as a traditional bank account is just as useless to the countless people who can't access traditional consumer finance options today. Tokens, on the other hand, can be accessed by anyone with a computer, smartphone, or even a plastic card. They are egalitarian in a way that accounts are not, because every person—not just the powerful and privileged—can possess a private key. Mathematical functions, unlike KYC procedures, don't discriminate.

If the primary objective of a CBDC is to restore the freedom, privacy, and universality of physical cash, and to prevent tech companies from leading the way, then tokenized CBDCs win. Everything else is just conjecture.

Most central banks are exploring the topic. Their leaders speak openly about the potential benefits and risks of overhauling money and urge caution. The motivation to build something varies by country, depending on the current pace of digitization and the overall use of cash. The more cashless a society, the greater the need for a CBDC that reintroduces public money into the economy. Here the variance between countries can be stark. Cash usage in Denmark is already below 15 percent, but in neighboring Germany it remains above 60 percent.[90] Despite its techno-logical sophistication, Japanese society still relies on physical cash as its preferred form of payment. South Korea, on the other hand, is almost entirely cashless.[91]

Different countries also have different opinions on whether payment systems should be run by the private sector or run as a public good. The Federal Reserve has often gone out of its way to let private companies lead the way in building new payment systems. Indeed, America's early success with checks and credit cards has led it to fall behind most other advanced countries in developing any kind of digitally native payment infrastruc-ture, including CBDCs. The European Central Bank, on the other hand, speaks openly about the need to diversify away from foreign payment pro-viders such as Visa and Mastercard with some kind of public option, and hopes to introduce a digital euro by 2025.

Some central banks may decide to develop digital currencies for more practical reasons. Countries with a big geographic footprint, or ones that are stretched across a chain of islands, may look to CBDCs as a more effi-cient means of moving cash, sending digital tokens through a blockchain, as opposed to putting paper bills on a boat. Many Caribbean nations are exploring the issuance of a CBDC and the Bahamas has already issued one.[92] Developing countries that have yet to build a national payment system, and developed countries whose existing central-bank operated systems are reaching the end of their natural life cycle, might see a CBDC as a logi-cal investment.

Others might use digitization as a means of increasing the prominence of their money. That seems to be a key part of China's rush to deploy a digital renminbi—the most aggressive CBDC effort of any major coun-try. Despite its economic dominance, China's currency is not a major player on the global stage. It accounts for a small fraction of reserves held by other central banks and is seldom used in trade that doesn't involve China. There are many complex reasons for this discrepancy having to do with the country's relatively recent rise in economic prominence, the strict capital controls that restrict the flow of money across its borders, and a general distrust of its political system abroad. Rapid digitization of its money might be one way to offset some of those factors, especially if tied to regional expansion programs such as the Belt and Road initiative.

China's central bank, officially known as the People's Bank of China (PBOC), is a pioneer in digitization. It set up an independent unit to research digital currencies years ago and was one of the first to embrace the underlying technology that enables Bitcoin, apparently unencumbered by the usual biases against blockchain technology found elsewhere. The PBOC's "Digital Currency/Electronic Payment" solution (DCEP) is not a pure blockchain per se, but borrows many features from it. It uses a distributed database hardened with cryptography and cryptographic keys to initiate transactions. It also enables programmability, though perhaps only by the central bank itself. Digital yuan are to be distributed mostly through existing financial intermediaries, but members of the PBOC have made it clear that each unit will still be considered public money, even when distributed by the private sector.

While it remains to be seen whether a digital yuan will make a run at the dollar or euro, it will directly impact the dominance of the country's domestic payment providers. Cash usage in China is already way down, thanks to the popularity of mobile payment solutions such as Alipay and WeChat Pay. The rush to deploy a CBDC is, in part, meant to blunt the power of the companies behind those solutions as part of the Communist Party's broader crackdown on domestic tech companies.

Regardless of intent, the successful launch of a CBDC in such a large and important country is bound to reverberate in economic and geopolitical circles. Politicians in the United States and Europe are already concerned with China's mercantilism in developing countries throughout Asia, Africa, and South America. Integration of its own digital currency in bilateral trade agreements could make that power grab more potent. The world needs only so many reserve currencies, and any adoption of the renminbi for trade will come at the expense of the dollar and the euro.

On a long enough timeline, the ascent of the renminbi could pose a serious threat to the economic vitality of the West. The United States and Western Europe increasingly rely on debt to grow their economies and will continue to need low interest rates to sustain their profligate ways. Being a global reserve currency helps that cause—especially at a time of record money printing—as it increases demand for their money. Should a Chinese CBDC chip away at that demand, then politicians in America and Europe have a serious problem. Indulging in the free-rider temptations of money is more dangerous when there's an alternative, and this particular competitor can theoretically be zapped across the world faster than an American or European banker can type a SWIFT message.

The final wrinkle in the geopolitical implications of central bank digital currencies is de-dollarization. A substantial percentage of global trade is settled in dollars, even when neither party is based in the United States. This is partly because industrial commodities such as oil are usually bought and sold in dollars, regardless of where they are produced or consumed (protecting regimes that price their commodities in dollars is a major function of the US military). Thus, a disproportionate amount of global payments are routed through American intermediaries, giving the government that regulates those companies a unique kind of soft power. Anyone whose actions run counter to America's interests can simply be kicked out.

CBDCs are increasingly viewed as a potential answer to American hegemony, a development that is, in turn, forcing the Fed to consider issuing its own. The decision to digitize public money will be as much a political and geopolitical one as it will be economic, much to the chagrin of the world's commercial banks and payment providers.

An Unbundling of Banking

CBDCs could bring an end to one of the most successful marriages in monetary history, the one between banking and payments. It is a marriage that goes back centuries, to the days when the first European travelers and Chinese merchants began depositing their coins with the local goldsmith, bank, or money changer. The inefficiencies of doing business in physical cash enabled financial institutions of all kinds to offer both payments and credit, sometimes within the same instrument. A goldsmith who custodied a lot of client coins was in prime position to lend some out. A money changer who interacted with the same merchants on a regular basis knew who he could safely lend to. A correspondent bank that enjoyed deposits from smaller banks had a cheap source of funding.

So long as money has no choice but to move through a private system of interconnected ledgers, the centralized intermediaries that facilitate the movement are in prime position to lend. CBDCs could unbundle that relationship since payments that move inside of a government-run blockchain are by definition *outside* the banking system. Central bank digital currencies create a direct link between the top of the monetary pyramid and the bottom, cutting out the middlemen. Put differently, digital euros that live on a platform operated by the European Central Bank are the equivalent of a direct deposit with the ECB. What deposits a commercial bank doesn't have, it cannot lend.

This transition is great for depositors and savers. Why keep your money at a fallible commercial bank that often pays no interest when you can keep it with an infallible central one (that also doesn't pay interest)? Today, the answer to that question is to make payments. But soon, there might be a government-run blockchain for that. Not only is a CBDC a safer type of money, it's also a better payment instrument. No more slow and expensive movement of money across the payments pyramid. No more opacity and pointless delays. No more walled gardens, discrimination, or fees. No more friction. The relative safety of public money combined with the convenience of tokenization. Fiat money, evolved.

But this unbundling would not come without consequences. The money that consumers and corporates deposit with commercial banks for payments is a significant source of funding for the banking system.

If it leaves, banks will have less money to lend. They'll have to either pay higher interest rates to attract money or rely on alternative sources of funding, most of which are bound to be more expensive. The current marriage between banking and payments is a de facto subsidy for lending—a reality to which anyone who has ever had a checking account that doesn't pay interest can attest. Mobile-wallet solutions and even fiat-backed stablecoins also fall into this category. Users put up with this setup because their need to make payments trumps their desire to earn interest. From the bank's point of view, deposits that don't earn interest are effectively a free loan. CBDCs introduce a public option for payments. The main reason anyone will want to keep money at a commercial bank once they are launched will be to earn interest.

Critics of central bank digital currencies point to this unbundling as a societal cost. They have a point—from a borrower's perspective. If credit creation is a social good, then so is the payments subsidy. In other words, it's okay that people who have checking accounts don't earn any interest because other people who are taking out mortgages get a cheaper loan. Central bankers looking into CBDCs are aware of this risk. As the high priests of the church of borrowing, they appear to take it seriously, and talk a big game about the need to only entertain CBDC designs that don't disintermediate commercial banks so credit can keep flowing.

One such design is a two-tier model where fiat tokens created by the central bank are only distributed through commercial banks, in the same way that central-bank-issued paper money today is only distributed through commercial bank branches and ATMs. Clever as this design might seem, it is a temporary solution and does little to prevent disintermediation of commercial banking in the long run. Unlike paper money, digital tokens are simple to store in large quantities and easy to transmit without the aid of a bank. A store owner who gets paid in CBDCs will not have to send them to his bank for safekeeping every night. He can just keep them in his own digital wallet, the same one he'll use the next day to pay his suppliers. Constantly moving the coins to and from his bank will be cumbersome and unnecessary, unless the bank pays interest.

Not everyone will want to keep *all* their money in their own wallet. Digital tokens can be lost or stolen, and digital wallets are in some ways riskier than physical ones because they can be picked from afar. Regardless of the type of money, people will often want the help of a trusted institution to protect it. Corporations, in particular, will need this kind of service lest the CFO of a multinational be forced to walk around with billions of digital euros on her smartphone. But that doesn't mean that users will return to banks, or the same banks they use today. They can employ the services of a crypto custodian instead. Such services already exist to help people protect their bitcoins and can easily be modified to do the same for central bank digital currencies. Some custodians directly hold the private keys that unlock user assets. Others provide software that helps clients manage their own keys. Regardless of approach, none lend customer deposits out to others, making them safer depository institutions from a counterparty standpoint than a traditional bank.

The ability to store large amounts of digital currency outside of the banking system might accelerate bank runs in a crisis. The easier it is for users to convert their private money to public money, the lower the fear threshold. Commercial banks have historically relied on the frictions of dealing with physical cash to mitigate bank runs. Consumers might be willing to deal with the headaches of keeping their money under the mattress, but corporations can't. The best they can do is move their money to a different commercial bank, so their deposits still stay within the banking system.

CBDCs introduce the possibility of instant mass-conversion from private money to public money—moving all of your money from a commercial bank to the central one—creating a new form of systemic risk. If all it takes to withdraw one's money from a bank is a few clicks of a mouse, then why not always do so at the first hint of trouble? The money could just as easily be returned if nothing happens. One could even argue that having a quick trigger finger is the responsible way to manage one's savings. But if too many people think that way at the same time, then just a whiff of fear will be all it takes to create a crisis.

Some of these issues could be mitigated by the central bank itself with special rules enforced at the network layer. Commercial banks could be given special powers to restrict large withdrawals during a crisis, or the tokens themselves could be programmed to penalize storage outside of the banking system via withdrawal fees or negative interest rates. Either way, so long as central banks don't want to take on too big of a role within the economy, and their managers are content staying the humble technocrats they claim to be, then commercial banks have nothing to worry about.

But therein lies the rub.

For all the talk of preserving as much of the status quo as possible, most central bankers are too ambitious to let this unique moment in monetary history pass them by. CBDCs represent a dramatic shift in power within the monetary system, from the middle of the pyramid to the top, and the many to the few. Central banks might appear to have a lot of power already, but they are mostly paper tigers under the current architecture. Their ability to influence the economy is blunted by the need to transmit monetary policy through the commercial banking system. The complexity of the money pyramid doesn't just prevent the bottom from accessing the top, it also prevents the top from directly influencing the bottom efficiently or effectively. Central bankers try to drive things by tweaking short-term interest rates or manipulating the bond market, but most of what they do gets diluted by the vagaries of commercial banking. Case in point: multiple central banks have attempted to implement negative interest rates to punish savers, but the commercial banks that offer savings accounts have hesitated to pass those rates to their customers.

A Monetary Death Star

Central bank digital currencies enable policy tools that previous generations could only dream of (and future generations may have nightmares about). They arrive at a time when the existing levers of economic control have lost all efficacy—assuming they ever worked in the first place. Decades of low rates and easy money have almost fully etherized the economic patient, hardly registering an economic response at the next iteration. A more humble policymaker would simply admit that there's only so much that can be achieved with printing and borrowing. Today's technocrats are anything but.

In the mind of the economist cum policymaker, if billions of ordinary people refuse to change their behavior on account of theories concocted long ago, then it's clearly the people who are in the wrong. If lower interest rates don't create enough growth, then surely zero interest rates will. And if that doesn't work, then negative rates must! At no point, across the span of decades, has anyone questioned the link between monetary policy and sustainable growth.

Remarkably, the rest of the financial establishment always goes along with this obdurateness. For example, no one questioned the Federal Reserve when it decided to cut rates in 2019, a full year before any sign of the pandemic. Why the US economy needed stimulus at a time of record high stock prices and record low unemployment was beside the point. Our economic overlords decided to act, and the only thing left to do was to make up a justification. Here's the *Wall Street Journal*, in an article titled "Why the Fed Is Cutting Rates When the Economy Looks Good":

> Federal Reserve Chairman Jerome Powell is leading his colleagues to cut interest rates this week for the first time since 2008, even though the economy looks healthy, partly because it isn't behaving as expected.[93]

The central bankers who devise these theories portray themselves as scientists but given the lack of evidence of their effectiveness, they are more driven by faith. Like other true believers, they start with the conclusion and work their way backward. To them, it doesn't matter that easy money has failed to deliver for a long time. Nor do they care about the unintended consequences, like an exploding wealth gap, or rising populism on both sides of the political spectrum, driven by the (correct) suspicion that most people don't benefit from any of this. To the professionals who work at places like the Bank of England or European Central Bank, the only reason why their policies haven't been effective is because they didn't have the proper tools. Soon there'll be a (government-run) blockchain for that.

CBDCs represent a significant shift in power, and not just because governments could zap printed money directly to whoever they want. Roman emperors also issued their metal coins directly to the people, but their money took a long time to travel throughout the empire and was not programmable. The sky will be the limit once digital dollars, yen, and euros hit the economy. Gone will be the days when central bankers have to fiddle with interest rates and the bond market to create inflation. The next time there is a banking crisis, recession, pandemic, or climate emergency—all events that mainstream economists believe can be cured with higher inflation—then the bureaucrats will simply program their money to grow. Parisians who go to bed with 100 digital euros in their smartphone wallets will wake up with 102 and, *voilà!* instant inflation. Baguette prices will rise, the oceans will recede, and there will be economic peace for our time.

Whether the long-term consequences of such actions end up being more of the intended or unintended variety is beside the point. The tokenization and programmability of government-issued money will be a game changer. CBDCs diminish the sovereignty of cash, allowing radical new policies like stimulus payments programmed to disappear if not spent within a proscribed time period (and at pre-approved merchants), or excess reserves granted to banks with restrictions on how (and to whom) the money can be lent. Since every payment takes place on-chain, governments will also have a powerful real-time snapshot into the economy. No more delayed reports or quarterly surveys that try to estimate what has happened in the economy. CBDCs will tell a compelling story of what is *happening.*

Some of these practices will push the boundary of what is considered legal, particularly in Western-style democracies where freedom of choice in economic matters is considered a right. Central bankers will campaign for them and continuously push the envelope. They've been doing it for years anyway, so why not do technologically what they've already done teleologically. Momentum is clearly on their side.

For decades, central banks the world over have used every crash or crisis to assume more power, using the fallout from the last crisis to grant themselves more tools for the next one. In 2008, the Federal Reserve refused to issue an emergency loan to no less a troubled company than Lehman Brothers, for fear that doing so was outside of its legal authority. Twelve years later it did not hesitate to provide financing to a ski lodge or to prop up the junk bond market.

Without anyone asking, the Fed also took it upon itself to buy bonds issued by Apple and Microsoft, despite the fact both companies had billions in cash and stood to benefit from the pandemic. Why a central bank needed to lend money to the world's richest companies at a time when food banks that serve the poor were running out was beside the point. America's central bank had declared itself the lender of *first* resort, and the economic (and political) establishment barely shrugged. Remarkably, the Fed was only playing catch up to other central banks by enacting these policies. The ECB has been financing private businesses for years and the Bank of Japan already owns a substantial part of the Japanese stock market. The billionaires and investment funds who own the vast majority of these assets should be grateful.

All of this makes sense from a historical point of view, particularly to anyone with a skeptical view of government involvement in the private economy. The ability to issue money is power, and the decision to untether national currencies from metal backing was bound to end badly, because power corrupts, even if the people wielding the power have good intentions. That's why it's a curse, not a choice. Central bank digital currencies are the next logical step in that corruption. What happens afterwards remains to be seen, but if history is any guide, then we can speculate that programmable fiat money will corrupt absolutely. Satoshi Nakamoto's technological stew, originally used to create a more trustworthy kind of money, will be co-opted to create the opposite.

There Will Also Be Benefits

Not all the consequences of tokenized government-issued money are bad, or dangerous. Some are clearly beneficial, starting with the total elimination of the payments tax. Whatever progress in reducing fees private stablecoins would have made by then will be driven home by the launch of digital dollars, euros, and the like. The countless dollars in economic value that gets captured by transaction fees today will be recycled back into the economy, generating growth. The economic inclusion of every single individual into the digital economy beyond those who today qualify for a bank account will also benefit society. What the unbanked lack in individual wealth they more than make up for in aggregate numbers so onboarding them into the digital economy will be a boost to the private sector. There are plenty of poorer people who'd also like to take advantage of digital platforms and shop online. Today, they must go out of their way to pay in cash or get a prepaid debit card, which erodes their buying power. Tomorrow they'll use digital fiat money.

Thanks to CBDCs, that money will become available to them as soon as they are issued a paycheck, without the wait time of hours or days the current architecture requires. CBDCs will not only save people money in the form of fees, they will also save them time in terms of settlement delays—yet another burden currently suffered disproportionately by the less privileged. No more waiting for paychecks and Social Security payments to clear for individuals, and no more waiting on batch processing or end-of-day payouts for small businesses. While we are at it, no more absurd closures on the weekends or ridiculous messaging in preparation

of a payment. Everyone will have digital tokens in a wallet (or with a custodian) and will be able to send instant payments to anyone else.

These efficiencies will be particularly useful in cross-border payments
where both fees and delays are still stuck in the analog era. Here, too, the
greatest benefits will accrue to the less fortunate. Whatever the fees transnational corporations pay their banks to process a million-dollar wire,
they are dwarfed in percentage terms by the absurd amounts migrant
workers pay remittance services to send a little bit of money back home—
even more victims of the current system's presumption of guilt, and the
resulting "de-risking" that's led some financial institutions from exiting
the handling of cross-border payments. Those willing to try are still constrained by the so-called last mile problem: how is the money being sent
back going to be converted to local currency or physical cash once it gets
there? CBDCs solve that problem because they won't have to. A Mexican
citizen working in North America won't have to take his or her dollars to
a local money transmitter only to have their family members back home
collect 5 percent less. They'll just send digital dollars from one smartphone to another.

Since most central bank digital currencies will be some kind of a token,
and all tokens are natively programmable, then central bank digital currencies will also be integrated into DeFi. Indeed, the commercial bankers'
argument that the disintermediation of commercial banking will cripple
credit creation is based on the false assumption that only commercial
banks create credit. That argument is a weak one to begin with, as even
today plenty of credit gets created by other types of private companies, the
government, or financial securities. The mortgage-backed security market
is a good example of this phenomenon, as trillions of dollars' worth of
home purchases are financed by the investors who purchase these products, like pensions funds. DeFi represents a newer, and ultimately better,
source of credit creation.

Today, that ecosystem relies on private money in the form of stablecoins to function. In the future, such protocols could easily switch to

public money in the form of CBDCs. We can't be certain whether central banks will want to issue their digital tokens directly into public blockchains such as Ethereum, but so long as they make their own platforms programmable, they won't have to. Since all code in DeFi is open source, it can easily be ported to some other blockchain. Even if it can't, cryptography will build a bridge. There are already multiple bridges between the biggest public blockchains, allowing users to transfer their assets from Bitcoin to Ethereum or other decentralized platforms. They vary in design and level of decentralization but eliminate the need to build everything on a single platform. CBDCs could also be used to act as the reserves for private stablecoins, further diminishing their counterparty risk. Unlike a stablecoin such as Tether, whose reserves may or may not exist inside opaque bank accounts, CBDC-backed stablecoin issuers will be able to display their reserves on-chain.

Cryptographic bridges could also be built across different government-run CBDC networks, allowing for direct foreign exchange transfers. Along with transaction fees and delays, the cost of converting fiat money from one currency to another is another major inefficiency of the current system. If multiple governments issue their own digital currencies, then most people will be able to easily swap one for the other, forgoing the friction of the airport money changer or correspondent bank. Such markets may still require the services of liquidity providers willing to buy one currency and sell another, but they won't have to be the same institutions that provide foreign exchange services today. Re-architecture not only changes the nature of the game, it also changes the players.

Putting It All Together

CBDCs will be the ultimate manifestation of a broader digitization thesis for money, one that already includes halfway innovators such as Fintechs, cryptocurrencies like Bitcoin, and newer innovations such as private stablecoins. By moving money online, all these solutions diminish the importance of geographic borders for money. How central banks deal with the prospects of their money being as easily accessible in a foreign country as it is domestically is an open question. Some will see this as a benefit because the more demand for their money abroad, the more they get to print at home. Others will try to impose draconian restrictions to preserve artificial economic policies such as currency pegs and capital controls. Regardless, the world is about to experience a period of significant currency competition, the likes of which has never been seen before.

This phenomenon, which has been unfolding slowly for years, has been accelerated by the fallout from the Russian invasion of Ukraine. Indeed, future generations may record the monetary and economic response by the West as a milestone in the history of fiat money. The overnight expulsion of major Russian banks and corporations from global payment systems, along with the freezing of the Russian central bank's foreign exchange reserves—however much deserved they may have been—represent a leap in the weaponization of fiat money. Other governments surely took notice, and will now have to think twice about which currencies they will sell their exports for or save their reserves in. CBDCs will empower this weaponization thanks to their natively digital and programmable architecture. To transact or save in another country's currency always entailed being vulnerable to their monetary policy. Now it also means being vulnerable to their political process. There will be many losers from this monetary shift, and one clear winner.

Which brings us back to the question of whether Bitcoin is money. To answer it we must ask another question: compared to what? Given the current global obsession with printing money, and the continued fragmentation of the existing monetary order, the coming arms race to issue CBDCs is likely to be a race to the bottom. Economists and politicians are a stubborn bunch and tend to stick to their beliefs until the bitter end. The first wave of inflationary pressure from their actions was brushed off as healthy. The second wave is being called temporary, and the third wave will be addressed with even more radical policies, potentially as enabled by programmable fiat money.

Meanwhile, Bitcoin will continue to behave as originally intended: remaining apolitical, providing access to all, and having its inflation ratchet down. One kind of money will be politicized and inflated away as dictated by a central committee, and another will remain neutral and deflate as guided by a decentralized community. The economic establishment can mock this new kind of money all they want, but trust—it is worth repeating—is not so gullible. Money exists to serve people, not the other way around. The more traditional currencies devolve into digital tools for economic surveillance and political control, the greater the appeal of a decentralized currency that does neither. Money that liberates its users will always triumph over the kind that shackles them.

Like most things (including societies and people) neither the birth nor the death of a currency is ever elegant. Anyone shocked by the meteoric ascent of Bitcoin, or its ongoing volatility, should take a look at the collapse of failing currencies such as the Venezuelan bolivar and Iranian rial, or study countless other monetary collapses throughout history. If the death of a once-mighty form of money can be so violent, then so must the birth of a future one.

7
RESPECT

respect   noun.
that which has been lost, but can now be restored.

If we had to pick one way to explain the problems of the digital economy, a catchall explanation that applies as much to the financial system as everything else, it would be a simple lack of respect. The dictionary describes *respect* as "a feeling of deep admiration for someone or something elicited by their abilities, qualities, or achievements." That our online existence is sorely lacking in it is apparent everywhere you look, from platform companies that abuse their users to users who abuse each other.

Respect is a second derivative of trust. It takes time to build and is only possible under certain conditions. Like most things that matter in life, it's hard to gain but easy to squander. It has a nostalgic quality to it, as indicated by the etymology, from the Latin "to look back on, to regard." The nostalgia is fitting for those of us old enough to remember the initial promise of the web, back when we naively believed that all information would soon be democratized, and the world's gatekeepers demolished. We remember our first experiences on social media, and the ability to reconnect with old friends. We remember the promise of a new way for artists and musicians to connect to their fans, and the early economic liberation of the gig economy.

Those were the halcyon days before bad incentive structures and a lack of sustainable trust ruined everything. We were naive and didn't see what was coming. We switched to digital music without realizing what it would do to our favorite artists. We surrendered our data to centralized services without realizing the dangers of surveillance capitalism. We stood by as a new generation of gatekeepers rose to power.

The backlash to the inevitable conclusion of incentive structures gone wild is well underway, but the proposed cures are often just as bad if not worse than the disease. Streaming music offered by yet another intermediary is not good for musicians, and social media censorship as enforced by the same companies that radicalized people in the first place is not good for anybody. The absence of digital respect cannot be solved with more disrespect. There has got to be a better way, and it can't be backward looking. The Pandora's box of digitization has been opened, so we must plow forward.

To understand how the decentralized approach pioneered by platforms such as Bitcoin and Ethereum might help, we need to closely examine exactly how they managed to achieve digital trust in the first place. Only then can we speculate on whether a similar model might be used to build digital respect.

What Did Bitcoin Achieve?

Bitcoin changed the world. Not in the theoretical (and often hypocritical) way most Silicon Valley startups talk about, but in multiple, tangible ways. Tempting as it might be to lionize its inventor as a prophet, the intellectual foundation was laid by others, and the network itself survived adolescence thanks to the passion of its earliest adopters. What they knew then—and everyone else is starting to realize now—was that Bitcoin solved two fundamental drawbacks of the information age: the lack of digital scarcity, and the difficulties of organizing online communities.

These drawbacks are interrelated, but the first one is easier to comprehend. Before anything was digital, everything was physical, and that which is physical is naturally scarce. Even something as evanescent as information had a corporeal quality to it because the only way to share it at scale was through a physical object. Write a book, print a bunch of copies, and send them to bookstores. Physical distribution was expensive for producers and inconvenient for consumers, but nobody complained because there was no other way. Publishing houses had to worry about a supply chain and bibliophiles had to worry about a desired title being available at their local bookstore. Music, newspapers, and magazines faced similar challenges.

As frustrating as those limitations may have been, they enabled an elegant business model: take some kind of information, put it on a physical device, then sell the device. Consumers wanted stories and songs, but what they paid for were books and records. The physical scarcity of those objects guaranteed a profit for creators. The need to manufacture them had its own drawbacks—elevating the importance of publishing houses and record labels—but writers and musicians could earn a living. As an added bonus, physical scarcity created repeat customers. A lost book could only be replaced by purchasing a new one, and music lovers who wanted to share their favorite album had to buy multiple copies, or at least buy a cassette tape and take the time to make a copy.

The internet changed all of that, for better and for worse. From the consumer's point of view, digitization was mostly upside. Information that was freed from the shackles of physical distribution could now be accessed immediately by anyone, anywhere. Book lovers could download ebooks as soon as they came out and music fans could share a new album by sending a link. Some of the charm of the original experience was lost— no more dog-eared paperbacks or artful album covers—but the trade-offs were worth it. No more scratched or lost CDs, either.

Producers, on the other hand, suffered because the economics of digital were not very good. Digital information may have been easy to distribute, but it was also easy to replicate. That super fan who could now share a link was no longer buying multiple copies of the same album. The recent time period after the invention of digital, but before the achieving of digital scarcity, was a paradox for creators: more exposure to a bigger audience, but less money and, initially, higher costs. Nowhere was this phenomenon more pronounced than in the music business.

Music sales in the United States doubled in the decade leading up to the mainstreaming of the web thanks to insatiable consumer demand for the superior sound quality of digitally pressed (but physically delivered) compact discs. Sales peaked in 1999, right around the launch of the Napster file-sharing network. They then collapsed by over 50 percent, despite soaring consumption. Consumers loved downloading new music instantaneously and storing all their music on a portable device like an iPod. But the lack of digital scarcity made charging for that convenience difficult. The music industry thrashed about in search of a solution, but nothing worked. Suing Napster out of existence did not slow the revenue decline (but did alienate fans). Porting their catalogues to iTunes was somewhat effective, but more to the benefit of Apple, the company, than Fionna Apple, the musician.

The industry eventually settled on the current subscription-based streaming model, but services such as Spotify are arguably the worst of both worlds. The economics are dreadful—there are now more intermediaries than ever—and a handful of corporate platforms (along with their opaque algorithms) control the careers of the world's musicians. Spotify might talk a big game about serving both musicians and their fans, but it must extract value from both for its shareholders. A lot of people are frustrated but nobody knows what to do because the alternative is going back to the bad old days of free. In the absence of digital scarcity, selling out to a seigniorage-seeking intermediary is the lesser of two evils.

One Network, Two Kinds of Scarcity

Bitcoin proved that there could be a better way: the convenience of digital ownership and transfer, combined with the value-preservation of physical scarcity. Each unique bitcoin is scarce in and of itself, because individual coins are practically impossible to counterfeit—arguably even harder than $100 bills. Crypto experts categorize this as protection from double-spending, or the impossibility of the same coin being spent twice. But just as importantly, *all* the coins in existence are also scarce, because inflation is controlled by the protocol, and the protocol is managed by a decentralized community. Bitcoin owners trust the system to both protect the integrity of the coins in their wallets and to not print too many more. In other words, they expect the supply of their money to have integrity, now and forever.

Digital scarcity of the first order—the micro protection against double-spending—is easily achieved in a centralized setting, but is less desirable because putting an authority in charge is likely to lead to violation of the second order, at the macro level. The Federal Reserve runs a payment system for commercial banks, and the existing dollars preserved within it can't be double spent. But the Fed can always violate aggregate scarcity by printing new ones, which it does.

TWO TYPES OF SCARCITY

	WHEN PROTECTED	WHEN VIOLATED
FIRST ORDER (MICRO)	EXISTING UNITS CAN'T BE COUNTERFEITED OR DOUBLE SPENT	FAKE $100 BILLS BOOTLEG CDS DOUBLE-SPEND ATTACK
SECOND ORDER (MACRO)	NEW UNITS ARE DIFFICULT TO CREATE	QUANTITATIVE EASING NAPSTER BADLY DESIGNED CRYPTO

For digital scarcity to be sustainable, the network atop which it exists must also be decentralized, a precondition of lasting trust that applies as much to music as it does to money. Bitcoin would not have worked as money if some corporation was in charge of maintaining the ledger. A corporation can easily prevent users from double-spending their money, but what's to stop it from enriching itself by printing more (for proof in action, see airline miles). Bitcoin wouldn't have worked if a fixed group of individuals were in charge, either. Any amount of centralization would have eventually led to corruption given the astronomical rise in value. Digital scarcity that's meant to stand the test of time could only be achieved through an open and democratic community—people ruled by a protocol, not the other way around.

Building that kind of community is hard, especially on the internet. Mere distribution is not enough. The Bitcoin blockchain might exist across tens of thousands of nodes all over the world, and that redundancy might be great for transparency and resilience, but it doesn't solve the fundamental problem of transaction validation. How do disparate users all over the world agree on which transactions are valid and the order in which they should be written? Here the openness and censorship resistance of any decentralized network is a liability because thieves and hackers could run their own nodes and cause havoc.

This being a democracy, one option is to hold a vote. Since everyone has their own copy of the ledger, and the content is locked down with cryptography, determining the validity of each proposed transaction is easy. In fact, the blockchain's use of hash functions to create a digital fingerprint of every single block makes validating new transactions against the historical record computationally trivial. Software could be used to automate this process at the user level, and the protocol itself can tally the votes. Thieves and hackers could still lie—proposing bogus transactions then voting them as legitimate—but as long as the majority of participants are honest, then the truth will prevail.

But therein lies the rub because majorities are not what they seem online. Voting is great so long as each participant gets only one vote, but there is no way to enforce that limit in a permissionless network where anyone can do anything—including run multiple nodes. For all we know, more than half the nodes out there could be operated by a single individual, or a group of hackers colluding to attack the net-work. Simple democracy, as it turns out, is nearly impossible in a decentralized setting.

In network science, the problem of one participant pretending to be many is known as a Sybil attack, named after a famous book about a woman with multiple personality disorder. Sybil attacks are a big problem on the internet because anyone can pretend to be someone else—an idea memorialized by a famous *New Yorker* cartoon published in 1993 depicting one canine explaining to another that, "On the internet, nobody knows that you're a dog." The simplest solution to this problem in voting is to require everyone to identify themselves. That's why parliaments have roll calls and communities require voter registration. But identification is not possible in a decentralized setting. Giving one group of users the responsibility of validating others—a responsibility that must come with the ability to reject some people—is a form of centralization. It puts all the power in the hands of a few people, placing us squarely back on the road to platform hell.

Sybil attacks are not just a problem of blockchain networks. They are a risk in almost every online activity and have been slowly ruining the internet for a long time. Everything from phishing scams (is this email really from the IRS?) to fake reviews (did this person actually eat at that restaurant?) to fake followers on social media (does this person truly have a million subscribers?) can be placed in the category of problems that arise when one person can pretend to be another, or many different people. Stuffing the ballot in an old-fashioned paper ballot election takes some effort, as the fraudster has to fill out many forms. Digital fakery can be automated with software, so it scales easily. Part of the problem is the decentralized nature of the internet itself, where devices—and not individual users—are identified. One person can have many devices.

Existing web applications try to solve this problem by surrendering to central authorities. Amazon supposedly prevents fake reviews and YouTube supposedly deletes fake subscribers. But here we have an incentive problem because Amazon would rather every product have a lot of reviews, real or fake. Google is even worse because it's an advertising company that makes money from selling page views and clicks. Users might want it to vigorously crack down on the fake ones, but shareholders do not. Advertisers pay for everything, and on the internet, nobody knows that you are a bot.

This inherent conflict of interest leads to the comical charade now unfolding before us. Facebook and Twitter claim to cut down on fake accounts but leave enough back doors open for new ones to appear. Amazon deletes obviously fake reviews, but only after a significant lag.[94] There are marketplaces where anyone can buy as many subscribers as they want, companies that give away free products for five-star reviews, people who'll like your posts if you like theirs, and mercenary influence peddlers. If aliens arrived from another world and visited our internet, they would assume that every $5 tchotchke on Amazon and every small restaurant on DoorDash is of the highest quality, thanks to the prevalence of five-star reviews. The platform companies know about all of this. They have the money and resources to stop it. But they don't, because doing so violates a basic tenet of the Unholy Trinity. So, the web devolves.

Generic LED String Lights
78,000 Reviews
★★★★★ 5.3 out of 5

About this item
Made poorly inside a dirty factory
using cheap and unreliable materials.

The Influencers Dilemma

The prevalence of digital fakery is an underrated contributor to the breakdown of respect in every online setting. It leads to a toxic environment where the worst behaviors are rewarded. To see why, we must first recognize that online influence is valuable. Having a lot of likes, retweets, positive reviews, and followers is an asset, one that increasingly impacts the offline economy. A restaurant that has a lot of five-star reviews is more likely to get new customers and a pundit who has a lot of Twitter subscribers is more likely to get a book deal. The digital attestations of likes and followers and so on are a form of social capital, and everyone is motivated to acquire as much as they can. The question is how.

Some people try to acquire their social capital by doing something useful, like running a quality restaurant or putting out valuable content. They hustle, put in long hours, and work to earn every like, retweet, positive review, and follower. This is the social capital equivalent of proof of work: do the work, earn the reward. Other people cheat. They don't put in the hours or hustle, they instead buy enough fake followers and reviews on the black market to make it look like they did. This is the social capital version of a Sybil attack. On any centralized platform such as Seamless or Twitter, the second group is guaranteed to win. As the comedian Groucho Marx once said, "the secret of life is honesty and fair dealing. If you can fake that, you've got it made."

To understand why, recall that the target audience—the consumers who order food from an app, watch TikTok videos, and subscribe to Instagram feeds—have no idea what's real and what's fake. Facebook doesn't tell them what percentage of an Instagram influencer's likes were generated by a click farm (if it did, advertising revenues would plummet). This lack of information puts every would-be influencer in a bind. If viewers can't tell the difference between what's real and what's fake, then what's the best strategy for becoming popular? Should they work hard to earn real users or pay up to acquire fake ones? The answer is both. After all, those who decide to both build and buy will always be more popular than those who only do one. In game theory, this is known as the Nash equilibrium. In real life, it's a race to the bottom.

But now we have a new problem because Instagram users aren't that gullible. They understand that some chicanery is going on. There are too many content creators who are suspiciously popular, and the numbers only ever go up, sometimes too quickly. There are also academic studies and media reports that confirm their suspicions.[95] But there is no obvious tell, so the most reasonable response from the users perspective is to assume that everything is a little fake, and to discount every number—every like, retweet, five-star review, and follower count—accordingly. Since tomorrow will bring more fakery, then discount a little more with each passing day. It helps that the human brain is uniquely adept at performing this invisible calculus. People have been doing it for millennia. Not with social capital of course, but with money.

Online social capital in any centralized setting is an inflationary currency. It does not enjoy scarcity of any kind and is easy to counterfeit so its purchasing power falls on a daily basis. That's why it takes much higher numbers to impress users today than it used to. Here the world's centralized platform operators are even more irresponsible than central banks. The Federal Reserve might be profligate with its printing, but it at least tries to preserve the integrity of its currency after it's been issued. That's why $100 bills are difficult to counterfeit. One hundred (or one hundred thousand) likes on any social media platform, on the other hand, are easy to counterfeit.

In economics, Gresham's Law is the phenomenon by which "bad money eventually drives out good." It's more of a principle than a law but explains why lower quality representations of the same currency, like diluted coins with less gold that still have the same face value, tend to force higher quality money out of circulation. It's best understood from the perspective of ordinary people making sensible decisions. In any economy where legal tender laws force citizens to treat coins of different metal content as having the same value, people are going to try to spend the diluted coins (to get rid of them) and save the denser ones. Maybe the laws will be changed, or the currency will fail, and all coins will have to be melted down to capture their pure metallic value. A similar phenomenon also explains why Bitcoin is increasingly viewed as a store of value, not the medium of exchange it was invented to be. The more fiat money that is printed by the world's central banks, the greater the perception that fiat is a form of bad money, leading people to want to spend their dollars and hoard their bitcoins.

Kabessa's Law is the social capital equivalent of this dynamic, named after a popular crypto pundit who first postulated the dilemma that every would-be influencer faces in a centralized setting—to build or to buy. This law states that counterfeit online social capital eventually drives out the quality kind, taking over. The higher the percentage of fake activity on any platform, the lower the incentive to bother trying to create the real deal. Put differently, the easier it is to buy one thousand Twitter followers, the lower the incentive to try to earn one.

And so, the same lack of digital scarcity that doomed the music business is also a problem with social media. The constant stream of controversies coming out of places like Facebook and Twitter is no accident. Bad social capital that is easily acquired by bad actors is an enabler of bad behavior. Good actors who want to reach the top of the discourse by earning the respect of their community don't stand a chance against provocateurs willing to buy their way to the top of the search results. To paraphrase the poet William Butler Yeats: *the best lack all conviction, while the worst are full of passionate intensity.* Digital trust is in desperately low supply and trending in the wrong direction, so things fall apart, and the center cannot hold.

But thankfully, there's a blockchain for that.

Sybil Resistance to the Rescue

Bitcoin solved the problem of fakery on the internet in an anonymous setting, at least as far as simple payments are concerned. Not by anointing some kind of dictator—as frustrated users of social media platforms increasingly demand—but by going in the opposite direction. Bitcoin consensus is highly democratic, and everyone effectively votes on every transaction. To eliminate the risk of Sybil attack, the Bitcoin protocol makes voting expensive. As stated in the original paper:

> The proof-of-work also solves the problem of determining representation in majority decision making. If the majority were based on one-IP-address-one-vote, it could be subverted by anyone able to allocate many IPs. Proof-of-work is essentially one-CPU-one-vote.

Most of the messy and confusing sausage making known as Bitcoin mining is a form of Sybil resistance. By requiring participants to "do work" before voting, the system weeds out a whole lot of fakery. A participant who runs thousands of nodes is no closer to stuffing the ballot than a user who runs just one, because the network doesn't care about the outward appearance of participation. It cares about sweat equity, in the form of the computational contribution that separates the mighty miners from mere nodes. Miners have a lot more skin in the game, so they get more of a say. Imposing a cost on voting allows the network to not care about the legal identity of its voters—like a democracy that lets anyone vote as often as they want but makes them walk a mile each time. Stuffing the ballot is theoretically possible but exhausting. Hackers and thieves might be clever, but they are lazy.

Proof-of-work mining builds integrity in an anonymous setting. Bitcoin's much-maligned energy usage is a litmus test for honest intent. Miners who expend a lot of money on electricity are doing so to earn the trust of the community. They can still choose to attack the network—doing the work, then voting for bad transactions—but why would they? They'd be spending money to steal coins that are now crashing in value because the network has been attacked.

Newer blockchains have simplified this process (and eliminated the electrical usage) by using a newer form of Sybil resistance known as *proof of stake*. Nodes that want to vote on transactions post coins in escrow with the rest of the network. If they vote honestly, they earn a reward. If they don't, they lose their collateral. Incentives are aligned by paying participants in the currency of the network.

And so, the problems of digital scarcity at the micro level, where the coins in your possession cannot be counterfeited, as well as at the macro level, where the network can't mint new coins like a drunken central banker, are solved simultaneously. Miners don't approve counterfeit transactions because they want to earn more coins, and they want to earn more coins because new supply is limited. If protocols such as Bitcoin and Ethereum could not guarantee limited inflation in the future, then their miners would have more of a reason to cheat users today.

Few people, perhaps not even Nakamoto himself, could have been certain that such a radical approach to trust building would actually work. That the price of bitcoin remained below a dollar for the first few years of its existence is one indication that there was plenty of doubt. But the years since have proven that an incentive-based approach to building Sybil resistance and enforcing digital scarcity at all levels is a smashing success. The very existence of the Bitcoin platform today is almost unfathomable when compared to the rest of the internet: a close to trillion-dollar platform that is owned by nobody, open to everybody, secured by anonymous miners, and still capable of flawlessly handling billions of dollars' worth of transactions per day. Trust, reinvented.

Ethereum and other smart contract platforms have expanded that success to many other functions beyond crypto transfers, including fiat payments and decentralized finance. All have proven that math combined with incentive alignment is a powerful thing. They protect against threats while elevating the best approach. The question now is whether this new approach to trust building can be applied to everything. Can blockchains and cryptocurrencies solve the other problems of the internet? Can they enable musicians to earn more money and save social media? Can they make it harder to fake social capital, reining in the chronic inflation that chases away honest actors? Put differently, can they introduce the one thing on the internet that's currently even more scarce than bitcoins? Can they create digital respect?

```
It might make sense just to get some in case it catches
on. If enough people think the same way, that becomes a
self fulfilling prophecy. Once it gets bootstrapped, there
are so many applications if you could effortlessly pay a
few cents to a website as it easily is dropping coins in
a vending machine.
```

Satoshi Nakamoto—two weeks after Bitcoin launched[96]

Into the Great Wide Open

If solving respect was a simple yes/no question, then the answer would be an emphatic yes. Permissionless blockchain networks have clearly succeeded in producing digital scarcity and a narrow form of digital trust. Cryptocurrencies like BTC and ETH would have never appreciated as much as they have if millions of people didn't trust the value proposition of their underlying networks. The same could be said for straightforward tokens like stablecoins or simple decentralized applications such as Uniswap.

But expanding those capabilities from generic platforms to specific applications, and therefore communities, is hard, which is why there are more generic platforms like Ethereum than there are specific decentralized applications. Success in restoring digital respect would look more like the opposite: a few platforms, lots of dApps. After all, part of the charm of any blockchain network that can handle tokens and smart contracts is its ability to have many different solutions leverage the same security framework while interoperating with each other. Proof of work and proof of stake are both expensive to operate on a global scale, in terms of energy or cost of capital. Better to deploy as many dApps as possible on the same platform.

One area that has seen traction is digital collectibles. Digital scarcity of the first order—protecting a specific item from counterfeiting—is a relatively straightforward problem to solve on any blockchain that can handle tokens. Indeed, just as the owner of a cryptocurrency derives trust by tracing the history of their coins, so can the owner of a digital work of art. Here the process is made even easier by something called a *non-fungible token* (NFT).

NFTs are true originals, blockchain tokens that can be thought of as *one of one*. This is in contrast to fungible tokens like Bitcoin and Ether (or stablecoins and governance tokens) that are *one of many*. The owners of those tokens don't distinguish between individual units, in the same way that people don't distinguish between individual dollar bills. Non-fungible tokens, on the other hand, are closer to baseball cards or works of art.

NFTs were first introduced on the Ethereum platform in 2017 in the form of an experimental digital art project known as CryptoPunks, one where ten thousand different cartoon characters were generated as images by an algorithm and given away. The project generated both excitement and confusion, two emotions that still pervade the NFT world today. Users who believed in the power of digital scarcity were eager to snag up verifiably scarce digital art. A secondary market managed by smart contracts sprang up and collectors began bidding up their value, with the rarest characters fetching the most money. The skeptics wagged their fingers and shook their heads. How valuable could a digital collectible be if the image that represented it was easily replicated?

As it turned out the answer was millions of dollars. In the case of a work of art known as *The First 5000 Days*, a visual collage by an artist named Beeple that was the first natively digital work to ever be sold by a major auction house, it was $69 million, despite the fact the digital image being sold was as replicable as any other. Indeed, the headlines generated by the shocking price tag probably made it more downloaded and copied than most. But for the first time in the history of digital, a single individual could still claim ownership, thanks to an NFT that was issued by the artist, vetted by the auction house, and transferred to the buyer's Ethereum address. The bragging rights that came with being the one true "owner" turned out to be all that mattered.

Just as Bitcoin had reinvented money, and Ethereum had redefined the digital platform, non-fungible tokens rekindled excitement around digital art, an excitement that had arisen decades prior when computers first hit the scene but gone quiet once creators realized there was no way to preserve the scarcity of their work. Not the scarcity of consumption—that activity was liberated by the web—but rather the scarcity of ownership. Understanding this distinction is important, as it hints at the coming revolution in art, media, and pop culture.

With physical art, every unit is both scarcely owned and consumed. There is only one Mona Lisa, and it can only be viewed at the Louvre. There might be thousands of prints hanging in people's apartments, or millions of photographs on the web, but those are cheap knockoffs. They don't look, feel, or even smell the same. Digital art by way of NFTs shatters that model, because only the ownership bit is scarce. Consumption and enjoyment of the original, on the other hand, is open to anyone, anywhere. Case in point, Christie's, the auction house that sold the Beeple work, put an ultrahigh-resolution version of the image on its web page to promote the sale, meaning that people who didn't pay a penny for it (along with those who bid millions, but still lost) could consume "the original image" just as much as the winner of the auction. A skeptic could refer to this as the ultimate "winner's curse." That skeptic would be wrong.

The belief that only the owners of fine art (or those who can afford trips to Paris) should be able to enjoy it at its highest quality is rather gauche. It's also elitist. Most artists do not want only a privileged few to have access to their work. They want everyone to be able to enjoy it at its highest quality, regardless of their location, wealth, or circumstances. That's why musicians go to recording studios and use expensive equipment to record themselves. Otherwise, only the small subset of fans who have the luxury of attending a live concert would get to enjoy their music at its highest quality. Art elevates us all, and there should be no limit to the consumption of beauty. But the artists who provide that beauty shouldn't have to starve either. Historically, the easiest way to monetize art has been by selling to a collector. NFTs represent the best of both worlds: art that is universally enjoyed yet singularly owned. Their existence on a programmable platform ruled by code opens the door to other innovations that benefit artists, such as tokens programmed to always send a percentage of their resale price back to the original artist. Gone are the days when a work of art originally sold for $10,000 now trades for millions, but with all the additional value accruing to wealthy collectors.

Such features are not available to traditional artists working in the physical domain. For all we know, the fact that a digital work of art could be enjoyed by anyone, anywhere, in a fashion that continues to financially benefit the creator, could ultimately make digital art more desirable than the physical variety. Indeed, young people who go out of their way to snatch up NFTs are happy to pay up for videos and images that have gone viral. The reason why is status.

Signaling social status has always been an important driver in the domains of art and collectibles. From Cezanne paintings to Swiss watches to limited-edition sneakers, people like to own rare and coveted objects to indicate a certain place within society. But not all objects are good at signaling status. The first requirement is that the item be provably scarce. The second requirement, counterintuitively, is that it *lack* day-to-day utility. The fact that a $5,000 Gucci leather handbag is less useful than a $50 canvas equivalent is part of its appeal. Wastefulness is the ultimate form of conspicuous consumption.

Non-fungible tokens are the ultimate status-signaling mechanism. The blockchain makes verifying the scarcity and authenticity of each one easy, far easier than with a handbag. Since they are often nothing more than bits of data, there is little utility beyond signaling status. This is why owners of the most coveted NFTs such as the CryptoPunks often use them as their profile picture on social media. The digital domain was always going to be the ultimate place for status games, but not without the invention of digital scarcity. Now, there's a blockchain for that. Not surprisingly, many of the world's biggest luxury brands, including Gucci, have begun selling NFTs. Those who criticize the high amounts paid for these virtual items miss the point. Why bother with the pretense of a physical item when the only thing anyone cares about is the logo on it.

The Games We Play

In terms of mass appeal, NFTs have turned out to be one of the more popular applications of blockchain technology, second only to pure cryptocurrencies meant to serve as a form of money. Their popularity is partially driven by their flexibility as a non-fungible token that can be used to upgrade everything from visual art to music to gaming. Here we should give credit to the pre-blockchain video game industry as it normalized the concepts of virtual currencies and in-game collectibles long before anyone had ever heard of an artist named Beeple. Some of the most popular video games in history have made the bulk of their revenues from the sale of in-game items—proto-digital collectibles that usually have no bearing on gameplay. There are card games where users purchase digital packs to compete, and massive multiplayer online games (MMOs) that have their own self-contained economies, complete with their own virtual currencies.

All the value stores that exist in these pre-blockchain games are supposed to be at least somewhat scarce, but have often not been, thanks to the usual drawbacks of assets managed by centralized issuers on opaque databases. Users have no way of confirming how many units of any particular item already exists or how many more will be created in the future. Sybil attacks in the form of a practice known as "gold farming" are common, and there are entire businesses dedicated to exploiting loopholes to generate as much in-game currency as possible. A lighter version of Kabessa's Law applies here as well, as the virtual currency generated by gold farms and sold on the black market slowly crowds out virtual currency earned by hardworking players. The result is something known as mudflation, the virtual world's equivalent of hyperinflation.

Much like the world's central banks, the corporate operators of these communities try to counter mudflation with strong-armed interventions. They fix prices, ban certain kinds of open-market activity, and constantly tweak their policies. Also like the world's central banks, their interventions have limited utility, and only treat the symptoms, not the disease. Video game companies suffer from a lighter version of the Unholy Trinity, and the hard decisions that would benefit the players have to be filtered through the lens of what's also good for shareholders.

A better solution would be to incorporate the benefits of transparency and code, allowing users to track the provenance of every valuable in-game item, and to take comfort in programmable inflation. Porting online gaming onto some kind of a blockchain platform can help preserve digital scarcity at all levels, improving trust. Doing so would also allow the operation of the game to be decentralized, returning power to the players. After all, every virtual world is a platform, and the fact that so many people play these games all over the world make them among the most valuable digital platforms on earth. The only way to achieve lasting trust is by collapsing the Unholy Trinity into one.

Not surprisingly, there are already entire virtual worlds that exist primarily on decentralized platforms such as Ethereum. Like most dApps, they are launched in a more centralized manner, with a road map toward total community ownership down the line. Some of these games replicate the same exact gameplay of their traditional counterparts, and use the token and smart contract functionalities to improve the provenance and trading of in-game assets. Others go a step further and invent brand-new ways for people to compete.

One of the pioneers in this nascent movement was CryptoKitties, an Ethereum-based game released in 2017 that let users buy, sire (breed), and collect their own digital cats. Each cat had its own unique attributes, as determined by a simplified DNA stored in an NFT. Cats that were bred together had kittens that would have a combination of their traits, and the kittens with the rarest traits were the most sought after. CryptoKitties was arguably the first Ethereum-based project to have any kind of adoption, and will be remembered for the painful congestion (and resulting spike in fees) it caused on a then-young Ethereum blockchain.

The introduction of digital scarcity into the world of gaming and entertainment represents an important leap forward in the virtualization of everything. People have been talking about the arrival of the Metaverse— a post-internet virtual domain that combines cyberspace, virtual reality, and augmented reality—for decades. Previous attempts to build it, as led by social media companies and gaming platforms, have fallen short. Too many people have reservations about investing heavily in virtual realities that are controlled by corporations and built on surveillance capitalism. They prefer communities that are organized by their members, meritocratic, and transparent, as is standard in the crypto domain. The alternative is the kind of dystopian worlds often portrayed in science fiction.

Virtual worlds built atop permissionless blockchain networks allow for interesting and unexpected developments, because that which isn't centrally planned is free to flourish. They enable a place like Decentraland, an online world where people buy plots of land and put up their own establishments, places that range from shops to schools to NFT-based art galleries. Its success in resembling the real world was apparent early on when feisty entrepreneurs began shilling video lessons on flipping virtual land.

Permissionless platforms also enable unique entertainment propositions such as Zed Run, a virtual horse-breeding game in the spirit of CryptoKitties, but with the added twist that players can enter their characters into races where they can win prizes. The races are action-packed and livestreamed. Skeptics argue that a game like that is nothing like real horse breeding. What they don't understand is that being different is the point. Physical horse racing is a dying sport that is dominated by a handful of ultrawealthy investors. Zed Run is open to anyone, anywhere, and you don't need to be able to afford a Bob Baffert to compete. As an added bonus, the smart contracts that operate the game don't allow doping.

As in the domains of money and banking, permissionless networks also allow gaming that's censorship resistant. In fact, eSports has almost caught up with traditional sports in terms of viewership and prestige, and its success has had political consequences. In 2019, the gaming giant Activision Blizzard penalized an eSports competitor for voicing support for democracy protestors in Hong Kong while he was being interviewed during a tournament.[97] The company's decision was widely believed to be motivated by fears of a Chinese government reprisal against its business interests—proving once again that bad things happen when platform operators have to pick between people and profits.

Not to be left behind, digital currencies and NFTs have started infiltrating traditional sports. Many of the human tendencies now playing out within the crypto domain—playful versions of tribalism, loyalty, and status—first found a home in sports fandom a century ago. Back then it was the social and economic changes resulting from the industrial revolution that drove people to find new forms of entertainment, ones that provided inspiration, a sense of belonging, light competition, and status. We might take it for granted today, but people wearing the jerseys of their favorite football players or paying millions of dollars for a piece of cardboard with a player's picture on it would have seemed ridiculous a few centuries ago. And yet, professional sports is one of the biggest industries on earth today.

Not surprisingly, many professional sports leagues have already recognized the power of this new tool for fan engagement. The NBA was a pioneer in selling NFT-based "Moments," video clips of actual in-game events that fans could purchase in packs and trade on the secondary market. Some European football clubs have issued fungible fan tokens that help organize modern fan clubs, and leagues are developing NFT-based tickets to live events that have collectibles embedded within them.

Not only do such items reinvent the notion of the bobblehead give-away, but they will eventually reinvent ticketing itself. Indeed, of all the markets in desperate need of re-architecting, the one for tickets of sporting events and concerts might be the most inefficient (to put it politely). Today, dominant providers such as Ticketmaster and StubHub can get away with charging exorbitant fees because they provide the most crucial ingredient needed in that market: trust. Without them, counterfeits would be difficult to spot. A ticket that grants access to a specific seat in a particular venue on a certain date is nothing more than an analog non-fungible token. Once venues begin issuing their tickets on a blockchain, then the secondary market for them can be ported over to DeFi. The value currently extracted by intermediaries like StubHub and SeatGeek will return back to performers and their fans. Each ticket can even be programmed to send a portion of every resale back to the venue, introducing a novel solution to the problem of scalpers and ticket brokers.

Now Comes the Hard Part

Speculating on all that could now be built using this new approach to organizing groups is easy. Executing on those dreams is a whole other matter. Building new communities is hard, and building decentralized communities is even harder. Ingredients like transparency, scarcity, and financial incentives can help, but by no means guarantee success. Digital respect is the sort of thing that must be coaxed into existence, gently and slowly. It must grow organically, in an environment fertile with trust. It can't be contrived. The success of narrower applications like Bitcoin has proven that it's possible, but that success has only upped the stakes for everything else.

Bitcoin had the luxury of coming of age at a time when almost nobody was watching. Ethereum too was initially mostly thought of as an interesting experiment. Uniswap was just a young man's excuse to learn how to code, and the CryptoPunks were an artistic side project.

Their success, along with the success of other protocols and dApps, has increased expectations. People now talk openly about whether decentralized cloud storage can eventually take on Amazon Web Services, or if decentralized social media can replace Facebook.

Part of the challenge of achieving these feats is technical. Storing data inside a gigantic data center managed by a single company is a solved problem. Storing that same data across countless hard drives offered up by individuals who want to earn a token is not. There are engineering issues that have to be overcome and more advanced forms of cryptography that need to be invented. These are the easier problems to solve.

The economic, social, and governance problems are more challenging. What kind of consensus mechanism should be used? What should the token supply be? How will the community handle illicit use? There are no obvious answers to these questions, only guesses. Every project needs to experiment to see what works, constantly tweaking their approach. Some need to make radical changes to their original design, as is the case for many startups. But pivoting is harder to do when there is nobody in charge. Indeed, for all the drawbacks of the centralized approach, the one thing it excels at is change. Corporations are more decisive than communities. Crypto projects have to execute major decisions within some kind of a governance framework, and there too everything is experimental.

Decentralized governance is a new field of study. It borrows from the domains of political science, game theory, and organizational psychology. It's highly experimental and grapples with fundamental issues, like the trade-offs between decentralization and decisiveness. It asks serial questions, like whether everything should be put up for a vote, and if yes, whether every token holder should be given an equal vote, and if no, whether those who earned their tokens should be given more of a say than those who bought in.

Here too Bitcoin has the advantage of being older, and by extension, simpler. Bitcoin governance is done via defection. The protocol hums along doing what it has always done, and those who don't like it leave—sometimes to create a competitor via a fork. This *lack* of formal governance is one reason why it hasn't changed much over the years. That's fine for Bitcoin as many consider its obdurateness a virtue. Newer projects, and those trying to solve more niche problems don't have the same luxury—they have to iterate to find success.

Then there is the need for a go-to market strategy. Traditional start-ups hire ad agencies and run marketing campaigns to attract customers. Decentralized protocols don't have it so easy; picking a marketing strategy is the kind of thing a CEO does. While many start out in a more centralized fashion—with some kind of a foundation or even corporation in charge—the leaders of these affiliated bodies have to deal with unique constraints, like the now-collapsed distinction between users, owners, and operators. Anyone who launches a dApp has to stay mindful of the fact that their future customers will also be their bosses. The good news is that decentralization also enables new tools for attracting users, some of which can be quite powerful. Unlike a company, a community gets to issue its own currency. Or rather, it gets to issue a *trustworthy* currency, one that offers guaranteed scarcity at both the micro and macro levels.

The Flywheel

Kicking off a project by first issuing a token is like using the kick-start lever on an old-fashioned motorcycle, an initial jolt of energy that gets the flywheel of trust going. The project still needs to execute, but that first jolt, the initial coin offering, is important. Despite the bad reputation these crowdfundings developed after the 2017 bubble, they remain an integral part of the crypto ecosystem. New offerings bring attention and energy.

A crypto-skeptic might argue that this is not new, and corporations have been issuing stock to fund new ventures since the days of the VOC. But there is a difference, because the shares of a company can't be used to buy its (eventual) product. Decentralized projects can intentionally blur the line between equity and currency in a powerful way, attracting new users and accelerating the adoption curve in the process. People who want to use the service tomorrow have an incentive to buy the token today, and those who invest in the token today have a reason to try the solution in the future. The project still needs to solve an actual problem to succeed, but the circular flow of tokens helps build momentum toward becoming a viable ecosystem.

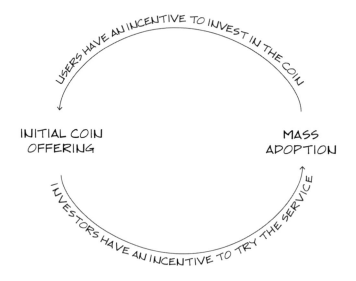

THE FLYWHEEL OF DECENTRALIZED ADOPTION

USERS HAVE AN INCENTIVE TO INVEST IN THE COIN

INITIAL COIN OFFERING

MASS ADOPTION

INVESTORS HAVE AN INCENTIVE TO TRY THE SERVICE

Not every decentralized project needs to follow this playbook. The fly-wheel analogy is only an approximation and applies most directly to projects that deploy a utility token to intermediate between those who provide a service and those who want to use it. Utility tokens are popular in non-financial applications that have well-established centralized counterparts, such as cloud storage and video transcoding. Most DeFi applications opt instead for a simpler governance token. These tokens, which unlike their utility counterparts, are not needed to use the service, are closer to equity than currency. Their owners get to vote on important decisions in exchange for a portion of the project's profits.

Regardless of its function, any token can be programmed to grow its supply over time. The resulting inflation is a powerful go-to market strategy, enabling younger projects to bootstrap adoption by channeling additional supply to different parts of the ecosystem. Bitcoin and Ethereum pioneered this approach by sending newly minted coins to miners, incentivizing more computing power deployed in mining and, by extension, security. DeFi protocols like Compound and Aave have at various times targeted inflation toward borrowers and savers, driving liquidity.

Every dApp can have its own inflation curve, and deciding the shape of that curve, along with the recipients of the resulting coins, is one of the most important decisions that the founders of a project must make. Inflate too much and a token can collapse under its own weight before the application gets going. Inflate too little and the project may not attract enough users. Many projects follow in the steps of Bitcoin and launch with an aggressive initial inflation schedule that flattens out over time. Indeed, of the 21 million bitcoins that will ever be created, half were mined in the currency's first four years. Some projects opt for a deflationary approach, starting with a finite set of tokens and using a burn mechanism to diminish the supply over time. This approach might work for governance tokens like MKR but is unlikely to succeed for a utility token. Currencies that are meant to be used need to grow to remain useful, a fact of economic life that is as true for fiat money as it is for Filecoin.

To see why, let's start with the simple observation that successful populations, economies, or ecosystems tend to grow over time—more citizens for a nation, and more users for an application. If the supply of money doesn't grow concurrently, then the currency becomes increasingly scarce, and by extension, more valuable. This price appreciation of money might be preferred by those who already have some, but not by those who don't. Newcomers will have to pay up to get their hands on any, while those who already have some will be reluctant to spend theirs.

We know this cycle to be true because it's already taken over the Bitcoin economy. Thanks to its anemic inflation schedule—currently running at less than 2 percent per year—growing adoption has resulted in skyrocketing prices. That's all well and good for its perceived role as digital gold, but the same dynamic has slowed adoption as a medium of exchange. People who own bitcoins don't want to spend them. This dynamic is also why Ethereum was originally designed with a more linear inflation schedule, with the supply growing steady forever. Unlike BTC, ETH is meant to be spent, to pay for token transfers or smart contract operations. That said, its inflation schedule has been ratcheted down by the community on several occasions, further testament to the experimental nature of all of this.

Inflationary rewards can play an important role in the establishment of digital respect. Not only do they increase the appeal of a new project to early adopters, they also help preserve a sense of meritocracy as a project matures. If not for the constant minting of new coins, then power would remain in the hands of those who either invested in the original coin offering or are wealthy enough to buy some on the open market. To paraphrase Ralph Waldo Emerson, inflationary rewards help make sure that those who do some good also do well. Newcomers who don't have a lot of capital, but do have a lot of value, can still contribute, acquiring more coins as they do, and getting more of a say in governance.

And Away We Go

These key ingredients—digital scarcity, Sybil resistance, initial coin offerings, and inflationary rewards—can theoretically be applied to any kind of problem from online gaming to decentralized social media. They can also be applied in entirely new ways. The Helium network is constructing a fully decentralized telecommunication network. Designed to be the first decentralized and organically built *physical* network for IoT devices, Helium deploys a novel consensus mechanism known as *proof of coverage*. Network contributors spend money up front to purchase hotspots they can install at their home or office, contributing their existing internet connection to become an outpost for the network. These hotspots are then pinged by IoT devices that need to establish their location or communicate some other kind of data to the internet. The Helium token is a full-on utility token. Users must purchase it to access the network, and hotspot owners earn it in the form of both transaction fees and inflationary rewards.

Unlike a traditional telecommunication network that requires a centralized operator to raise large amounts of capital and design a network topography based on the whims of central planners sitting in an office somewhere, the Helium network uses tokens to organically build itself, literally growing like weeds. Proof of coverage gives the highest rewards to the hotspots that generate the most utility for the network. Devices that are added in areas that are already covered by other devices earn little inflationary rewards and must compete for transaction fees. Hotspots that extend the edge of the network, on the other hand, are rewarded handsomely. Sybil resistance is achieved by a combination of the cost of installing a new hotspot, and the devices constantly challenging each other to prove their location and availability.

Inflationary rewards have allowed Helium to build significant supply in anticipation of future demand. If hotspot owners were only compensated by fees paid by IoT devices, then there would be little incentive for anyone to install one because the investment would take years to pay off. But thanks to an aggressive inflation schedule, tens of thousands of hotspots were deployed in the span of a year, with the earliest adopters earning back their original investment in a matter of days.[98] Their participation was entirely speculative, as was Bitcoin mining in its first year of operation. There was no guarantee that the network would succeed, or the tokens become valuable. But the promise of that potential success, combined with the flywheel effect of a verifiably scarce token, was reason enough for volunteers to try. The resulting supply can now induce demand. The cart before the horse, in a good way.

This organic approach to building new infrastructure is now being applied to all sorts of services, from cloud computing to video processing. These services are colloquially referred to as Web3, a loosely defined term applied to blockchain-enabled solutions that feature some combination of transparency, censorship resistance, and user control. There is no guarantee that any of them will succeed, and the history of technology teaches that most of the earliest attempts probably won't. But the lure of catching that next big thing is appealing enough for lots of people to try. Whereas traditional technologies often rely on the passions of their early adopters, blockchain ones tap into the greed of early suppliers.

But What About Social Media?

Here we should pause to ask arguably the most pressing digital respect question of all: can the tools discussed so far be used to build better social media? So many of the world's problems seemingly trace back to platforms such as Facebook, Twitter, and YouTube, and controversies around radicalization or censorship pop up with increasing frequency. The problem is the bad incentives of the Unholy Trinity. Social media companies make money from selling ads, and ads require eyeballs, so the platforms go out of their way to make people addicted to their content.

The politically correct term for this addiction is engagement, but we should not be naive about the toxicity, it can be just as destructive as heroin or meth. Human nature being what it is, the most effective way of hooking people's attention is by showing them content that evokes negative emotions like shock, fear, and outrage—a sad reality as true in the pre-web era as it is today, thus the old newspaper motto of "if it bleeds, it leads." Social media platforms practice something similar by designing their algorithms to prioritize provocative content. If it offends, it trends.

This phenomenon, which has been long speculated about by critics, has been confirmed by outside research and internal whistleblowers.[99] The critics who accuse these platforms of being too tolerant of radical or misleading content miss the point. It's not that Facebook and YouTube inadvertently welcome radicals and extremists, it's that they create them. Like any good drug dealer, they understand that the only way to ensure steady demand for their product is by creating new addicts—take one (offensive post) and call me in the morning. That radicalization is further fueled by each platform's constant slicing and dicing of user profiles into marketable categories. This is done to increase ad rates, because advertisers pay more for ad campaigns targeted to specific types of people. So do political operatives and foreign agents.

The executives of these companies pretend to care about these problems. They give podcast interviews (and increasingly, congressional testimony) about the steps they are taking to rein them in. They create oversight panels and censor certain kinds of content, sometimes even taking the extreme step of banning people. Their interventions are inconsistent at best and politically biased at worst. Either way, they are guaranteed to fail, because they go against the core mission of every centralized social media platform, which is not—as their sappy TV commercials claim—to bring people together, but to extract value from other people's work. Like the allegorical scorpion riding the frog, Facebook and YouTube can't help but cause social disharmony. It is in their nature.

To see how a decentralized alternative might be better, it helps to study the closest thing to one that exists today: Wikipedia. Despite having millions of crowdsourced articles that touch on everything from the efficacy of vaccines to Donald Trump, the encyclopedia is seldom the subject of any controversy, an impressive feat by modern online standards.

Wikipedia is not built on a blockchain and has nothing to do with crypto, but its architecture resembles projects that are, starting with its business model, or lack thereof. Wikipedia is run by a nonprofit and funded via donations, so it does not suffer from the Unholy Trinity. It doesn't need to sell ads, so the service doesn't care about engagement. In fact it might be one of the few places on the internet that measures success by how little time anyone spends on the site, because short visits mean users found what they were looking for. Quality over quantity, and satisfaction over engagement.

If Wikipedia did care about engagement, it would go out of its way to create chaos. Every article would highlight the most contested edits and have a sidebar designed to bait people into clicking on topics that had nothing to do with why they came to the site in the first place. Its homepage would be a horrific collection of pointless listicles designed to hijack people's attention. But Wikipedia doesn't care about engagement, so it deploys many crypto-like techniques to achieve the opposite: digital respect.

Wikipedia has its own consensus mechanism, one that relies on outside sources such as newspaper articles or academic papers for building trust. It achieves Sybil resistance by blocking anonymous contributions to controversial articles, and even deploys its own version of proof of work. Editors who want to work on controversial articles must prove honest intent by first working on a series of uncontroversial ones.[100] Like any blockchain (and unlike every centralized platform) most of the code is open source, and the site's search algorithm is transparent.[101] Wikipedia also has a distributed power structure, so the admins who have the power to restrict editing on a certain article are different from the ones who work on content.

None of these features may have come about if not for the project's benevolent dictator, one who made the unlikely decision to not become personally wealthy by turning on monetization. Society is seldom that lucky, so any attempt at building a decentralized version of Facebook or Twitter must begin with a simple question of governance: in the absence of a Jimmy Wales, how are the most important decisions made?

The answer, for any token-enabled solution, is with voting. If the flywheel of a blockchain-based social media service involves a utility token designed to encourage positive behavior, then that same token could be used to vote on protocol-level decisions. Smart contracts can even be programmed to give certain tokens, like the ones earned by users who provide valuable content, more weight than others, like ones purchased on the open market.

Voting is impractical for all but the biggest decisions, so everything else would have to be embedded in the tokenomics of the project. Here a great deal of experimentation will be needed to see what works. For example, how many tokens should be given to users who create original content versus those who curate existing material? A successful service needs both. And what should the business model be, if any? Advertising is still an option, but in a less toxic way. Since the users of these platforms are also its owners, they don't need to prioritize quantity over quality, they can strike a balance of both.

Regardless, a decentralized approach will enable better outcomes. Users and content creators who are also owners take pride in their contributions and are more active in governance. They are less likely to tolerate radicalism and more capable of reaching a consensus on what kind of content is desired and what isn't. They won't have to resolve to strong-arm tactics to keep out bad content, because the tokenomics of their platform would disincentivize bad behavior from the get-go. Critics of an open internet falsely assume that digital platforms must use force to keep out bad actors. Bitcoin proved that there is a better way: let the bad guys try, but incentivize the good ones to try harder.

Applying a similar formula to social media is a lot more complicated, but not impossible. Figuring out the right formula will take time and a lot of experimentation but will happen because so much is at stake. To their credit, several centralized social media platforms are beginning to explore their own blockchain-enabled solutions. Facebook tried (and failed) to issue a stablecoin. Twitter now allows users to verify ownership of the NFTs they display as profile pictures, and TikTok has partnered with a Web3 music streaming service. How genuine these activities are remains to be seen, as all three companies face a potential loss of power should decentralization win. In the social media platforms of tomorrow, it will be the content creators and curators who make the money and wield the power, not the operators or shareholders.

Putting It All Together

Anything that is worth doing is worth doing with other people, a fact of life as true for procreation as it is for a payment system. But organizing groups of people is hard, especially if that group is meant to include more than a handful of people who already trust each other. Until the invention of Bitcoin, the primary vehicle for organizing people around an economic objective was the corporation, a centralized and rigid structure that has changed little since its invention centuries ago. The industrial era blossomed under the structure of the corporation. It's the perfect architecture for organizing people who interact with objects. But it's not very good for organizing people to interact with each other.

Bitcoin introduced a novel organizational system, ruled by code and empowered by a currency. Despite its financial success, it remains first and foremost a community. The success of that community has inspired many imitators, some of which are quite different from the original. But the one thing they all have in common is a lack of rigidity. Investors, developers, and validators come and go. Users, owners, and operators exchange hats. Prices fluctuate. Despite all the fluidity, or maybe because of it, the community persists. People trust it in ways that they would not trust a corporation, because communities respect and empower individuals in ways that corporations can't.

These benefits are encapsulated in the notion of a DAO, or decentralized autonomous organization. Upon first glance, DAOs are the blockchain version of a corporation. They are designed to organize groups of people to fulfill a specific function, like investing capital or running a decentralized bank. They replace shares with tokens and rely on smart contracts executed within consensus to operate, as opposed to operating agreements enforced within the legal system. They are democratic in ownership and management, and meritocratic in terms of who gets to contribute ideas or labor. But defining DAOs by comparing them to what came before is limiting, akin to describing email as more efficient faxing.

DAOs are one of the most revolutionary innovations in community creation to come around in a long time. By existing exclusively online, they are global and borderless, in ways that corporations are not. By existing on censorship-resistant platforms such as Ethereum, they are nondiscriminatory in ways that corporations can't be. Since all the heavy lifting is done by transparent code executed within consensus, they are more trustworthy. A lending facility designed as a DAO can't violate trust the way banks occasionally do, its code wouldn't allow it. A social media service designed as a DAO can't hide behind opaque algorithms and ad hoc censorship, all of its programming would be open source.

Any service currently buckling under the perverse incentives of an Unholy Trinity could theoretically thrive as a DAO, with a token acting as the measurable unit of digital respect. But designing successful ones is far from trivial, because building lasting communities is hard. DAOs straddle the relatively clean world of computing and code with the messier one of humans. Each community has its own dynamics and internal politics, and the most important decisions cannot be automated. Then there is the open question of how these communities intersect with existing laws and regulations, almost all of which were created for the analog era.

The first official DAO (confusingly named *The DAO*) was a sort of decentralized venture capital fund organized on Ethereum, one where investment decisions were meant to be democratically decided by way of a governance token sent to anyone who contributed capital. Despite a successful ICO in 2016, it quickly collapsed due to a vulnerability in its code that was exploited by a hacker. Even if it hadn't collapsed, it would have eventually ended up in the crosshairs of regulators such as the SEC which later concluded its token was an illegal security. Despite its unfortunate ending, the ideals and ambition of that first effort proved irresistible and contagious.

With hardly anyone noticing, DAOs have quietly become some of the most valuable entities on earth, at least when compared to their more traditional corporate counterparts. There are DeFi DAOs such as Aave and Uniswap whose market caps run in the billions, and NFT creation and curation DAOs that are more valuable (and when measured by user count, more popular) than prominent art galleries. There are DAOs dedicated to specific artists. They raise money by issuing their own token then use the proceeds to buy expensive NFTs, giving their token holders a fractional share of the art and a say on what to purchase next. There are DAOs dedicated to creating decentralized versions of Patreon and Substack, turning the most popular content creators into platform owners who get a say in governance. There are DAOs dedicated to the most idealistic social causes, but also ones simply meant to make their token holders money.

DAOs have gained enough traction that certain jurisdictions have begun accepting them as registered entities, in the same way that governments have done for corporations for centuries. But their global nature, censorship-resistant makeup, and ability to issue their own currencies make them potentially far more impactful. On a long enough timeline, the most successful DAOs might be more comparable to nation-states than companies.

As hyperbolic as that may sound, we should remember that nation-states are a relatively new idea in the context of history, one that came of age in the industrial era. Like DAOs, they are first and foremost a coordination mechanism meant to build trust. They start with a set of core principles, like individual liberty (or the lack thereof) enforced via a legal system. They have their own money and use it to incentivize desired behavior, like working hard, or not committing crimes. They have their own form of censorship resistance, as anyone born into a certain country is automatically a citizen, and their own consensus mechanisms, such as representative democracy.

Nation-states are beginning to show their age. The physical borders by which they define themselves are not as relevant in the digital era, and the standing armies through which they attack others (or defend themselves) are not as useful in the information age. Unlike the old days, when one country could invade another to steal its natural resources or appropriate its factories, intangible assets such as brands, fan bases, and copyrights can't just be taken. The mere act of co-opting them can collapse their value, diminishing any incentive to try in the first place. Put differently, a foreign army can always occupy Disneyland, but it wouldn't be very good at making Marvel movies.

Like other transitional periods throughout history, these shifting dynamics open the door to different ways of building trust and organizing communities. But the transition will take time. Where DAOs fit in with broader society, and how the existing power structures react to their continued ascent, is one of the great unknowns of the coming decades. Many are already responding. Look past the headlines of every regulatory threat or governmental crackdown against crypto, and read between the lines of every expert takedown of decentralized platforms and the applications built on top of them, and what you'll find is a group of vulnerable people acting out of fear. The fear of change and diminished importance, but also, progress.

But that progress will prevail, for the same reason it always has. The strongest trust frameworks, the ones that have a fighting chance at outrunning the curse for the long run, win out because the people who subscribe to them become stronger by doing so. That's why the crypto community continues to grow, against all odds and despite constant criticism. Bitcoin, along with a multitude of smart contract platforms and the applications built on top of them, has successfully demonstrated how the decentralized approach can help restore respect to digital interaction. It can take power away from intermediaries bound to be corrupted by perverse incentives and return it to the people who made the internet interesting in the first place: our friends, family members, and the kinds of strangers we still root for. Whereas the centralized approach goes out of its way to reward the outrageous and the outraged, the decentralized approach elevates the righteous. Given all that we've learned, and everything that we long for, now is the time to make the leap.

EPILOGUE

Omnia mutantur, nihil interit

Everything that's old is eventually new again, and the oldest things are seldom what they set out to be. Take "Respect." Not the concept, but the song, the iconic one made famous by Aretha Franklin long ago. Over fifty years later, it is still recognized for its relatable themes of protest and personal empowerment. But that's not how it began. The original version, which was written and recorded by Otis Redding, was less ambitious. It told the story of a frustrated man who felt neglected by his woman, and was more a reflection on traditional gender roles than a challenge to them.

Aretha's version is noticeably different. It's less subtle and more demanding—she literally spells out what she wants. It also reverses the usual gender tropes, with the woman being the breadwinner. Female singers who celebrate their sexuality are a mainstay of modern music, but a black woman doing so at a time of great racial and gender inequality was revolutionary. No wonder then that it was her version, and not the original, that would become recognized as one of the greatest songs of all time.

But it didn't get there purely on its merits, for the simple reason that nothing does. Art is an extension of culture, and the songs that seep into the zeitgeist are as much a product of what society needs as they are their own composition. Aretha Franklin's cover of "Respect" was released in 1967, a tumultuous year that included race riots in some American cities, the Supreme Court ending restrictions on interracial marriage, and a woman being attacked during the Boston Marathon. What better time to release a song about respect than a year simultaneously remembered as the Summer of Love and the Summer of Rage.

History has a funny way of deciding what becomes historical, and the same song released a decade earlier or later might not have been as impactful. For all we know, similar songs were recorded even earlier but never heard, either because record companies refused to release them or audiences didn't accept them. That's not to take anything away from the Queen of Soul, but to concede something that every creator knows: timing is everything. For songs, jokes, memes, technologies, and ideas. On a long enough timeline, it matters little what an Aretha Franklin (or Satoshi Nakamoto) intended when they released their creation. What mattered more was that society had a need and latched on to that which filled it. Timing is everything, and to quote Victor Hugo, "Nothing is more powerful than an idea whose time has come." [102]

The crypto industry as we understand it is very young, but most of its components are decades old and predate the modern internet. The notion of using a continuously updated chain of cryptographic fingerprints to timestamp digital events and documents was introduced in 1991, at a time when little was digital. Few people noticed, and fewer still cared. A presentation put together by its inventors—ironically created on paper, not PowerPoint—listed several potential applications such as notary services and stock trading.[103] Today, we call that solution a blockchain, and it is already being applied to almost every application listed on that faded slide, sometimes with billions of dollars' worth of investment capital. It took thirty years, but one application in particular—then listed innocuously as "funds transfers"—is now a multitrillion-dollar industry. For Stuart Haber and Scott Stornetta, being early was almost as bad as being wrong.

The idea of using cryptographic identity to shield people from government surveillance and corporate control dates back even further, to the 1980s. It was developed by a group of like-minded outcasts who were paranoid enough to realize the surveillance threats of the digital economy and smart enough to conceive of solutions rooted in the then-sleepy field of cryptography. Known as the cypherpunks, this eclectic group of programmers, mathematicians, and civil libertarians found inspiration in the ideas of a computer scientist named David Chaum, a pioneering thinker whose 1982 dissertation proposed several of the concepts that would enable Bitcoin decades later.[104] Chaum's contributions to the crypto industry have by now been mostly forgotten, an experience to which Otis Redding might relate.

The practice of filtering out bad behavior on the internet by forcing participants to do some kind of difficult computation was first conceived of in 1993 as a way of combatting spam email. It would not be called "proof of work" until six years later, in a now-forgotten paper on micropayments.[105] It would be adopted by several different cryptocurrency proposals around the turn of the millennium however, most of which bore a striking resemblance to Bitcoin. Some were launched, but none made it. Before disappearing, Satoshi Nakamoto was forthright about Bitcoin's reliance on these earlier projects.[106] We'll never know if Bitcoin was just better, or also better timed.

———

In *The Sun Also Rises* by Ernest Hemingway, one of the characters asks another how he went bankrupt. "Two ways," replies his counterpart, "gradually, then suddenly."

Bitcoin was proposed in the middle of a financial crisis, at a time when the curse had afflicted many important intermediaries, not to mention the governments that propped them up. Some of its earliest adopters believed that it would disrupt the financial system quickly. They were wrong. Despite the cryptocurrency's material appreciation in price and prominence since, the centralized intermediaries it hoped to upend are more powerful than ever. Things change, but often not as fast as we'd like, and sometimes not in the order we'd expect.

Despite the hopes of Tea Party members and Wall Street occupiers, the 2008 financial crisis did not start an economic revolution. What it did do, however, was to plant the seeds for a social and political one. The current design of our monetary system—with public central banks issuing fiat currencies, the ownership and transfer of which is controlled by an elite club of commercial banks—is very old. It is neither egalitarian nor elegant, and regressing. At a time when technology is liberating other industries from the shackles of over-the-hill gatekeepers and returning power to users, money and banking continue their march toward even greater concentration, with the too-big-to-fail banks now bigger than ever. Not to be left behind, the central bankers who sit atop this increasingly vertical hierarchy amass more power every day.

Banking is not so much an industry as it is an agreement. We grant a select group of professionals and their institutions special powers and *hope* that they do the right thing. The proof of whether they've done so is in the socioeconomic pudding: an ever-growing wealth gap fueled by central bank activism, a clunky commercial banking sector that can't get out of its own way, failure to expand inclusion despite growing awareness of the problem, and confused regulators more concerned with protecting the industry in their charge than reinventing it.

When an existing trust framework breaks down, it does so in two ways: gradually, then suddenly.

The economist Rüdiger Dornbusch, who may or may not have been a fan of Hemingway, once postulated that economic crises take longer to develop than you think they will, then unfold faster than you thought they could. The reinvention of our existing frameworks for money, banking, and other types of digital interaction may seem imminent, but it's felt that way for a while, so it's hard to say when the surge will begin. Nevertheless, progress has been made.

Like Bitcoin, gold is often viewed as a trustworthy store of value, a function it has dutifully served for thousands of years. All the gold that has ever been mined is estimated to be worth just over ten trillion dollars.[107] Bitcoin is only a dozen years old, yet its total market cap is close to one trillion. One-tenth of the market cap in a fraction of the time is an accomplishment.

Bitcoin will never replace all the functions of gold, but there are things it can do better, as it can be stored cheaply and transported easily. For governments looking to opt out of the dollar-dominated international payment system, and individuals looking for an alternative to the pseudo-governmental commercial banking system, Bitcoin is an appealing alternative. The critics who accuse these independence-minded users of having some kind of ill intent should recall the basic principle of the curse of history: the more dominant any trust framework, the greater the incentive for someone to abuse it. Few superpowers in history have had as much power as America does today.

Fortunately, not everyone will have to switch to crypto to enjoy the resulting benefits, and most people never might. The mere optionality of this new and more trustworthy opt-out mechanism might be all the world needs. Central bankers who don't respect their own money and financial companies that don't respect their own clients will now have to grapple with a new kind of alternative, one that is decentralized and less co-optable by design. Sometimes, the mere threat of competition is all it takes to keep the authorities in check.

Sometimes.

Like the existing payments industry, stablecoins exist to enable every other kind of economic activity. But unlike their predecessors, they don't demand a pound (or dollar or euro) of flesh for every transfer. No wonder then that despite being only a few years old and the subject of endless controversy, stablecoins on Ethereum already move more value than every Western Fintech and e-money provider combined. Years from now, the idea of paying a fee to move money will seem as preposterous as paying per minute to talk on the phone. Just as all data currently moves on the public internet, all money will eventually move on public blockchains—effectively for free. Many of the world's top payment experts disagree with this thesis. Most of them work for a traditional payment provider.

The American writer and activist Upton Sinclair liked to say that it is difficult to get a man to understand something when his salary depends on his not understanding it.

The notion of using private blockchains for enterprise applications dates to the first bull market in Bitcoin. For almost a decade, corporate executives skeptical of cryptocurrencies and the public networks atop which they reside have campaigned for private alternatives, controlled by them. Rebranded to a more banal sounding "distributed ledger technology" (DLT) and deployed among a handful of companies, these networks offer incremental improvements for incumbents. They also preserve the existing power structure. In their defense, private networks are easier to deploy and harder to hack. They also fit within existing regulatory and compliance frameworks.

But so were the private intranets that were once offered as an alternative to the public internet. Some, like America Online in the United States and Minitel in France, were wildly popular. But none exist today. All were vanquished by the more decentralized, and therefore more trustworthy, public internet. That said, it's difficult to get corporate executives to understand something when their stock price depends on their not understanding it.

Like the existing financial system, DeFi exists to enable people. But unlike the traditional system, DeFi is also owned and controlled by those people. That's why it is faster, cheaper, and more transparent. It's also more innovative, an admittedly low bar given the obdurateness of the legacy financial industry. Despite being in its infancy, DeFi as a sector is already bigger than 95 percent of American banks by balance sheet and will grow exponentially once off-chain assets such as government bonds and tokenized real assets are onboarded. The traditional financial system may require a great deal of manual processing to function, but only because it's inefficient, not because there is a lot of discretionary decision-making on the part of its intermediaries. On a long enough timeline, the people and companies who intermediate loans and trades today will seem as preposterous as the telephone switchboard operators of antiquity.

As will a financial system built on exclusion. Remarkably, at a time when every other industry is going out of its way to eliminate discrimination, finance, as empowered by government, encourages it, supposedly because assuming the worst about everyone prevents crime. There are two problems with our current acronym-based (AML, KYC, CFT, OMG) approach to compliance. The first is that it punishes the good guys. The second is that it doesn't catch many of the bad ones. Crypto is different, and assumes most people are not criminals, for the simple reason that they aren't. The bankers and politicians who refuse to accept this reality are only protecting the status quo—and their position within it.

This controversy mirrors the one over electronic communication in the 1990s. Indeed, much of the fearmongering that goes on about an open financial system today—that it will enable terrorists, drug dealers, and child pornographers, unless the government is granted special powers—is a copy and paste of the hyperbole from the early days of digital communication. Today, the US government is trying to force everyone to report the content of every digital wallet. Back then, the National Security Agency wanted every computer to be manufactured with a built-in snooping device. But it failed, thanks to the realization that it's foolish to make everyone less secure just to catch a few crooks.

The same goes for money. Imposing primitive anti-crime rules on this new approach will only perpetuate the injustices of the past and worsen inequality. In wealth, and dignity. Governments concerned about illicit activity should go after criminals directly and stop turning financial-service providers into Keystone Cops. Any compliance approach that locks out a billion people just to stop a few begs the question of which is the worst crime. Now is the time to build an inclusive alternative.

Thankfully, there's a blockchain for that.

———

Everything that's old is eventually new again, and some of the attributes of the old architecture will show up in the new. The decentralized systems of tomorrow will be better than what we have today, but they won't be perfect. Those who push a utopian vision of the future are just as ignorant as the skeptics who defend a flawed past.

Thanks to their decentralized architecture, most blockchain platforms —particularly Bitcoin and Ethereum—have a capacity problem. They cannot process enough transactions to keep up with demand, leading to occasional queues and high fees. Ethereum will have more capacity due to the transition to proof of stake, but it's not a given that more throughput will result in lower fees. The upgrade might motivate even greater adoption, in the same way that new highways can lead to more traffic by incentivizing more people to buy a car. This problem of induced demand is likely to inflict every decentralized platform, even the newer ones with higher capacity.

The most likely solution is a return to hierarchies of settlement, the decentralized version of our now-familiar pyramid of trust. Indeed, most of the scaling solutions being developed for both Bitcoin and Ethereum move smaller transactions to secondary networks that occasionally reconcile themselves to the main one. Batching and netting are once again deployed to allow more transactions at a lower cost.

Returning to a hierarchy makes practical sense, even in a decentralized setting, due to the importance of security. Security is a scarce asset, and like any other coveted object is ultimately sold to the highest bidder. The more secure blockchain platforms become, the higher the fees users moving large amounts are willing to pay to get their transaction processed first. Not that the smaller players who get priced out by this dynamic should care. As these platforms mature, wanting base-layer security for micro transactions is increasingly overkill, like hiring an armored truck to send someone a few dollars.

Executing smaller payments (or in the case of Ethereum, code executions) on a secondary layer is a more efficient use of the infrastructure. The risks of not using the primary layer are offset by lower fees and faster processing times. So are the risks of using some of the newer and faster (but also less secure) layer-one blockchains being developed, most of which are building bridges back to Bitcoin and Ethereum. In time, the blockchain ecosystem will resemble the existing one, with value moving horizontally and vertically across a system of interconnected decentralized ledgers, one where all users get to pick their place on the perennial spectrum of convenience versus trust.

Despite being hierarchical, the new system will still be better than the old. It will be natively digital and programmable, running around the clock and across the world. It will also be transparent and immutable, free for all to see but for none to change. Best of all, it will be censorship-resistant and permissionless. The fundamental failure of the legacy system isn't that it's hierarchical, it's that by virtue of being both centralized and censorable, the hierarchies never change, leading to stasis and rot. It's not that our current payments or market pyramids can't be better. It's that they don't have to be because the authorities who sit at the top restrict competition among the intermediaries in the middle.

The decentralized hierarchies of tomorrow will be more dynamic. Unlike a DTCC or Federal Reserve, base protocols like Bitcoin and Ethereum have no say over who builds on top of them. Due to their open and censorship-resistant architecture, anyone can build their own aggregation service or Layer 2, and many teams are, sometimes to provide the same service as another. This constant competition will keep everyone honest, and the curse at bay. Users who mistrust a secondary layer can always move their assets to Layer 1, yet another incentive for the maintainers of secondary layers to remain trustworthy.

Which brings us to the final drawback of this brave new world, one so inherent to money that it was foolish to assume we could ever escape it. Despite the many benefits of the decentralized approach, most people arrive on the shores of crypto for one reason: its presumed scarcity. Things like mining, DeFi, and NFTs might be difficult to understand, but money with fixed inflation is not, especially at a time of record monetization all over the world. Indeed, if there's one attribute that almost anyone can appreciate about Bitcoin, it's the currency's finite supply. Too bad it's not true.

Or at least, not the total truth. While it's accurate to say that the Bitcoin protocol will only ever mint 21 million coins—almost 19 million of which have already been distributed—the total supply of bitcoins will always be higher, because credit creates money. Just as American banks somehow hold far more dollars on deposit than ever created by the Fed, the exchanges, lending protocols, and digital banks that deal in crypto will always hold more of it than what's recorded on the blockchain.

This is not a failure of the technology, but an extension of human psychology. Bitcoins deposited at a crypto bank—like dollars kept in a savings account—are not the same as bitcoins held in a private wallet, for the simple reason that the bank may lend some of those coins out to other people, and the crypto will reside in *their* private wallet. As far as the blockchain is concerned, the borrower is the true owner because they control the private key. The depositor only owns a promise, one that may be broken.

And so, the same money magic that has befuddled ordinary people forever has now arrived on the shores of crypto, muddling the discussion about what is truly inflationary and what's not. This phenomenon is even observable in DeFi, where the amount of stablecoins like Dai deposited with lending protocols such as Aave is already more than the total amount minted by the smart contracts of MakerDAO.

At issue is our tendency to conflate the promise of something being returned tomorrow with possession today, a tendency that no technology can cure. Bitcoins deposited with a crypto exchange or Dai deposited in a DeFi protocol are no different than dollars kept in a checking account, or gold florins deposited with a Florentine money changer, for that matter. All result in more money supply than whatever was originally minted. As the crypto economy gets built out, and coins and tokens get loaned and borrowed (then loaned and borrowed again), the broad supply of everything will grow, above and beyond the limits enforced by the protocol. Just as the Fed has limited control over the total supply of dollars, the blockchain can only do so much to control the total supply of bitcoins.

Like most inflation, whether this lending-induced increase in the money supply is good or bad is in the eye of the beholder. Credit increases adoption, and Bitcoin will need its own credit system to become a global standard. Part of the appeal of the US dollar as a reserve currency is the ease with which it can be borrowed and lent. But credit confuses the supply issue. The more places willing to accept deposits in crypto in order to lend some out, the higher the practical supply. Good for adoption, but not great for scarcity, at least on the way up. Just as economic expansions increase the synthetic supply, market contractions will shrink it, in the same way it used to for fiat currency until the central bankers assumed control.

The long-term impact of this ancient money madness on the price or prominence of crypto remains to be seen and is beyond the scope of this book. Unlike the stewards of the old system who we have frequently critiqued, we should be humble enough to admit what we don't know, which is a lot. What we do know is that crypto is still unique in that its base inflation, the number of coins originally minted, will always be controlled by a protocol, as opposed to people.

Maybe this basic restriction is enough, especially at a time when the world's central banks take the opposite approach. Or maybe not. Without a central bank empowered to smooth out the credit cycle and act as a lender of last resort, crypto's broad money supply (and ultimately its price) is bound to be more volatile than traditional forms of money. Maybe that's OK, or maybe not. Maybe the crypto clearinghouses currently being set up to make it easier for Bitcoin exchanges and custodians to trade with each other will assume the role of private protector, just as the banker's clearinghouses did in the days before central banking. Or maybe wealthy individuals rich in coins will help return confidence during a crisis, just as private bankers like John Pierpont Morgan did long ago.

Crypto might be different, but the human nature with which it interacts will remain same. To paraphrase one famous writer, the history to come may not repeat, but it will probably rhyme. And to quote another, *omnia mutantur, nihil interit*, Latin for "everything changes, but nothing dies."

Including the curse of history. The crypto cure for money, markets, and platforms is real and already underway. It has attracted people and capital and will attract more in the years to come. Things will be better, but they won't be perfect. To claim otherwise is to mimic the mistakes of our predecessors. But either way, it will be one hell of a ride. So buckle up, back up your private key, and prepare for liftoff.

Acknowledgments

Understanding something new and complex is a journey, and I've never enjoyed traveling alone. Thanks to my co-instructor and intellectual sparring partner Gur Huberman, a tenured professor with decades of teaching experience brave enough to take a chance on someone with none. Your informed skepticism keeps me on my toes and makes me smarter, so please don't ever stop asking me whether a solution actually needs a blockchain. Thanks also to my students at Columbia Business School and the broader Columbia crypto community. Teaching is a privilege and your curiosity and open enthusiasm drive me. The business world is full of cynics, so don't ever change.

Thanks to all my friends and former colleagues at Citi Ventures. You gave me the freedom to speak my mind even when most people didn't want to hear what I had to say. Anyone who wants to become an expert at something should do a stint at a place where they are surrounded by skeptics. I'm also grateful to the broader Citi community for teaching me more about traditional financial services than I ever managed to teach them about crypto. Last but not least, thanks to all the lunatics and degens within the bank's crypto underground. We are all going to make it, even if they are not.

Many of the ideas within this book were developed through ongoing conversations with a handful of industry experts, most of whom I'm proud to also count as friends. Thanks to Nir Kabessa for understanding Web3 before the term existed; to Greg Di Prisco for knowing more about banking than most bankers; to Itay Tuchman, Shobhit Maini, Austin Campbell, Alex Kriete, Greg Girasole and David Zanette for seeing how the new would invade the old; to Lewis Cohen for teaching me to think like a lawyer; and to Alex Price for seeing all the moves before everyone else. Also, thanks to Flavia Cymbalista for pointing me in the right direction almost a decade ago.

Thanks to my friends and family who put up with me in the two years it took to write this book. Writing is a solitary affair but is made easier when you know that the people you are neglecting are rooting for you. None of the risks I've taken in the past few years would have been possible if not for the constant support of my immediate family—Edna, Naz, and Az (the original professor Malekan) and a handful of loving cousins and close friends. My gratitude to DeeDee, who understood me even when she didn't understand my work, and to Victoria, who told it like it was, even when I didn't want to hear it.

The best writing advice that anyone ever gave me came from my longtime friend Pamela Van Giessen, who once told me that every writer thinks they need more words than they actually do. That was more than twenty years ago. The second-best piece of advice came from my current editor Pamela Van Giessen, who told me not that long ago that it was time to cut myself off from writing and finish. Every aspect of this book, from the content to the illustrations to the cover design, was influenced by her decades of experience as a publisher and book lover, more potent now than ever, despite her primary focus being on baking. If you ever find yourself passing through central Montana, be sure to look up daisy donuts. Mention this book and she might let you pay in crypto.

This book was self-published in the spirit of decentralization. That means it took a small army of freelancers, artists, and professionals to create it. My thanks to Karen Minster who, for the second time, brought it all together with a beautiful design. To Paul McCartney who understood what I hoped to convey with the cover art better than I did, and to Dorie Herman for her crisp illustrations. Thanks also to Debra Nichols for her attention to detail.

Last, but not least, my renewed gratitude to all the thinkers, tinkerers, entrepreneurs, engineers, developers, degens, hackers, and hodlers who gave me something fascinating to write about. You've managed to create something that is both impactful and original, and that's a rare thing. I am but a traveler in this world.

There, I finished.

About the Author

Omid Malekan is the Explainer-in-Chief of blockchain technology. He's the author of *The Story of the Blockchain: A Beginner's Guide to the Technology That Nobody Understands* and an adjunct professor at Columbia Business School where he lectures on blockchain and crypto.

An eight-year veteran of the crypto industry, he spends most of his time as a consultant, educator, and advocate for this new way of building trust. He advises individuals, investors, and seed-stage startups to Fortune 100 companies. His essays on crypto and related topics have appeared in the *New York Times, Wall Street Journal, Financial Times, Spectator* magazine, various industry publications, and his blog at Medium.com. Prior to his work with crypto, he was best known for several viral videos in the heyday of YouTube, an animated one of which found its way into the financial zeitgeist, possibly to the chagrin of former Federal Reserve Chairman Ben Bernanke, aka *The Bernank*.

Malekan has spent years being confused about crypto so you don't have to be. When not writing or teaching, he plays the part of ambassador, sitting between the people who push the envelope on what is possible and those who will be impacted should they succeed. He resides in a quiet corner of the Metaverse. Learn more about his work at www.explainer -in-chief.com.

Endnotes

PREFACE

1   Bitcoin.com, Satoshi's Archive, emails/cryptography mailing list, Bitcoin P2P
    e-cash paper, https://www.bitcoin.com/satoshi-archive/emails/cryptography
    /1/#selection-29.0-29.470

0. TRUST

2   "Indenture," Wikipedia, https://en.wikipedia.org/wiki/Indenture

3   "Social contract," definition from Oxford Languages, https://www.google.com
    /search?q=social+contract&rlz=1C1CHBF_enUS931US931&oq=social+&aqs
    =chrome.0.69i59j69i57j69i60j69i61j69i60.1407j0j7&sourceid=chrome&ie=UTF-8

1. MONEY

4   *Sapiens: A Brief History of Humankind,* Yuval Noah, Harari, Harper Perennial, 2018.

5   "The Parable of the Wedding Banquet," Matthew 22, *New Revised Standard
    Version,* Bible Gateway, https://www.biblegateway.com/passage/?search=Matthew
    +22&version=NRSV

6   "Imperial Roman Army," Wikipedia, https://en.wikipedia.org/wiki/Imperial
    _Roman_army

7   "Dixie," Encyclopaedia Britannica, https://www.britannica.com/place/Dixie-region

8   "Silver Certificates," Bureau of Engraving and Printing, U.S. Department of
    Treasury, Silver Certificates, https://web.archive.org/web/20140403223347/http:
    /moneyfactory.gov/silvercertificates.html

2. PLATFORMS

9   "TCP/IP," Lee Copeland, Computerworld, January 17, 2000, https://www
    .computerworld.com/article/2593612/tcp-ip.html

10 "TCP/IP vs OSI Model: What's the Difference," Lawrence Williams, Guru99.com,
    October 7, 2021, https://www.guru99.com/difference-tcp-ip-vs-osi-model.html

11 "The Anatomy of a Large-Scale Hypertextual Web Search Engine," Sergey Brin and Lawrence Page, Computer Science Department, Stanford University, http://infolab.stanford.edu/~backrub/google.html

12 Ibid.

13 "The Flourishing Business of Fake YouTube Views," Michael H. Keller, August 22, 2018, *New York Times*, https://www.nytimes.com/interactive/2018/08/11/technology/youtube-fake-view-sellers.html

14 "Ad Blocking User Penetration Rate in the United States from 2014 to 2021," Statista, https://www.statista.com/statistics/804008/ad-blocking-reach-usage-us/

15 Facebook, Inc. Form S-1 Registration Statement, February 1, 2012, United States Securities and Exchange Commission, https://www.sec.gov/Archives/edgar/data/1326801/000119312512034517/d287954ds1.htm

16 Uber Technologies, Inc. Form S-1 Registration Statement, April 11, 2019, United States Securities and Exchange Commission, https://www.sec.gov/Archives/edgar/data/1543151/000119312519103850/d647752ds1.htm

17 "The Gender Earnings Gap in the Gig Economy: Evidence from over a Million Rideshare Drivers," Cody Cook, Rebecca Diamond, Jonathan V. Hall, John A. List, and Paul Oyer, May 2020, Section 2.4, p. 10, https://web.stanford.edu/~diamondr/UberPayGap.pdf

18 Lyft, Inc. Form S-1 Registration Statement, March 1, 2019, United States Securities and Exchange Commission, https://www.sec.gov/Archives/edgar/data/1759509/000119312519059849/d633517ds1.htm

19 "Facebook Reports First Quarter 2021 Results, Meta, April 28, 2021, https://investor.fb.com/investor-news/press-release-details/2021/Facebook-Reports-First-Quarter-2021-Results/default.aspx

20 "SEC Filing Shows American Airlines Loses Money Flying, All Profit Comes from Frequent Flyer Miles," Gary Leff, View from the Wing, October 26, 2018, https://viewfromthewing.com/sec-filing-shows-american-airlines-loses-money-flying-on-loyalty-program-earns-profit/

21 *The Credit Card Catastrophe: The 20th Century Phenomenon that Changed the World,* Matty Simmons, Fort Lee, NJ: Barricade Books, 1995. https://books.google.com/books?id=otBIAAAAYAAJ&q=credit+card+catastrophe&dq=credit+card+catastrophe&hl=en&newbks=1&newbks_redir=0&sa=X&ved=2ahUKEwi69e_u7-fnAhUxmHIEHYqUBU8Q6AEwAHoECAAQAg

22 "Twitter Officially Kills Off Key Features in Third-Party Apps," Casey Newton, The Verge, August 16, 2018, https://www.theverge.com/2018/8/16/17699626/twitter-third-party-apps-streaming-api-deprecation

23 "Investing in the Best Twitter Experience for You," Rob Johnson, blog.twitter
.com, August 16, 2018, https://blog.twitter.com/official/en_us/topics
/product/2018/investing-in-the-best-twitter-experience-for-you.html

24 "Amazon Admits to Congress That It Uses 'Aggregated' Data from Third-Party
Sellers to Come Up with Its Own Products," Lauren Feiner, CNBC.com,
November 19, 2019, https://www.cnbc.com/2019/11/19/amazon-uses-aggregated
-data-from-sellers-to-build-its-own-products.html

25 "Network Effects," Jessie Romero, Richmond Federal Reserve, *Econ Focus*, second
quarter 2018, Richmond Federal Reserve, https://www.richmondfed.org/-/media
/richmondfedorg/publications/research/econ_focus/2018/q2/pdf/jargon_alert.pdf

26 "Read the Full Transcript of Mark Zuckerberg's Leaked Internal Facebook
Meetings," Casey Newton, The Verge, October 1, 2019, https://www.theverge
.com/2019/10/1/20892354/mark-zuckerberg-full-transcript-leaked-facebook
-meetings

27 "OnlyFans' Policy Switch Is the Latest Victory in Big Banking's War on Sex,"
Daniel Cooper, Engadget.com, August 20, 2021, https://www.engadget.com
/onlyfans-big-banks-war-adult-content-174041161.html

3. PAYMENTS

28 "Payment Intermediation and the Origins of Banking," James McAndrews and
William Roberds, Federal Reserve Bank of New York, Staff Reports, September
1999, No. 85, https://www.newyorkfed.org/research/staff_reports/sr85.html

29 "Central Banks and Payment Systems: The Evolving Trade-off Between Cost and
Risk," Charles Kahn, Stephen Quinn, and Will Roberds, Norges Bank
Conference, Oslo, June 5–6, 2014, https://www.norges-bank.no/contentassets
/3fba8b3a3432407d929ae9218db1ffc4/10_kahn_quinn_roberds2014.pdf

30 Ibid.

31 *The Rise and Decline of the Medici Bank, 1397–1494,* Raymond de Roover, New
York: W. W. Norton & Company, revised ed. edition, April 17, 1966.

32 "Those Medici," *The Economist*, December 25, 1999, https://www.economist.com
/finance-and-economics/1999/12/23/those-medici

33 "Victorian Data Processing," Martin Campbell-Kelly, Communications of the
ACM, October 2010, Vol. 53, No. 10, pp. 19–21, https://cacm.acm.org/magazines
/2010/10/99495-victorian-data-processing/fulltext?mobile=false

34 Ibid.

35 Ibid.

36 New York Clearing House Association Records, 1853–2006, Columbia University Libraries, Archival Collections, https://findingaids.library.columbia.edu/ead /nnc-rb/ldpd_7094252#history

37 Diners Club International, The Story Behind the Card, dinersclub.com, https: //www.dinersclubus.com/home/about/dinersclub/story

38 "Visa, Inc.," Wikipedia, https://en.wikipedia.org/wiki/Visa_Inc.#History

39 Ibid., https://en.wikipedia.org/wiki/Visa_Inc.#cite_note-Thomas-8

40 "Western Union," Wikipedia, https://en.wikipedia.org/wiki/Western_Union #cite_note-16

41 "Paypal Inc. History," fundinguniverse.com, http://www.fundinguniverse .com/company-histories/paypal-inc-history/

42 "Tracking the Sources of Robust Payments Growth: McKinsey Global Payments Report," Sukriti Bansal, Philip Bruno, Olivier Denecker, and Marc Niederkorn, September 22, 2019, https://www.mckinsey.com/industries/financial-services /our-insights/tracking-the-sources-of-robust-payments-growth-mckinsey -global-payments-map

43 "Its IPO Document Shows the Massive Extent of Uber's Card Business," Jim Daly, Digital Transactions, April 12, 2019, https://www.digitaltransactions. net/ipo-document-shows-the-massive-extent-of-ubers-card-business/

44 "Swipe Fees (Interchange)," NACS, Advancing Convenience & Fuel Retailing, January 8, 2021, https://www.convenience.org/Advocacy/Issues/SwipeFees

45 "Financial Inclusion on the Rise, but Gaps Remain, Global Findex Database Shows," The World Bank, press release, April 19, 2018, https://www.worldbank .org/en/news/press-release/2018/04/19/financial-inclusion-on-the-rise-but-gaps -remain-global-findex-database-shows#:~:text=Globally%2C%201.7%20billion %20adults%20remain,help%20them%20access%20financial%20services

46 "House Lawmakers Officially Ask Facebook to Put Libra Cryptocurrency Project on Hold," Makena Kelly, The Verge, July 2, 2019, https://www.theverge .com/2019/7/2/20680230/facebook-libra-calibra-crypto-maxine-waters -congress-regulation-investigation-halt

47 "At 7½ Cents a Minute, Who Cares If You Can't Hear A Pin Drop?" Steven V. Brull, Bloomberg, December 29, 1997, https://www.bloomberg.com/news /articles/1997-12-28/at-7-1-2-cents-a-minute-who-cares-if-you-cant-hear-a -pin-drop

48 "Global Coalition to Fight Financial Crime," World Economic Forum Centre for Cybersecurity and Shaping the Future of Financial and Monetary Systems, https://www.weforum.org/projects/coalition-to-fight-financial-crime

49 "Payment Card Fraud Losses Reach $27.85 Billion," Annual Fraud Statistics Released by The Nilson Report, November 21, 2019, https://www.prnewswire.com /news-releases/payment-card-fraud-losses-reach-27-85-billion-300963232.html

50 "The Sinister Side of Cash," Kenneth S. Rogoff, *Wall Street Journal*, August 25, 2016, https://www.wsj.com/articles/the-sinister-side-of-cash-1472137692

4. MARKETS

51 *The World's First Stock Exchange,* Lodewijk Petram, Columbia Business School Publishing, 2014.

52 *The Ascent of Money: A Financial History of the World,* Niall Ferguson, Penguin Books, 2009

53 *The World's First Stock Exchange,* Lodewijk Petram, Columbia Business School Publishing.

54 "John Law's Banque Royale and the Mississippi Bubble," John E. Sandrock, http://www.thecurrencycollector.com/pdfs/John_Laws_Banque_Royale.pdf

55 *Memoirs of Extraordinary Popular Delusions and the Madness of Crowds,* Charles Mackay, Project Gutenberg, Money Mania—The Mississippi Scheme, https://www.gutenberg.org/files/24518/24518-h/24518-h.htm#miss_scheme

56 "The Mississippi Bubble: Money for Nothing: A History of Mania in John Law's Mississippi Company Stock," Winton, April 29, 2019, https://www.winton.com /longer-view/the-mississippi-bubble

57 "The Rise and Effects of the Indirect Holding System—How Corporate America Ceded Its Shareholders to Intermediaries," David C. Donald, SSRN, September 27, 2007, https://papers.ssrn.com/sol3/papers.cfm?abstract_id=1017206

58 Ibid.

59 "Study of Unsafe and Unsound Practices of Brokers and Dealers," Report and Recommendations of the Securities and Exchange Commission, December 1971, http://3197d6d14b5f19f2f440-5e13d29c4c016cf96cbbfd197c579b45.r81.cf1 .rackcdn.com/collection/papers/1970/1971_1201_SECUnsafe_01.pdf

60 See endnote 57.

61 "A Conversation with Mike Bodson, CEO of DTCC," Frank Chaparro and Ryan Todd, The Block, April 23, 2019, https://www.theblockcrypto.com /post/20135/mike-bodson-dtcc

62 Ibid.

5. FINANCIAL SERVICES

63 "The Failure of the Bank of the United States, 1930," Anthony Patrick O'Brien and Paul B. Trescott, *Journal of Money, Credit and Banking*, August 1992, Vol. 24, No. 3, pp. 384–399, Ohio State University Press, https://www.jstor.org/stable/1992725?origin=crossref

64 "The Banking Crisis of the Great Depression," The FDIC: A History of Confidence and Stability, https://www.fdic.gov/exhibit/p1.html#/10

65 Ibid.

66 "The Failure of the Bank of United States, 1930," Anthony Patrick O'Brien and Paul B. Trescott, *Journal of Money, Credit and Banking*, August 1992, Vol. 24, No. 3, pp. 384–399, Ohio State University Press, https://www.jstor.org/stable/1992725?origin=crossref

67 "Real Estate Prices During the Roaring Twenties and Great Depression," Tim Nicholas and Anna Scherbina, December 17, 2009, https://www.web.fordham.edu/download/downloads/id/3461/2010_spring_2_annapdf.pdf

68 "Streetscapes: The Bank of the United States in the Bronx; The First Domino in the Depression," Christopher Gray, *New York Times*, August 18, 1991, https://www.nytimes.com/1991/08/18/realestate/streetscapes-bank-united-states-bronx-first-domino-depression.html

69 "False Rumor Leads to Trouble at Bank," *New York Times*, December 11, 1930. https://timesmachine.nytimes.com/timesmachine/1930/12/11/118200963.html?pageNumber=5

70 See endnote 63.

71 *A Monetary History of the United States, 1867–1960,* Milton Friedman and Anna Jacobson Schwartz, Princeton University Press, 1971.

72 "Bank Rumor Mongers Called "Worst Traitors," *New York Times*, December 29, 1930.

73 "Why Did FDR's Bank Holiday Succeed?" William L. Silber, Economic Policy Review, Federal Reserve Bank of New York, July 2009, Vol. 15, No. 1, https://www.newyorkfed.org/research/epr/09v15n1/0907silb.html#:~:text=Why%20Did%20FDR's%20Bank%20Holiday%20Succeed%3F,-July%202009%20Volume&text=The%20contemporary%20press%20confirms%20that,Chat%20on%20March%2012%2C%201933

74 *Reframing Financial Regulation: Enhancing Stability and Protecting Consumers,* Hester Peirce and Benjamin Klutsey, eds., Chapter 3, 2016, Arlington, VA: Mercatus Center at George Mason University, https://www.mercatus.org/system/files/peirce_reframing_ch3.pdf

75 "GAO Estimates Final Cost of S&L; Bailout at $480.9 Billion," Robert A. Rosenblatt, *Los Angeles Times*, July 13, 1996, https://www.latimes.com /archives/la-xpm-1996-07-13-fi-23615-story.html

76 "Stealing Deposits: Deposit Insurance, Risk-Taking and the Removal of Market Discipline in Early 20th Century Banks," Charles W. Calomiris and Matthew Jaremski, March 2016, https://www0.gsb.columbia.edu/faculty/ ccalomiris/papers/Stealing%20Deposits.pdf

77 "Subprime Nonsense," Daniel Gross, *Slate*, August 6, 2007, https://slate.com /business/2007/08/the-fed-chairman-and-treasury-secretary-say-the-subprime -mess-has-been-contained-are-they-joking.html

78 "Banks' Self-Dealing Super-Charged Financial Crisis," Jake Bernstein and Jesse Eisinger, ProPublica, August 26, 2010, https://www.propublica.org/article /banks-self-dealing-super-charged-financial-crisis

79 "Bear Stearns CEO Says Liquidity Strong," Reuters Staff, Reuters, March 12, 2008, https://www.reuters.com/article/sppage012-n12172869-oisbn -idUSN1217286920080313

80 "Ex-Lehman Officials to Pay $90 Million to Settle Suit," Peter Lattman, *New York Times*, DealB%k, August 25, 2011, https://dealbook.nytimes.com/2011/08/25 /former-lehman-officials-to-pay-90-million-to-settle-suit/?mtrref=undefined&gwh =0160126A0AEAF99AFDA440B6D4FA7687&gwt=pay&assetType=PAYWALL

81 "Wall Street Pay: A Record $144 Billion," Liz Rappaport, Aaron Lucchetti, and Stephen Grocer, *Wall Street Journal*, October 11, 2010, https://www.wsj.com /articles/SB10001424052748704518104575546542463746562

82 "What's the Fed Doing in Response to the COVID-19 Crisis? What More Could It Do?" Jeffrey Cheng, Tyler Powell, David Skidmore, and David Wessel, Brookings, March 30, 2021, https://www.brookings.edu/research/fed-response -to-covid19/

83 "What Drives Insurance Operating Costs?" Björn Munstermann, George Paulus, and Ulrike Vogelgesang, McKinsey & Company, July 1, 2015, https://www.mckinsey.com /industries/financial-services/our-insights/what-drives-insurance-operating-costs

6. MONEY, AGAIN

84 A Century of Lawmaking for a New Nation: U.S. Congressional Documents and Debates, 1774–1875, Statutes at Large, 2nd Congress, 1st Session, The Library of Congress, American Memory, pp. 248–755, http://memory.loc.gov/cgi-bin /ampage?collId=llsl&fileName=001/llsl001.db&recNum=371

85 "US Dollar Share of Global Foreign Exchange Reserves Drops to 25-Year Low," Serkan Arslanalp and Chima Simpson-Bell, International Monetary Fund,

May 5, 2021, https://blogs.imf.org/2021/05/05/us-dollar-share-of-global
-foreign-exchange-reserves-drops-to-25-year-low/

86   "The Island of Stone Money," by Milton Friedman, February 1991, Working
Papers in Economics, No. E-91-3, Stanford, CA: Hoover Institution Press,
https://miltonfriedman.hoover.org/objects/56723/the-island-of-stone-money

87   "Bitcoin: Money or Financial Investment?" Scott A. Wolla, Economic Research,
Federal Reserve Bank of St. Louis, March 2018, https://research.stlouisfed.org
/publications/page1-econ/2018/03/01/bitcoin-money-or-financial-investment

88   "The Fed Is Looking into Facebook's Libra Cryptocurrency as Powell Flags
'Serious Concerns,'" Kate Rooney, CNBC.com, July 10, 2019, https://www.cnbc
.com/2019/07/10/powell-says-facebooks-libra-cryptocurrency-raises-serious
-concerns-such-as-money-laundering.html

89   "Mario Draghi, President of the ECB, Luis de Guindos, Vice-President of
the ECB, Frankfurt am Main," July 25, 2019, European Central Bank, Press
Conference, https://www.ecb.europa.eu/press/pressconf/2019/html/ecb
.is190725~547f29c369.en.html

90   "Estimate of the Share of Cash in Total POS Payment Transactions in
38 Countries in Europe in 2019," Statista, https://www.statista.com
/statistics/1112656/cash-use-in-europe-by-country/

91   "Japan Wants to Go Cashless, but Elderly Aren't So Keen," Tetsushi Kajimoto
and Izumi Nakagawa, Reuters, November 4, 2019, https://www.reuters.com
/article/us-japan-economy-cashless/japan-wants-to-go-cashless-but-elderly
-arent-so-keen-idUSKBN1XF0BT

92   "Central Bank Digital Currency: The First Nationwide CBDC in the World Has
Been Launched by the Bahamas," Vipin Bharathan, *Forbes*, October 21, 2020,
https://www.forbes.com/sites/vipinbharathan/2020/10/21/central-bank-digital
-currency-the-first-nationwide-cbdc-in-the-world-has-been-launched-by-the
-bahamas/?sh=30fa0a34506e

93   "Why the Fed Is Cutting Rates When the Economy Looks Good," Nick Timiraos,
July 29, 2019, *Wall Street Journal*, https://www.wsj.com/articles/why-the-fed-is
-cutting-rates-when-the-economy-looks-good-11564392600

7. RESPECT

94   "The Market for Fake Reviews," Sherry He, Brett Hollenbeck, and
Davide Proserpio, SSRN, August 6, 2021, https://papers.ssrn.com/sol3
/papers.cfm?abstract_id=3664992

95   "Fighting Instagram's $1.3 Billion Problem—Fake Followers," Emma Grey Ellis,
Wired, September 10, 2019, https://www.wired.com/story/instagram-fake
-followers/

96 "The Quotable Satoshi, Bitcoin Economics," Satoshi Nakamoto Institute, https:
    //satoshi.nakamotoinstitute.org/emails/cryptography/17/

97 "One of America's Biggest Gaming Companies Is Acting as China's Censor,"
    Zack Beauchamp, Vox, October 8, 2019, https://www.vox.com/2019/10/8
    /20904433/blizzard-hong-kong-hearthstone-blitzchung

98 "The Helium Flywheel," Tushar Jain, Multicoin Capital, March 17, 2021,
    https://multicoin.capital/2021/03/17/the-helium-flywheel/

99 "Facebook Tried to Make Its Platform a Healthier Place. It Got Angrier Instead.,"
    Keach Hagey and Jeff Horwitz, *Wall Street Journal*, September 15, 2021,
    https://www.wsj.com/articles/facebook-algorithm-change-zuckerberg
    -11631654215?mod=article_inline

100 "Wikipedia: Protection Policy," https://en.wikipedia.org/wiki/Wikipedia
    :Protection_policy#semi

101 "How We Collaborated to Build a New Open Source Plugin to Improve Search
    Results Across Language-Wikis," Melody Kramer, Diff, October 17, 2017,
    https://diff.wikimedia.org/2017/10/17/elasticsearch-learning-to-rank-plugin/

EPILOGUE

102 "Victor Hugo," Wikipedia, https://en.wikiquote.org/wiki/Victor_Hugo

103 Scott Stornetta and Stuart Haber, email message to author, July 17, 2021.

104 "On the Origins and Variations of Blockchain Technologies," Alan T. Sherman,
    Farid Javani, Haibin Zhang, and Enis Golaszewski, Cyber Defense Lab,
    University of Maryland, October 14, 2018, https://arxiv.org/ftp/arxiv/papers
    /1810/1810.06130.pdf

105 "Proofs of Work and Bread Pudding Protocols (Extended Abstract)," Markus
    Jakobsson and Ari Juels, IFIP—The International Federation for Information
    Processing Book Series (IFIPAICT, Vol. 23), https://link.springer.com/chapter
    /10.1007/978-0-387-35568-9_18

106 "They Want to Delete the Wikipedia Article," Bitcoin Forum, bitcointalk.org,
    July 20, 2010, https://bitcointalk.org/index.php?topic=342.msg4508#msg4508

107 "Gold holdings," Wikipedia, https://en.wikipedia.org/wiki/Gold_holdings

Index